Happy Never After

why the happiness fairytale
is driving us mad
(and how I flipped the script)

Jill Stark

SCRIBE
Melbourne • London

Scribe Publications
2 John St, Clerkenwell, London, WC1N 2ES, United Kingdom
18-20 Edward St, Brunswick, Victoria 3056, Australia
3754 Pleasant Ave, Suite 100, Minneapolis, Minnesota 55409 USA

Published by Scribe in Australia 2018
Published by Scribe in the UK and North America 2019

Typeset in Adobe Garamond by the publishers
Printed and bound in the UK by CPI Group (UK) Ltd, Croydon CR0
4YY

Scribe Publications is committed to the sustainable use of natural
resources and the use of paper products made responsibly from those
resources.

9781911617587 (UK edition)
9781925713107 (Australian edition)
9781947534704 (US edition)
9781925693225 (e-book)

CiP records for this title are available from the National Library
of Australia and the British Library.

scribepublications.co.uk
scribepublications.com.au
scribepublications.com

For Chris, Jason, and Nonie, who brought me back to life

CONTENTS

AUTHOR'S NOTE

When I was a kid, outspoken and chatty, Dad would proudly tell people that his daughter knew her own mind. But I didn't really—I had no clue. It was only when it started to malfunction that I came to know it intimately. And even now, after a spectacular breakdown that nearly killed me, my mind is still revealing its secrets. Every day a new subplot emerges; there are more twists and turns than a daytime soap.

The experiences of the last few years have taught me a lot. They have shaken up my perception of happiness and given me a greater insight into the universal struggles we all face. The journey has helped me identify the things I can do to make life easier, and the things that make it more challenging.

But our brains are wonderfully complex and unique. The myriad forms of emotional distress we experience can't be shoehorned into one homogenised story. What works for me may not be right for someone else. So this is not meant to be a prescriptive guide. I'm not a doctor, a counsellor, or a psychologist. I'm not a spiritual guru or a happiness expert. I'm just a person who lived through some tough times and learned a few things along the way. Those lessons form the backbone of this book. Whether our stress is a minor irritant or a clinical disorder, the key to understanding it comes from figuring out what lies beneath.

My hope is that my story will resonate with anyone who has chased their happy-ever-after and found it lacking. It's for anyone who knows what it feels like to struggle, even if their life, on paper, is 'perfect'. It's for every person who feels 'abnormal' or worries that their troubles define them. It's a book for people who wonder why they're stuck in the same old unhealthy patterns and want to change. It's for anyone who feels strung out by a hectic modern world and all its challenges, or worries about the pressures on the kids in their lives. It's a book for those who want to change the script.

The events described move around in time but largely occurred over a period of years directly preceding or following an emotional firestorm that came to a head in October 2014. Some chapters contain edited extracts of articles that first appeared in *The Age*, *The Sunday Age*, or *SBS Life*.

While I believe my story is ultimately one of hope, it also documents some dark and difficult times. This content may bring up issues for some readers. If you need help, turn to the back of the book for further information. You don't have to go it alone.

The
Neverending
Story

1

FALLING APART

It was a chat with a philosopher that finally tipped me over the edge. He was sharing his wisdom on the power of solitude. 'It's the capacity to confront and accept your own existence without needing others around to entertain or distract you,' he said cheerfully, as I gripped the phone, my knuckles whitening.

Suddenly, that familiar sense of dread engulfed me. He was still talking, but I was no longer listening. The only sound I could hear was the thundering of blood rushing to my head. My heart hammered. I was trapped on this phone call with a modern-day Socrates, schooling me on 'human complication' and the calm that comes from truly knowing yourself, and I was being buried by an avalanche of panic. My mind raced in time with the pulsing in my chest as I applied his words to my life. *I'm not calm. I don't know myself at all. What the fuck is wrong with me?*

The anxiety only intensified with every catastrophic thought. It was a death roll, and I felt powerless to stop it.

My brain tried to save me by faking a coughing fit. I hung up the phone mid-sentence. And then I was on the newsroom floor, gasping for breath like a freshly caught fish flip-flopping on the deck of a boat.

My friend and colleague Chris stood up from the desk opposite mine. 'Jesus, Starkers, you alright?'

'I can't breathe.'

Dying felt like a certainty. In these moments it often feels as if that would be a better option than living through another minute. It's like a scene from a horror movie where the petrified girl is running down a darkened corridor in her nightgown. Except the predator is my own mind. I tried to breathe deeply, in and out, in and out. Science tells us that it's impossible to panic if you practise diaphragmatic breathing: the body and mind are so interconnected that breathing deeply has an automatic calming effect. But that's not always easy to believe when it feels like insanity or cardiac arrest are real possibilities. Electric shocks surged from the tips of my toes to the crown of my skull. I was petrified. I wanted to slam my head against the wall just to make it stop.

It was Saturday, the quietest day of the week. My bosses at the news desk couldn't see my meltdown from where they sat. Only Chris bore witness. He'd never seen this side of me. I didn't dare look at him for fear of what I would see written on his face. Anxiety had been with me since I was child, but few people knew the extent of my history. It had been years since I'd experienced anything like this. And never at work.

I lay on the floor in child's pose, face down, knees tucked beneath my chest, arms by my sides, willing myself to keep breathing. I couldn't stay here. I stood up, my hands trembling as I inhaled and exhaled. Slow, deep breaths. I picked up the phone and redialled the philosopher's number. 'Hi, Damon. Sorry about that. I've got a really bad cough at the moment. Just had to get some water.'

I finished the interview. The piece I wrote about the lost art of solitude ended up as a front-page story the following Sunday. The headline read 'Why Being Alone Means Keeping Good Company'. The image underneath was of a pigtailed girl in a flannel shirt, jeans, and hiking boots sitting cross-legged on a rock in a darkened forest, her face illuminated by the tablet in her hands. Take away the digital device and she looked like a 15-year-old me.

This story would be the last one I wrote for almost five months. It was October 2014, and I had reached my life's peak. But I had fallen apart.

In February the previous year, my first book, *High Sobriety*—a memoir about my tumultuous twelve months off the booze, set against a backdrop of Australia's binge-drinking culture—had been published. It soon became a bestseller and was even shortlisted for literary awards.

It came at a time when my career was flying. I was working in my dream job as a senior writer at *The Sunday Age*, writing long-form features and opinion pieces on issues that fired my passion for social justice. I was living the life I'd always imagined.

Publishing a book was all I'd wanted to do since I was a nerdy wee girl growing up in Scotland. And it was everything I'd hoped it would be. During a blissful few months that felt like it would never end, I had to pinch myself as I was thrust headlong into a whirlwind Festival of Me. Mum flew in from Edinburgh and joined me on a national tour, where I jetted around the country doing bookshop signings, TV appearances, and radio interviews with some of my journalistic idols. I gasped as I saw my memoir in an airport bookshop on the biography shelf right next to Bruce Springsteen's, his head tilted quizzically to one side, those dreamy bedroom eyes gazing at the letters of my name, which had been fashioned into the shape of a beer bottle. My emotions pinballed back and forth between rapture and delirium. My face ached from all the smiling.

It went on long after the book was launched. One day, a young man tapped me on the shoulder on the tram home from work and asked if I was Jill Stark. 'Oh my God,' he said. 'Your book is changing my life.'

I was giddy. At one point during those heady months — I think it was after a phone interview in my bikini on the beach in Noosa — I may even have gazed skywards like a character in an old black-and-white movie, drawing in a breath as I uttered the words, 'This is living.' It was a hedonistic hurricane of writers' festivals, launch parties, and awards ceremonies, where I sipped champagne and exchanged edgy banter with highbrow literary types I'd previously known only from the covers of books. I was in fantasy land, experiencing spikes of joy that felt intense enough to knock me over.

The buoyancy of success also invigorated my romantic life, and as the year progressed I fell into a series of hot-and-heavy flings with attractive young men who made me feel like a lovesick teenager. At the business end of the footy season I began dating an AFL player. Young and not much of a conversationalist, he liked to hunt wild animals in his spare time. He giggled as he made me watch YouTube montages of people falling off ladders and being hit in the face with basketballs. But I pretended not to notice any of this because he was kind and sweet, and his chiselled body was such a perfectly formed piece of art it would have been more at home in a modern sculpture gallery than in my bed.

On one particularly surreal evening, I found myself on assignment, six floors up, in the Grand Hyatt's diplomatic suite, waiting to interview Captain Kirk himself, Hollywood legend William Shatner. As the city lights cast an otherworldly glow on the Yarra below, I heard the world's most famous intergalactic traveller pad down the hallway. At that moment, my phone beeped. It was an explicit text message from my AFL player asking when he could next see his 'Scottish cougar'. A rush of euphoria washed over me. I rested my head against the notepad on my knees and grinned. This was surely the most ridiculous year of my life. I had reached it: the happy-ever-after.

But something wasn't quite right. In truth, my joy was a free-falling, anchorless kind of happy that at times bordered on mania. The more praise I got, the more I craved. I was like a crack addict chasing my next fix. And there was never enough. When people were emailing and tweeting and stopping me on the street to tell me they admired my work, it felt amazing. But once the euphoria wore off, something malignant began to grow. Just as I had once used the manufactured high of alcohol to fill the gap, praise had become my new drug. And just like drinking, those first few drinks were always the best. Then I'd try to recapture that buzz again and again, with ever-diminishing returns. I'd find myself refreshing Twitter and Facebook, replaying interviews, and looking up old reviews online as I scrabbled around for more adulation. There was never enough. My self-worth had been pinned to an external vision of my life that was so distorted it was like looking at my reflection in a carnival hall of mirrors.

As the months went on, friends and colleagues remarked on how awesome it must feel to have your dreams come true. I would proffer that ear-to-ear grin that people have come to expect of those who have reached the top of their game. Then I would nod, telling them that yes, it really was amazing and I'd never been happier. Privately, I was falling down the rabbit hole. I felt lost and alone.

I couldn't understand it. I should have been at peace with myself. The self-doubt that had been my companion for as long as I could remember should have been replaced by full-to-the-brim happiness. Instead, I was empty. This wasn't just the absence of something; it was a ravenous hunger — an emptiness so absolute I felt starved deep in my bones.

But I was faking it like a champion. On stage at Melbourne's Wheeler Centre, delivering a lunchtime lecture on the lessons I'd learned during my year off the booze, I had a full-blown panic attack in front of 100 people.

I watch the video on their website occasionally to remind myself of how so many of our struggles are hidden. At the eight-minute mark I pause, clear my throat, and reach for a glass of water. I am smiling, but inside, this is the exact moment where I felt like my heart might stop beating. The room swayed. My knees shook beneath the podium. Sweat trickled down my arms. But I kept going. I later asked a friend in the audience if she'd noticed my distress. Did she see my hands quivering as the voice in my head screamed *RUN! RUN NOW!?* She hadn't noticed a thing. Few people knew the truth.

Later that year I went to the United Kingdom, launching the book in Edinburgh, my home town, in front of old friends, colleagues, family, and my high-school English teacher. I spent most of my trip home accepting congratulations through gritted teeth, ravaged by anxiety. During a studio interview with *BBC Five Live*, the panic hit so hard my hands bunched into claws, gripping the edge of the desk in a bid to stop myself toppling off my chair.

I kept going until I couldn't anymore. A year and a half after the realisation of a series of dreams that I thought would be my happy-ever-after, I was plunged into the darkest period of my life. I couldn't work, I couldn't eat, I barely left the house. After months of panic, a deep depression descended and things became desperate. Close friends kept vigil as I clung on to a life I wasn't sure I wanted. They were seeing a part of me I had guarded so closely.

My internal crisis—unfurling in my mind like a bad stage play in which the protagonist has forgotten all their lines—had broken the fourth wall. The effort it took to keep smiling through the terror had pushed me to a breakdown. Here was incontrovertible proof of what I had long believed: I was bat-shit crazy.

For all my reporting on mental illness and the importance of breaking down stigma, I was terrified of what people would think. Outwardly, I was the outspoken firebrand—a journalist who started Twitter wars with homophobes and was as comfortable holding court in the pub as delivering a public lecture. The world hadn't seen the me that couldn't catch a tram for more than two stops without hyperventilating. Or the me that was googling 'how to kill yourself without hurting the people you love' in the middle of the night.

But there was no more hiding. I was a shell. A hollowed-out version of the three-dimensional person my friends had once known. The days dragged on at a glacial pace. Each morning, the weight of what lay ahead pinned me to the bed. It felt like a barbell crushing my chest. Sleep was fleeting; I snatched an hour or two at a time. The brief respite it provided seemed to fuel my anxiety—all that dormant time without a voice. Upon waking, it screamed at me everything that had been left unsaid while I slept. A pent-up jumble of my worst fears and insecurities spewed forth at warp speed, like the mutterings of a born-again Evangelical speaking in tongues.

As the months off work continued, my absence from the newsroom became more conspicuous. I considered concocting an elaborate backstory: a rich elderly relative had left me a generous inheritance and I'd gone home to Scotland to claim my castle in the Highlands. Or I was a contestant on *The Bachelor* and had been secretly filming hot-air balloon dates with a wooden-jawed Ken doll and 21 random girlfriends. The truth seemed an easier sell. I started to open up to colleagues, contacts, friends, and even strangers. Almost every person I confided in had their own stories to tell. Depression was common, anxiety even more so. One work friend told me how she'd taken months off work when her anxiety got so bad she was throwing up in the staff toilets every morning. I'd just presumed she was on holiday. Another said the panic attacks he'd suffered since his teens were still a constant feature. He seemed such a confident, laidback bloke. A friend shared the details of a breakdown that had forced her to move to the other side of the country rather than face the people who'd seen her fall apart. She was one of the fiercest women I knew. So many people were medicated: antidepressants, sleeping pills, relaxants. They all secretly worried they were not normal.

As I tried to rebuild myself, I started to see that there were struggles all around me. And it wasn't only those who were living with clinical depression or anxiety. When I scratched the surface I found a recurring theme: people were worn out. They spoke of unmanageable stress and an overwhelming sense of being 'always on'. The pace of modern life was exhausting. There was a listlessness — a collective sense of ennui — with the constant striving for success and satisfaction. It was the search for something that seemed tantalisingly close but remained forever out of reach, a frantic and often fruitless pursuit of happiness in an age of anxiety. Something about twenty-first-century living was making it harder than ever to stay calm.

People were wired, their brains like overheated laptops struggling to run dozens of open windows at once. Everything was just too damn fast and impossibly loud. The phones we clutched in our hands had become extensions of ourselves. We'd forgotten where the online version of ourselves stopped and the real selves started. Those I spoke to felt trapped in a constant feedback loop of digital distraction and white noise. It was almost impossible to switch off.

I could relate to all this. In the modern age, there is little downtime and always more to do. I reach for my phone to find escape only to face a barrage of atrocities and doomsday predictions every time I refresh the screen. How do you stay positive when an insatiable twenty-four-hour news cycle reminds you in graphic detail that we live in bitterly divided, post-truth times defined by global terrorism, catastrophic climate change, and the mass displacement of our planet's most vulnerable people?

On Instagram, a deluge of 'inspirational' memes jostle for space with images of shiny-faced fitspo bloggers #feelingblessed who offer hackneyed answers as they sit cross-legged against sunsets filtered to storybook perfection. On Facebook, achievements are curated into greatest-hits packages, bolstering the narrative that happiness comes from the key pillars of success—finding a partner, making babies, climbing the career ladder, and owning more stuff. Life's failures and disappointments are airbrushed out of the picture. So often it has left me feeling that I must do better. I must be better. And when I shared my worries with people around me, I found that so many of them felt the same. There was a sense of not being enough. A feeling that we are all failing in a world with impossible standards.

If the pursuit of happiness and perfection has become a competitive sport, I had played the game like a pro. I had bought the home, landed the dream job, written the book, dated gorgeous men, and generally lived the dream, documenting every step online because what's the point of success if you can't make people on the internet jealous? But all the achievements I thought would make me whole turned out to be red herrings. I could have had a Pulitzer Prize under one arm and Ryan Gosling under the other and it still wouldn't have been enough. My happy-ever-after had been built on quicksand.

When the wheels fell off, I had no idea what to do next. I was living in a world that promised me I could have it all, and here I was at the pinnacle, utterly bereft. But if I was broken, the culture that formed a backdrop to my disintegration had surely played a part in that fracturing. It's a culture that views sadness as abnormal, particularly when you've 'made it'; a culture so afraid of feelings that we think we can spend, drink, or click our way out of the blues. It's a culture frenzied by the constant need for online connection and external validation, with no room for solitude, silence, or switching off; an environment in which millions of us feel like we're drowning in an ocean of toxic stress but feel shamed for not being as happy as we should be by the very forces fuelling the problem. Could it be that the pursuit of happiness is making us miserable?

It can't be a coincidence that the worst period of my life followed one that was supposed to be the best. This book is an attempt to find out why. It is an examination of the enormous psychological challenges we all face in the modern era, but also an attempt to uncover what lies beneath so much of our discontent.

As I tried to put myself back together, I discovered that while my happiness fairytale had been a fantasy, and twenty-first-century living might be adding to my sense of feeling overwhelmed, these things weren't the sole cause of my anxiety. I looked into my past and found that this mental collapse had deep and complex roots stretching all the way back to childhood. And so I began to untangle the roots, embracing and understanding those messy, painful parts of me I'd long tried to deny. What I found forms the backbone of this story. It has been quite a journey. I continue to walk it daily, one step at a time. Often I stumble. Sometimes I feel like I'm going backwards. I have not been freed from pain or transformed into a barefoot guru, at one with the universe. But I am learning what drives my emotional suffering, tracing its history all the way back to a time before I could give it a name. And I am learning how to live well in our age of anxiety.

The process of unsnarling these roots has been illuminating, bewildering, and at times utterly terrifying. But ultimately, it has been lifesaving. It has taught me that happiness is not what we think it is, and that we all have struggles we worry we can't survive. Our challenge is to not run from that discomfort, but to make room for it and have the courage to hold it up to the light.

2

THE HAPPINESS HANGOVER

As a fretful, chronically anxious kid, when I worried about exam results or where life would take me, Mum and Dad would say, 'Jilly, we don't care what you do, just as long as you're happy.' They meant it, as so many parents do, as a statement of unconditional love. It was a way to take the pressure off. But every time I fell in a heap of worry or sadness, I felt that somehow I was doing life wrong. All they wanted was for me to be happy, and I wasn't.

Happiness is our society's holy grail. From the moment we hear that first bedtime story, 'happy ever after' becomes life's goal. In a spiritually malnourished Western world, happiness is a proxy religion.

In fact, the idea of happiness has become so central to our understanding of what makes a fulfilling existence that it is being prioritised in ways we could not have previously imagined. Since 2012, the United Nations has commissioned the annual *World Happiness Report*—a cheerfully coloured document filled with smiling faces from around the globe, which ranks Australia tenth in the international happiness stakes. UN secretary-general Ban Ki-moon said the index recognises that social, economic, and environmental wellbeing are equal pillars of a happy nation. It follows the lead of Bhutan—a peaceful Buddhist country that has replaced gross national product with gross national happiness as a measure of a thriving nation.

As a general philosophy, putting people over profits seems like a no-brainer. But when you're told that the cornerstone of personal and global success is happiness, and you routinely feel sad, frustrated, or unfulfilled, what then?

The tension between what we're expected to feel and our everyday reality has led to a desperate scramble to fill the gap. In the past few decades there has been an explosion of apps, websites, conferences, life coaches, and social media stars positioning happiness as the principal foundation for a good life. Books on how we can best achieve it rocket to the top of the *New York Times* bestseller list (and straight onto my bookshelf—there is nothing I haven't read about the quest for joy). Yoga and meditation studios have sprung up on every corner, and a booming 'wellness' industry promises to restore balance through detox cleanses, superfoods, clean eating, and ancient healing therapies. 'Do what makes you happy' and 'follow your bliss' have become meaningless totems in a movement that leaves us trapped in an endless search for contentment.

This spiritual chasm has been a boon for Big Business. From diet fads to home renovation, fashion magazines to luxury cars, we're sold the idea that the gap can be filled by pouring dollars into it. One of the world's most famous corporations, Coca-Cola, has co-opted happiness in a series of clever branding exercises linking the consumption of the soft drink to a fulfilled life. Its 'choose happiness' campaign involved the brand giving away cans of Coke at London's major transport hubs, and launching a 'happiness meter' on 300 digital billboards across the city to measure residents' happiness levels (based on the number of positive or negative 'mood words' used on Twitter). The corporate world's hijacking of happiness has been slick and effective, and ultimately designed to bolster its bottom line, with some major corporations employing 'chief happiness officers' to keep employees smiling and boost productivity. Over at Google, their CHO is known as the 'Jolly Good Fellow', whose job description is to 'enlighten minds, open hearts and create world peace'.

But for all that business is booming, the happiness industry is doing a pretty crappy job of delivering results. If it were a shonky car salesman, *Today Tonight* would have run it out of town a long time ago. In the past 50 years, rates of depression, anxiety, and suicide in the developed world have skyrocketed. In Australia, an estimated 45 per cent of people will experience a mental-health condition in their lifetime. If current trends continue, clinical depression will be the second most disabling condition in the world by 2020, behind heart disease. More people are medicated for mental-health problems than at any time in our history. In the absence of genuine contentment, we have learned to anaesthetise ourselves with manufactured highs, as rates of alcohol abuse, obesity, gambling, and drug addiction continue to climb. Anxiety is now the most common mental-health disorder in the world, with one in 13 people affected. In any given year, around two million Australians will grapple with the condition. It's more commonly reported in Western societies than in the rest of the world, even among countries experiencing conflict. At a time when we have become more affluent and aspirational, why do we appear to be more miserable than ever?

I grew up in an era when the self-esteem movement was king,

and 'positive thinking' was the cornerstone of psychological practice. These trends came to prominence in the 1980s as an antidote to rising rates of depression in Western society, borne out of a turbulent post-war period of social, economic, and technological change. For so long I believed that not being able to just think my way to happiness was the albatross of all failures. The positive-thinking movement taught me that all I had to do was repeat affirmations every day in the mirror until my psyche became bulletproof and my self-doubting inner monologue was silenced.

But my internal critic was prolific. Imagine a ball-breaking, bastard love child of Regina George from *Mean Girls* and Nurse Ratchett in *One Flew Over the Cuckoo's Nest*. She sneered and undermined and liked to loudly point out at every available opportunity that despite my wins, I remained a hopelessly broken loser who was destined to die alone under a pile of empty pizza boxes in a hovel reeking of cat wee. For every *I am strong, I am beautiful, I am happy* I parroted at myself in the mirror through gritted teeth, Regina would counter loudly with, *You are weak as piss, you are ugly, you are a misery whore.* It was like bringing a teaspoon to a gunfight. Nothing stuck. The harder I tried to convince my anxious mind that I was happy, the more I felt like a miserable failure. The obsession with positivity taught me that uncomfortable emotions were abnormal. I had come to believe in a divine right to live in a state of permanent bliss, which only made every minor setback feel like I was backsliding all the way to Sadsville: a desolate town with a population of one.

A 2017 University of Melbourne study of people with depressive symptoms found that the more societal pressure a participant felt not to experience the emotions of sadness or anxiety, the more likely they were to show an increase in these symptoms. The study's co-author, Associate Professor Brock Bastian, said this helped explain why countries that place a premium on happiness are experiencing higher rates of depression. 'In Eastern — particularly Buddhist — cultures, people aren't happier than their Western counterparts, but they are less depressed,' he told the university's *Pursuit* site. 'This over-emphasis on happiness we see here doesn't happen in those countries in the same way and they seem to embrace a better balance of the whole emotional repertoire. Feeling at times sad, disappointed, envious, lonely — that isn't maladaptive, it's human.'

And yet, in our quick-fix, consumer-driven society, we have come to believe that negative feelings need not be tolerated. Painful emotions are increasingly seen as unnatural and abnormal. We refuse to accept that we can't always get what we want.

In his book *The Happiness Trap*, British-born Australian doctor Russ Harris maintains that everything we've been taught about happiness is a lie. The notion that we should be happy at all times and any deviation from this is an aberration is a major driver of angst and misery. Harris told me ahead of a happiness conference I covered for *The Age*, 'So many people now think, *if I'm not happy, there's something wrong with me.* We seem to have forgotten that feelings are like the weather — changing all the time. It's as normal to feel unhappy as it is to have rainy days.'

The crash that followed the release of my book was not just a mental collapse; it was in many ways an existential crisis as I struggled to reconcile my depressed mood with society's expectation that I should be fulfilled. Not only had I achieved my childhood dream to write a book, but that book was a critical and commercial success. It completely blindsided me that reaching this goal, along with the other strides I had made in my professional and romantic life, would not only not deliver the happiness I'd anticipated, but make me question the entire purpose of my life. I had a very real sense that with my dreams realised, far from achieving the fairytale ending and basking in it, I had little left to strive for. My friend Kath, who had spent years completing a PhD only to feel empty and rudderless when it was finally handed in, had warned me of this looming pitfall. But I scoffed, thinking how could I possibly be anything but fulfilled when my book was on the shelves? And yet there I was, successful and miserable.

Compounding the angst was an overwhelming sense of guilt. I was a middle-class white woman with a good job, great friends and family, and her own home, complaining that the publication of her first book was making her sad. I was the living embodiment of #firstworldproblems. What right did I have to be so maudlin?

Exacerbating that guilt was my new unwanted role as the poster girl for sobriety. Readers were in regular contact, telling me my book could have been written about them. Most of the correspondence was quite lovely—touching tales of how the book had opened gateways to deep reflection. There were letters, emails, Facebook messages, and tweets from people all over the world, asking me to update them on the next chapter of my life. I sensed a quiet panic in some of the questions. Had I learned to drink in moderation? Had I found peace with my rate of alcohol consumption? Even though my book was about developing a healthier relationship with alcohol, and I'd never suggested I wouldn't drink again, I felt like I owed people an explanation. In a culture that makes moderate drinking such a challenge, I felt compelled to tell them that a year of sobriety had led seamlessly to a life of clean living, emotional clarity, and unbridled happiness.

In the immediate aftermath of my year off the booze I definitely did have a healthier relationship with alcohol. I was much more mindful of how and when I was drinking, and drank far less than I used to. It was rare for me to stumble home in the early hours of the morning or wake up with only hazy memories of the night before. But by midway through 2014, things were different. As my mental health deteriorated, old habits began to creep in. Maintaining a healthy balance became more of a challenge. Every time there was new research released about binge drinking, I'd be rolled out by the media to give my two cents' worth on the problem, and I'd wonder if maybe I should start to decline the requests. One night, I appeared on Channel Ten's *The Project* as an 'expert' talking head on Australia's alcohol culture. They filmed me sitting at my kitchen table drinking a pretend cup of tea and flicking through pages of my own book—because that's totally what authors do to relax—and even had me jogging around the local park to illustrate just how much day can be seized if you put down the bottle and get your shit together. The very next night I was downing Jäger shots and dancing on a bar at 3.00 am with two of my girlfriends.

I'd be in the pub with mates and a stranger would sidle up and ask, 'Aren't you that chick who wrote a book about not drinking?' while raising an eyebrow at the beer in my hand. On Instagram, I posted a picture of my delicious box of 'breakfast' doughnuts and confessed I was slightly hungover, only to be shamed by a follower for my lack of clean living after my year off the booze. Some people—like the UK radio presenter who said there was no point reading my book because ultimately I'd returned to drinking—had expectations about my abstinence that I couldn't possibly live up to. If I wasn't behaving like a nun, it was as if I had somehow let people down. The self-awareness was draining. I'd spent several years immersed in the issue of drinking, both personally and journalistically, and I was over it. I just wanted to be able to have more than one glass of wine without forensically examining my motivations from every conceivable angle or being branded a hypocrite.

I never claimed to have all the answers — for myself or anyone else. Yet I still felt pressure to be what people wanted me to be: sober and serene. But my life was moving in the opposite direction. I felt like a bride who'd planned for her big day for so long that when it was over there was nothing but hollowness.

A 2015 paper published in the *Journal of Family Issues* found that almost 50 per cent of brides suffer from postnuptial blues. One participant said: 'You ... think it's ... this fairytale, and the wedding is the climax, and then you come home and you have to go to work the next day. And nothing is different. Nothing is different at work, nothing's different with your friends, nothing's different.' Another told researchers, 'It's like life was punctuated by these really exciting, big events. Then it was like, "Well, this one's [the wedding's] over, so now what am I gonna do? It's over, and we have nothing to look forward to."' As Fairfax writer Kasey Edwards observed, the results are reflective of a culture that seduces women throughout their lives with the 'Hollywood perfect' wedding, from childhood storybooks all the way to reality TV shows and a booming bridal industry: 'For many women, "I do" is seen as the end point in a lifelong romantic narrative. It's therefore not surprising that so many brides wake up the next morning with a sense of grief and fear that nothing in their life will ever compare.'

This could apply to so many of life's milestones. Anticipation is often better than gratification. We're taught to plan for the wedding, not the marriage. The birth, not the baby. Buying a home, not servicing the mortgage. Reaching the goal is meant to bring the reward, and when it doesn't it can spark a psychological shitstorm.

I recently watched an ABC *Four Corners* investigation into the struggles faced by elite athletes post-success and found myself nodding furiously in recognition. It revealed widespread depression and substance abuse after the glory faded. Among the Australian sporting heroes to share their stories was retired cricketer Nathan Bracken, who was once the world's top one-day fast bowler. Now he works for his father-in-law, laying asphalt. He told the program that becoming a professional cricketer had been a childhood dream: 'It's a fairytale. It's probably more than you ever wished for. As a kid, you sit there and it's what you want to do and *aww, how great would this be?* And all of a sudden you're in a position where it's just bigger and better than you can imagine.' But when he was forced to retire in 2011 due to a knee injury, he lost not only his income but also his identity. Without the adulation of the crowds, his sense of self crumbled. Trying to prove himself again to the world, he became a contestant on the TV show *Dancing with the Stars*, only to be eliminated in the first round, compounding his sense of failure. It wasn't long before he could barely leave the house. He set himself the simplest of daily goals: getting out of bed, making breakfast. 'I remember times you'd just sit there and you'd think … I felt a failure. I went from "I [can] provide for my family" to all of a sudden, days where, yeah, I couldn't,' he said.

American swimming champion Michael Phelps had a similar experience when he fell into the 'darkest place you could ever imagine' after winning a record eight gold medals at the Beijing Olympics in 2008. At the same Games, Australian diver Matthew Mitcham won gold at the age of 20. Mitcham later told SBS's *Insight* program that he had spent his whole life wanting to be the best in the world at something. After retirement, he was completely unprepared for how to fill the gap left by the sporting accolades:

> My self-worth ended up being reflected back to me in the judges' scores. If I got an eight they liked me, if I got a nine they really liked me, and if I got a ten I was perfect, and my whole self-esteem was based on these numbers that I was getting from the judges or the feedback that I was getting from the coach or, you know, how many Twitter and Facebook followers I had. Like, all these external sources that are all really quite fragile.

You don't have to reach the dizzying heights of Olympic success or international fame to feel this boom-and-bust emotional cycle. The gulf between what we think we'll feel when we reach career and life goals and what actually happens when we get there can be vast enough to swallow any of us.

I'd long thought that publishing a book would symbolise success and recognition and provide evidence that I was not an imposter. But nothing changed. At some point in my past I'd set the benchmark so high I'd need stilts and a rope ladder to get within touching distance. Every achievement had come with a self-sabotaging inner dialogue, with my inner Regina George refusing to accept anything short of perfection. A career in the media, in which I had to present myself to the world for approval or opprobrium on an almost daily basis, had perhaps not helped. An editor once told me there are two types of journalist: the anxious and the useless. I suspected I had broken the mould by being both.

Living with Regina is exhausting. It's like being constantly tuned to You're Shit FM, and she's spinning all the tunes. When I'm in a good place, I know these statements in my head are not facts. I can turn the station down to a low hum and get on with my day. But as October 2014 approached, the noise was deafening. It should have been a warning of what was to come. It had been more than a year since my book had come out, and I was meant to be happy. Instead, I was running out of energy to combat Regina's missiles. Life felt like it was behind glass. Through the lives of people around me, I could see what it might be like to live freely, to find peace in the easiness of breathing in and out, of not being held hostage by my own brain. But I couldn't get there. Relief was fleeting. I always seemed to return to a horror show of hyper-awareness, an overarching sense of dread—to a world that existed only in the future and in the past, where I time-travelled at breakneck speed between what had been and what was still to come. I had whiplash from the back and forth.

Over the course of a week I began to write down every negative thought I had, just to get it out of my head. Committing these statements to paper, I was struck by how unspeakably mean I was to myself. I would never dream of directing these comments to my friends. And yet, I insulted myself in cruel and unusual ways, over and over again. The way I looked, the way I thought, the way I communicated: the very essence of myself was laid bare in an excoriating onslaught of self-flagellation.

One night after work I met Chris in the pub. He could tell straight away that something was wrong. I parroted a few of the journal statements, stringing them together in a seamless script of self-doubt. When I was done, I said, 'I just can't believe after all these years and all the things I've achieved I'm still this shit at life. I'm so pathetic.'

Chris, a chain-smoking, hard-drinking Canadian who likes to deliver me wisdom through a vehicle he calls the 'sledgehammer of truth', rolled his eyes and gave me his usual forthright assessment of the situation. 'You're so freaking harsh on yourself, Starkers. When are you going to give yourself a break?'

'You have no idea,' I answered, thinking of the notepad in my bag that contained the full extent of my shame. Then I thought, perhaps the only way to disarm the power of that shame was to share it with someone who could bear its weight.

'I want you to read something.'

'Of course,' he said, taking the A5 jotter with the appropriate pattern of skulls and love hearts on its cover.

It's a strange experience watching someone climb inside your head. At first there's a wry smile as they recognise your voice. Then, the wince of confusion as they try to reconcile their version of you with the distorted image outlined on the page. And then, worst of all, the moment they crumple as they realise just how much craziness you're housing. He cried. Just plain broke down and cried.

'Oh doll,' he choked, looking at me with an expression you never want to see on anyone's face.

'I don't want your pity,' I said with a sob.

He was out of his seat and on me, enveloping my diminished self. 'This isn't pity. This is love.'

And I knew then what it feels like to be seen — truly seen, deep into your being, for all that you are and all that you wish you weren't.

It would be Chris who made the phone call to the doctor not long after this, one Friday morning as I lay on my lounge-room floor, shaking. There was no more pretending. I needed help. It was the start of a five-month absence from work and an emotional journey that would turn everything I knew about happiness on its head. I had lived the dream. Now it was time to live the reality.

3

DON'T WORRY, BE HAPPY

I was, to say the least, a worrisome child. If my parents exchanged a terse word over the division of household chores, I was convinced divorce would swiftly follow. An evening news bulletin about nuclear weapons testing would have me investigating the logistics of building a fallout shelter in our back garden. Every setback was a disaster. When I was 10 and my gym teacher didn't pick me for the school netball team, I was in pieces. More than a decade passed until I could accept that being denied the wing-attack bib did not make me a failure as a person, and that despite having the hand–eye coordination of a milk-drunk baby trying to thread a needle in a sandstorm, I was still good at other things.

Mum would watch me getting lost in my thoughts and try to soothe me with helpful truisms such as, 'There's no point worrying about the day that'll never happen.' She may as well have been speaking in Mandarin. It was impossible to stay in the moment when there was always a chance of imminent doom. My glass wasn't half-empty: it was drained to the bottom.

In adulthood, the struggle continues. If you tell me to 'calm down', expect the same expression you might see on your dog's face if you asked him to explain the current geopolitical tensions in sub-Saharan Africa. Relaxation does not come naturally. I find the phrase 'go with the flow' baffling, like applied mathematics or the way that leggings have become acceptable stand-alone outerwear. When people say, 'Don't worry about it' or 'What will be, will be,' I want to shake them by their foolish, untensed shoulders and scream: 'AND JUST HOW DO YOU PROPOSE I DO THAT, MR MYAGI?'

If a friend is more than ten minutes late for a dinner date, I assume they've been involved in a terrible car crash. A call that goes straight to voicemail means they are almost certainly dead. Once, my Dad didn't reply to an email for a day and I was already making funeral plans. In my defence, he's ordinarily a very prompt messenger, so his tardiness was noteworthy. But even if it hadn't been, my go-to position is often the most catastrophic. It happens in an instant—like a bullet train reaching its destination before the luggage has even been loaded. I'll barely have time to consider whether Dad might be busy, or whether his server is down and he hasn't received the email—which, in this case, turned out to be what happened—before my brain goes straight to *dead*. If I get up in the morning and my cat, Hamish, isn't immediately visible or audible, I expect to walk into the kitchen and find his furry little corpse splayed out next to his water dish. So far, my track record for being wrong on these assumptions stands at 100 per cent. But this fact has done little to stop the thoughts. I worry about everything. Pain in my abdomen: early-stage ovarian cancer. Boss wants to catch up for a coffee: almost certainly getting sacked. Call from an unknown number: the possibilities are so varied and potentially awful I simply can't answer.

Recently, I was invited to a fancy cocktail reception at Victoria's palatial Government House. When I received the very official-looking envelope in my mailbox, marked with the seal of the Victorian governor, my immediate thought was that I was being deported.

I am the person who packs for an overseas holiday a fortnight in advance. If I could sleep at the airport check-in desk the night before my flight, this would be my preference. I am pathologically punctual to the point that I always take a book when meeting friends as there's a more than 80 per cent chance I'll arrive stupidly early. A weekend away requires days of logistics, lists, and all-weather wardrobe planning. The last, and only, overnight music festival I went to was in Glasgow in 1995 because the uncertainty of where I will sleep/shower/use the bathroom makes the whole prospect horrifying.

Over the years, when the anxiety has become more than I could manage, I've sought help from a range of medical professionals. I've tried doctors and drugs, cognitive behavioural therapy and mindfulness techniques, psychologists and anxiety counsellors and various meditation courses. I've exercised, changed my diet, followed strict gut-cleanse regimes, taken supplements and vitamins, and drunk freshly squeezed super juices. Some of it has helped. Much of it hasn't. Nothing has 'cured' me.

Unlike some physical conditions, there are no biomarkers for emotional pain we can pick up with diagnostic screening. You can't tell from an X-ray, brain scan, or blood test how much depression a person has. Treatment can be hopelessly inadequate or a gruelling process of trial and error. The dearth of solid evidence on what works and what doesn't can mean that, for people with continuing problems, there is no shortage of medical experts promising the quick fix. And although a problem may be psychological in nature, its effects can impact on the whole body.

I've seen respiratory specialists and taken tests to work out whether my breathlessness might be caused by an underlying lung-capacity problem. It isn't. In my early twenties, I spent two years visiting a specialist orthodontist who fitted me with a retainer to wear at night and gave me a biofeedback machine, which delivered an electric pulse to the back of my skull and my temples. He said the crippling headaches I'd developed were coming from a misaligned jaw, causing my muscles to spasm. They weren't. I've had ultrasounds to explore the cause of intermittent nausea, pelvic, and abdominal pain; blood tests to investigate my continued fatigue and to rule out immune disorders, thyroid problems, or inflammatory disease; stool samples to see whether my chronic gut problems are caused by bowel infections, coeliac disease, or Crohn's disease. All negative. I've spent a fortune on massage therapists, and visited osteopaths and chiropractors who said that my chronic body aches and sore head were due to neck and spinal misalignment. They pushed and pulled and cracked my back until it made a sound like a gun going off, telling me this would be the end to all my troubles. It wasn't.

The symptoms are real and at times utterly debilitating. But so far, touch wood, I have found no sinister underlying pathology. The dry mouth, body sweats, fatigue, and breathlessness I grapple with are not signs of an undiagnosed sickness. It's just my body set to fight-or-flight mode, bringing with it a constellation of aches, pains, and troubling sensations. When things are bad, I'm in a constant state of hyper-arousal, like a boxer ready to step into the ring. It amplifies every twinge and can trick me into thinking I'm dying.

The internet age hasn't helped. When I feel something in my body that I can't explain, Dr Google is on hand to fill in the gaps. Conditions I have diagnosed myself with include meningitis; stroke; heart attack; melanoma; tinnitus; alopecia; Crohn's disease; rheumatoid arthritis; glandular fever; type one (and two) diabetes; chronic fatigue; Parkinson's disease; multiple sclerosis; measles; motor neurone disease; endometriosis; vertigo; sleep apnoea; cancers of the brain, breast, bowel, cervix, lung and ovaries; and, for a brief period as a 14-year-old, an ectopic pregnancy — despite never having had sex — which perhaps says more about the Scottish education system than it does about my anxiety. When your default position is to worry about the sky falling in, hypochondria is a common problem.

My friend Edwina has similar problems. She messaged me recently to say, 'I almost parked in a doctors-only carpark the other day because I have convinced myself that Google is pretty much the same as a twelve-year medical degree.' There is nothing she doesn't know about all the ways in which the body can turn on itself. A mother of two with a doctor for a father and a mother who's a nurse, Edwina is no stranger to the medical system. She has always worried about her health, but when she was diagnosed with a benign brain tumour a few years ago, the anxiety escalated dramatically. The tumour — which can only be removed with delicate and needless neurosurgery — was picked up because she's hyper-vigilant to even the slightest change in her body. Three times she's ended up in the emergency department, convinced by a misbehaving brain that she was gravely ill. She's had colonoscopies, ultrasounds, MRIs, blood pressure monitors, mammograms, skin checks, and scans on almost every organ in her body. Working as a communications specialist at Cancer Council Victoria, where she has intimate knowledge of the most awful diseases and routinely tells the stories of the worst moments of people's lives, has been challenging, to say the least.

'It's a bit too easy to imagine yourself with ailments because maybe someone without anxiety can be very sensible and think, "Well, only one in 100 people get this," but I see that and I go, "Yeah, that one's going to be me. I see those ones in 100 every day at work, so what makes me so special?"' she told me once.

Like me, Edwina has battled her brain's faulty messaging for years. And she too has been inundated with advice from people who want to help. Her condition has gotten better and worse, and then better again. She describes herself as 'highly functional' but lives with her physical and emotional symptoms every day. One of her biggest frustrations is the unspoken expectation that she should be over this already. 'Even people who I love and who I'm super close to will say, "But you're all better now, aren't you?" And I'm like, "Yep, that's fine," but the reality is I'm going to need to manage this for the rest of my life. I will need to have strategies, or potentially medications in place, because if I don't I'll get sick.'

This is not the script we're given as kids. We're supposed to be happy; persistent emotional problems don't fit that story. My continued struggles with anxiety have often felt like proof that I'm unfixable—damaged goods. People are starting to talk more about mental ill health, but the stories I read are still so black and white. You're either mentally ill or you're mentally well. Emotional distress is viewed as an abnormality. Depression and anxiety are conditions you can develop, like a chest infection, and then you get help and go on your way. The narrative is a romantic hero's journey, with individuals emerging from their battles healed and bulletproof. When we're on the road to the fairytale ending, our troubles are supposed to be short-lived and resolved neatly—a linear path from sickness to cure. It leaves no room for a backward step. As I've careered back and forth throughout my life between bouts of depression, times of acute anxiety, and periods of relative calm, I've felt as if I was constantly failing.

My experiences with doctors have only amplified this feeling. In Scotland, after seeing me many times about my anxiety, the family doctor told me in my early twenties that it was time I 'snapped out of it'. Another GP, in Melbourne, treating me for depression recommended I 'stop being so gloomy'. It felt like the equivalent of asking someone with two broken legs to just make more of an effort and give walking a crack. Another time, again in Melbourne, when I began having blinding stress headaches, I visited my local medical clinic for help. Exhausted, barely eating, and feeling overwhelmed by the basic demands of life, I didn't know what I needed. But what I got wasn't it. As I walked into the consulting room, a silver-haired lady was hammering the keys on her computer, eyes fixed to the screen as she pushed a sheet of paper across the desk. Having been on the mental health merry-go-round for some years, the form was familiar to me. The Kessler Psychological Distress Scale is a universally recognised tick-box exercise designed to determine the severity of a person's depression. The questions are brutally direct and immediately focus the mind on just how fucked up one's life has become. *During the last 30 days, how often did you feel hopeless? … During the last 30 days, how often did you feel so nervous that nothing could calm you down? … How often did you feel so sad nothing could cheer you up?* There are ten questions, all in a similar vein, scored from one to five, with one being 'none of the time' and five 'all of the time'. Your number reveals your current state. Under 20 is well. Over 30 is a severe mental-health disorder.

The doctor totted up my scores. 'You got 25, which means you're only mild to moderately depressed, so there's not much to worry about.'

I was crying so hard that snot was dribbling from my nose. She didn't look up, and began scribbling on a prescription pad. I'd been on and off antidepressants since I was in high school. I wasn't convinced they had made much difference. This time I wanted an alternative. Or at least to discuss the options. My questions seemed to frustrate her. Medication would help, she insisted. I didn't have the energy to fight so I urged her not to prescribe the class of antidepressants I'd been on as a teenager, which had given me horrendous withdrawal symptoms when I came off them. For several weeks it felt as if electric shocks were zapping my brain as I grappled with crippling dizziness and tremors travelling up and down my body.

'They're the best antidepressants we have,' she said.

'Maybe not for me,' I mumbled.

She sighed and reluctantly agreed to put me on an older generation of antidepressant medication. But not before asking, 'Are you suicidal?'

I thought about it for a while and said no.

'Good,' she said. 'These ones aren't prescribed very often these days because they're much easier to overdose on. But you're not suicidal, so that's fine.'

The whole interaction was over in 15 minutes. And now, I had the knowledge that should I want to kill myself, the drugs she'd prescribed were well equipped for the job.

So on a hot October morning in 2014, when I realised I could no longer carry on without help, I was less than confident about finding it. By now, I was having daily panic attacks in even the most benign circumstances—with friends, on the tram, lying in bed staring at the ceiling at night. Being awake was becoming an exercise in unremitting terror.

I chose a medical practice that my friend Loretta, a free-spirited yoga teacher, recommended. She said the doctors were particularly good with mental-health issues and took an integrative approach that combined Western medicine with modalities such as meditation, Chinese medicine, acupuncture, and nutritional support. The clinic was described online as a 'wellness centre' and a 'community of healing', which made my sceptical health journo ears prick up. But despite my reservations, I was ready for a different approach.

Sitting in the doctor's waiting room, I felt as if the walls were contracting around me. This was the same sensation I had had in my early twenties when an acid trip went bad. Lying under the stars with friends, in the school playing field behind my parents' house, I had felt as if suddenly the sky was tightening around my head. It was as though the universe was crushing me — that vast expanse of nothingness wrapping around my limbs and squeezing the breath from my body. Almost 20 years later, the sense of helplessness was the same. But this time, I'd manifested the crazy without chemical assistance.

All around me, people were leafing through magazines and tapping on their phones. I longed for the ease they seemed to find in living. My sprinting thoughts were so loud I was amazed nobody could hear them; anxiety was a fighter jet roaring through my cells, dropping grenades from head to toe. I placed my hands flat on the fabric of my cheerful orange summer dress to stop them from shaking.

When the doctor called my name, I shuffled after her into the consultation room. Her name was Fiona — a woman about my age, with a blonde pixie cut and kind eyes. When she asked what she could do for me, I broke down. Then I braced for the judgement and the prescription pad. Instead, she handed me tissues and told me she could see I was in a great deal of pain. Together, she said, we would make a plan to get me to a place where living was not so hard. And then she asked me to start from the beginning. Not from the start of that week or even that year, but from childhood. She wanted to know everything. It was the first time in more than 20 years that a medical professional assessing my mental health had seen me as a whole person, not just as a collection of symptoms.

Fiona spent an hour and a half going through my family history, my friends, my school days, my working life. She listened attentively when I listed all the ways in which I was going mad. What made this doctor different was her willingness to share a piece of herself. She wasn't just a clinician; she was a woman who had suffered, just as I was now suffering. Fiona told me that in 2007 she had volunteered with her husband in Africa, and came home burdened by the awfulness of the world, carrying a sense of hopelessness about her ability to make a difference. They moved to Darwin and she threw herself into her work in emergency medicine. But soon her self-worth was tied to an ideal of what a 'great' doctor should be. The more she worked, the louder her inner critic became. She began comparing herself to colleagues but always pulled up short. She finally hit a wall when a two-month-old baby died during her intensive-care rotation. While other staff members expressed their grief, she felt nothing but anger. All she could think was *children are dying every minute in Africa and nobody cares*. Unable to sleep, and experiencing such intense anxiety that she had developed a tremor, she was on the fast track to burnout. Soon after, she quit emergency medicine, moved into general practice, and became a meditation teacher, with a mission to offer care that went beyond the physical and looked at psychological and spiritual wellbeing. It was her passionate belief that six-minute medicine was failing patients. So she started offering longer consultations, integrating conventional medicine with counselling, cognitive behavioural therapy, healing, and emotional support.

In the past, I'd felt that things were happening *to* me. Now I had a doctor who actively involved me in the decision-making process. A doctor who didn't expect me to be cured within a few weeks. She went through a range of possibilities in detail. Medication was discussed, but she stressed this was only an option. There were many other things we could try first. But as a matter of urgency she wanted me to see a psychologist. She jotted down some names. She also suggested that I cut out caffeine and alcohol, start taking a magnesium supplement, and try to get out of the house every day for some exercise, even if it was just a brisk walk. And she wanted to see me again in two days.

By the end of the consultation, it felt as if I'd been in therapy. I was grateful to Fiona for her care, but I was still daunted by the road ahead. My face was drained of colour, my body exhausted with the constant surging panic. I felt small, hunched over in my chair, a shrunken, child version of myself. I glanced down at the chipped polish on my toenails and wondered if there would ever again be a time when I could contemplate something as frivolous as painting my nails. When I looked up, Fiona was watching me. She had tears in her eyes. Before I left, she wrapped me up in a tight hug, and for a moment I felt that perhaps I might survive.

4

BEYOND THE PATCH-UP JOB

You know what's the best? When people say, 'Just don't worry about it' and my anxiety is cured forever. 'Have you tried wrapping an elastic band around your wrist and snapping it every time you have a negative thought?' is another gem. 'It'll pass, just think of something else,' is also a perennial.

'Do a 30-day detox,' says the Facebook commenter who just watched a documentary on the link between gut health and depression and is now qualified to treat psychological disorders in every person they meet with nothing more than a glass of kombucha and a jar of lacto-fermented pickles. Or shop on the Gwyneth Paltrow's Goop 'wellness' website and order a pack of wearable healing stickers to 'balance the energy frequencies' in your body.

A friend once offered assistance by patting me gently on the forearm one morning at work and handing me a book entitled *When Things Fall Apart*. It was the second gift she'd given me in a fortnight. The first was a DVD of the American comedy-drama series *Enlightened*, starring Laura Dern as 'a professional woman on the verge of a nervous breakdown'.

It all comes from a good place. People don't want to see the ones they care about in pain, so they look for ways to help. But sometimes there is no easy answer. Our psychological makeup is complex. What works for one person may not scratch the surface of another's angst. And it can change from day to day. Sometimes, I find meditation slows my brain down, but on other days, sitting quietly with my own thoughts is like trying to restrain a dozen feral cats inside a string bag.

An anxious mind can be difficult to understand for those who don't view 'pencilling in' a lunch date at a yet-to-be confirmed venue as a form of tortured chaos, can tolerate a rogue pimple on their face without automatically presuming it's a melanoma, and don't routinely lie awake at night worrying about whether a passing comment they made to their oldest friend in 1991 might be the reason she hasn't returned a text message. People are often tempted to offer solutions. But if someone's been battling these issues for decades, chances are there's pretty much nothing they haven't entertained to find relief. The entire happiness industry is predicated on this endless quest for respite.

It has led me to seek answers in all sorts of places. I've been to reiki therapists and tarot readers, floated on my back in a sensory deprivation tank listening to whale noises, and consulted energy healers, a transcendental meditation teacher, and a hypnotist who said she could trick my mind into calming down, but only left me $200 poorer for the privilege of sitting in an uncomfortable chair with my eyes shut for an hour while she walked me through the winding corridors of my dreams.

Sometimes the search for solutions has produced comical results. During my time as health reporter for *The Age*, a PR contact pitched me a story about a client who offered psychic services. I was, to say the least, sceptical. The contact told me that after a reading, I'd be won over. This woman, she promised, would change my life. She offered me a free session, pointing out that the usual rate was $300 and there was a very long waiting list, so this would be a unique opportunity with no obligation to write a word about the experience. So, like many anxious people before me, I thought, *what do I have to lose?*

When I arrived at the psychic's office, in a well-heeled bayside suburb of Melbourne, my cynicism only grew stronger. The waiting area, decorated in lavender tones, was filled with angels, moons, stars, crystals, and toadstools. The air was heavy with the musky smell of burning incense. A soundtrack of pan pipes and mountain breezes provided a musical backdrop that I did not find calming. I wanted to open my mind, but when the psychic emerged from a back room and responded to my extended hand by pulling me into an embrace and saying, 'We don't do handshakes here, we do hugs,' I felt like running for the door. Instead, I tried to remain impassive as she described my 'beautiful warm pink aura' and told me I'd led many interesting past lives.

She invited me to lie on the table as she placed crystals underneath and then began to read my soul. Much of what she told me made little sense. I had not known a boy called Peter who lived by the beach in a caravan park when I was growing up in Scotland. I could not see a future where I would work for *Madison* magazine—which folded not long afterwards—and I did not have a psychic aunt who shared the fortune-telling powers she said I was forced to hide from my family as a child. And yet, despite these false leads, when she spoke about the troubles I had had as a child, something inside me cracked open. 'There is so much pain,' she said, as I wept. 'You just wanted someone to speak up for you, to see you. But you were all alone.' The emotion poured out of me, like hot sticky lava.

She also told me that I would meet a man called Jason, who would be significant—it would not be a romantic relationship, but the connection would be important in other ways. 'He is going to change everything. His name keeps coming up.' She was right about that, too. When I met Jason Ball a couple of years later, and in *The Sunday Age* told his story of coming out as the first openly gay Australian Rules footballer, it was a catalyst for change. For Jason, it led to him spearheading a national campaign challenging homophobia in sport and lobbying the AFL to stage its first ever Pride Game, between St Kilda and Sydney, in 2016. His coming out was a game changer for acceptance and inclusion in the macho world of football. For me, it further fuelled my passion for equality and led to a series of articles advocating for social change, culminating in the honour of being named Victoria's Straight Ally of the Year at the GLOBE Melbourne LGBTI Awards—one of the proudest moments of my career. But beyond that, it led to a deep friendship. Jason has been by my side through the roughest times and played an integral role in my journey back to the living. I often think of that day, years ago now, when I was lying on a table in a dimly lit purple room, being told of the significance of this man I was yet to meet. Was it predestined?

Jason's response when I told him this, a long time afterwards, was to laugh out loud and roll his eyes so hard I thought he would do himself an injury. As an organiser of two global atheist conventions, his faith in psychic powers is limited. 'Jason is a pretty common Australian name,' he pointed out. 'And she also said you were a reincarnated Egyptian princess who had her throat cut by her father in a past life.' Meh. Details. I knew it was unusual stuff, but I certainly didn't feel like this woman was a fraud. She was warm, likeable, highly intuitive, and had a genuine passion for healing. After 20 minutes in her company I felt as if she'd known me a long time.

But there were moments when I had to stifle a laugh. Like when we discussed my love life and the feckless man-child I was entangled with, prompting her to 'remove his negative energy' and promise I would fall in love and have the best sex of my life with a wonderful man who would give me three children ('at least two from your womb'), and we would live in a place called Mermaid Beach. At one point she raised her hands above her head, pressed them against the wall, and rocked back and forth as she mimicked the mid-coital pose she was seeing in her mind. It was all a bit awkward, like watching a sex scene in front of your parents. Then, she came back to the table, hovered her right hand, palm down, over my pelvic region and said, 'I'm not going to touch you, but do you mind if I awaken your clitoris?'

What's that now? I wasn't aware my lady parts had been dormant. But I figured that an alert and conscious clitoris was better than one that was asleep at the wheel like a jobless dope-head in a '90s slacker movie, so I said, 'Sure. Why not?'

She began making circles with her hands above my pubic bone, breathing out sharply through an open mouth. 'There's no point in having it if it's not switched on,' she said with a smile.

When she was finished, I'm not sure I could say in all honesty that my downstairs region felt livelier than it did before. But in the years that followed, something unexpected happened. I dated some really fine men and had a lot of fun. The first was a comedian — smart, handsome, and hilarious, with a passion for death metal. Next I fell (hard) for a 25-year-old elite athlete who seemed to adore me. He was charming and attentive and smoulderingly good-looking. When not representing Australia on the world stage, my six-foot-three Jude Law lookalike was a professional model. He was so attractive I laughed whenever I saw him. He could have been cut straight from a catalogue, and, as I would later discover, his commitment to me was equally paper thin. But he had a smile that undid me. In the bedroom it took all my strength not to snap a sneaky selfie just to prove I hadn't dreamt him. Then, of course, there was the AFL player. My mojo had gone into overdrive. It was exhilarating. Chris had a theory to explain it. Just like Sir Ian McKellen's character Magneto in *X-Men*—an evil genius who has innate magnetic powers allowing him to bend immovable objects to his will—my vagina had somehow created a sexual magnetic field that was attracting all the hot guys within a 50-kilometre radius. My pants were electrified. I had become Magnovag. I couldn't help but think of the psychic. She had not only awakened my clitoris, she'd weaponised it.

Perhaps it was mystic powers, perhaps it was simply a single woman learning to embrace life again after recovering from the painful end to an unhappy relationship. Either way, it made me more open to trying new experiences, even if they were unconventional. When it comes to alleviating mental anguish, if you're at your wit's end, conventional medicine has failed you, and something, anything, gives a moment of light relief, you don't need peer-reviewed science to tell you it's real. You grab it with both hands and say thanks for the temporary peace.

Finding the right psychological help for yourself or a loved one in the midst of a crisis can also be a lottery. It's not like hiring a tradie, where you google all the plumbers in the area and a few hours later, a burly guy in Blundstones and flannel is elbow-deep in your cistern. When you're trying to reconfigure the displaced contents of your mind, finding the right therapist is more than just a search for who's readily available. The strength of that therapeutic relationship could be the difference between getting back on your feet or sliding further into the unknown. But when you're depleted, even the act of searching can feel like a hike to the top of Kilimanjaro. I've seen various psychologists and therapists over the years and at times it's felt like taking a smashed-up car to a panel beater. They beat out the visible dents and send you on your way, looking almost like the original version of you. But it's just a patch-up job. Underneath, the chassis is buckling and before long you've broken down again.

The healthcare system is set up to reinforce the narrative that our emotional distress should be transient. The Medicare-subsidised psychologist sessions I could access after ticking the GP's boxes were capped at ten per calendar year. There are few other areas of healthcare where judgement is passed so readily on the individual's inability to heal themselves.

Over the years, I've found some therapists to be empathetic and helpful. But others have done more harm than good. Not long after I arrived in Australia in the early 2000s, I discovered a counsellor who specialised in anxiety disorders, having recovered from one herself. Even though she lived in another state, I started doing sessions with her, and our weekly telephone calls were, for a time, enormously helpful. But when my troubles weren't eradicated after a few months, she seemed to grow frustrated. One day she stopped returning my calls. She left a voicemail saying 'I can no longer help you' without offering any further explanation. It was utterly bewildering. Nothing feeds an anxiety disorder quite like your therapist dumping you because you're too mad for therapy.

In 2009, my tick-box GP referred me to a psychologist who spent every session offering wisdom from the School of the Bleeding Obvious. At one point, as I was telling her how the anxiety was so acute it literally made my brain hurt, she produced a snow globe. 'Imagine life is this snow globe,' she said, holding it in her palm before she closed her hand into a fist and shook it up. 'Worries are like these snowflakes. They swirl around all over the place but eventually they all settle down.' She looked at me with a satisfied smile, handed me the globe, and said, 'You can keep that if you like.' It took all my powers of restraint not to throw it at her head.

This time, I needed someone who would go beyond the patch-up job. I needed someone who was qualified to deal with the full complexities of the human condition. So after seeing Dr Fiona, this staunch atheist prayed to unknown beings that the universe would present the right guide. And then she appeared. Jason had been visiting her for years, and credited her with transforming his life, relationships, and general sense of resilience. I had often marvelled at how this man who was 12 years my junior was more emotionally mature than many people my age — perhaps his psychologist was the difference. When I was at my lowest ebb, he called her up, unbeknown to me, and begged her to take me on as a client. Despite having a long waiting list, she agreed to an assessment over the phone. During our half-hour call, she said that if I was willing to put in the hard work, she would see me for as long as it took. I thanked her and promised I would put in all the work and be punctual for our first appointment.

I arrived 25 minutes early. When I pressed the buzzer on the wall of the red-brick terrace building in leafy, well-to-do East Melbourne, the door clicked open. I walked into a small waiting room with high ceilings, where a radio played ABC Radio Melbourne loudly enough to obscure the sounds of hearts being poured out in the adjoining room. When the door opened, a woman in a business suit emerged, clutching a receipt and avoiding eye contact as she hastily made for the exit. It was, I would learn over the years, a common reaction for the people entering and leaving this room. It was as if by not looking each other in the eye, we could pretend we were not both there because part of us was broken.

On that first day, I welcomed the anonymity. I wasn't there to make friends. I just wanted help. And yet, I wasn't convinced anyone could really help me. The hole was too vast. I wasn't quite at rock bottom, but I could certainly see the outline of its cold concrete floor just a few metres below me. I sat on the edge of a shiny leather couch, squeezing back tears, and waited.

A few minutes later, the door opened again and there was Veronica. A slender woman in her fifties with jet-black hair to her shoulders, smartly dressed in a knee-length black dress and heels, she welcomed me with a warm smile. I walked into the room that I would come to know so intimately and saw three chairs. One, a swivel chair next to a desk, was clearly hers. There were also two large leather armchairs — one facing hers, the other adjacent. I chose the one opposite and immediately regretted it. It was further away than the one adjacent to hers, and I worried that from this decision she would deduce I was an aloof weirdo with trust issues. Even when paying someone to help manage my mental breakdown, I still wanted them to like me. I treated it like an audition, trying to strike the right balance between fucked up enough that I needed immediate help but not so fucked up that she would view me as a lost cause.

In her hybrid South African–Australian accent, Veronica outlined what would happen. For this first session she would ask me a number of questions about my past — my childhood, my family history, and my relationships. Many of these might not seem relevant, but I should try to answer freely and honestly. This would be the one and only time Veronica would take notes in a session. She must have a near-photographic memory because her ability to recall names and details from my past that I've mentioned only in passing is staggering.

I took a different approach than I had with previous psychologists. From this very first session I jotted down bullet points, making sure I didn't miss a single salient detail and paying careful attention to my homework for the week. Veronica told me that she wanted commitment. I gave her the anxiety-disorder version of that — perfectionism to the point of obsession. I did everything bar shine her a crisp green apple and leave it on her desk.

But by the end of our first session, I was frustrated. I'd done all that Fiona had asked. I'd stopped drinking, cut out caffeine, and forced myself to get out of bed and move my body at least once a day. It hadn't changed things much. Most days I just wanted to be unconscious. Eating and sleeping had become almost impossible. The fear was overwhelming. It was that feeling you get when your plane hits really bad turbulence and for a few seconds you imagine what it might be like to plummet to your death — except that it wasn't just a few seconds, it was every waking moment. The thoughts were unyielding. It felt like a thousand angry fire ants were scuttling around my skull. I wanted to tip my head on its side and bang with the flat of my hand until they poured out like salt water after an ocean swim.

I begged Veronica to give me tools to stop my heart and mind from racing. She asked me to be patient. But it felt as though we were veering off on tangents, exploring issues from my past that bore no relation to what was happening in the here and now.

I told her about the therapist who abandoned me, and my suspicion that nobody could help because I was too crazy for therapy. She said that what had happened to me was unforgiveable, adding that she often despaired of her profession and the reductive way it views emotional health.

'But maybe it's not them. Maybe it's me,' I suggested. 'I'm just defective. Nothing can fix me.'

Veronica, in her gentle, considered way, told me it would be a long road, but she would walk it with me. 'The resistance is understandable. It's just you trying to protect yourself. You doubt the process for as long as you like.' She said she would happily give me strategies if that's what I wanted, but there was no quick fix. 'The strategies are the therapy,' she said. 'What we're doing is repairing damage to the soul.'

At first, I was reluctant to accept her long-game approach. I was still stuck in the happiness trap. I wanted instant gratification. It was the only way I'd known. But there was no denying it had failed me. Veronica made a promise on that first day that she wouldn't terminate my therapy if I didn't get better quickly enough. She stressed that the work we would do together would be an epic journey. This anxiety, and the way that I viewed myself and the world, had been 38 years in the making. It was going to take a lot of hard work to turn it around.

Veronica explained that the ancient, mammalian part of my brain, which controlled the fight-or-flight response, was vital to human survival. It acted as a threat detector, allowing cavemen and women to fend off attacks from wild animals. When danger was sensed, the mammalian brain kicked in automatically and the body reacted accordingly—the heart pumping faster to allow nutrient-rich blood to power muscles for fast escape. The skin started to sweat to keep cool, and adrenaline peaked to heighten thinking. Somewhere along the way, my brain had learned to see danger in situations that posed no threat to my survival. My body couldn't tell the difference: the physiological changes were the same as if a sabretooth tiger was at the door. And it had happened so often over so many years that my brain kicked into this mode automatically. Just as my brain had formed shortcuts so that I no longer had to consciously think about how to drive a car or make a cup of tea, my anxiety had become an automatic response to situations or stimuli of which I might not even be aware.

She told me that the maladaptive shortcuts or neural pathways in my brain had been formed through a process of repeatedly thinking, feeling, behaving, and reacting to these stimuli over decades. Those pathways were like a well-worn track heading deep into a forest, carved into the earth through the back and forth of hikers' footsteps. My job was to start forging a new path, walking it again and again until my mind followed the new way automatically. It was the process of making the unconscious conscious. She could give me strategies to deal with the physical symptoms of anxiety, but it would just be a bandaid. Underneath, there was a festering sore that had been left untreated for years. Therapy would be a process of untangling the roots of that wound. We would have to look to the past to find a path to the future.

It's a sentence I never thought I'd write, but the psychic lady was right—a man called Jason would be the conduit to a therapeutic relationship that would help me live again. Over the next few years I would work harder on this than anything I ever have in my life. It would not be an easy road. With every breakthrough there would be a setback. As I stripped myself bare, there were many times where I was left in a gravity-defying limbo—a purgatory where the old ways no longer worked but the new ways were not cemented enough to provide stable ground.

For every resurrection, something must die. I would have to burn myself to the ground before the shoots of renewal could flourish.

5

THE CHILD WITHIN

So much of our inner life is a mystery. We react in ways that make no sense, and sometimes in ways that are self-destructive. People descend into rage spirals on Twitter, erupt in righteous indignation in the comments section of an online news story, or fly into fits of apoplectic fury in an airport queue when a flight is delayed. They have the same fight with their family year after year, sabotage their own happiness, and fall into dysfunctional relationships that always produce the same results. Ask why they do it, and most people will draw a blank.

Throughout my life, I've found myself repeating the same impulsive behaviour in different situations. I often experience feelings of abandonment, isolation, and anger that are completely disproportionate to the situations that trigger them. The feelings come with a bewildering sense of being out of control, as if I'm being driven by unseen forces. It was only when my life collapsed around me that I began to understand what lay beneath.

I wanted answers immediately. Why was I falling apart when I had everything I'd ever wanted? Veronica had asked me to be patient. The only way to make my present more bearable was to look at the past. We would have to examine the unconscious drivers of my anxiety, and trace it all the way back to my early childhood. She told me that the way we learn to interact with the world is determined very early in life. The critical stage is in those first few years, before we have the verbal skills to communicate how we're feeling or the cognitive sophistication to rationally interpret how others behave towards us. Ninety per cent of the brain's development occurs before the age of five. It's during this time that we learn, on an unconscious level, our place in the world. Science has shown that our relationship with parents or caregivers in those first three years is pivotal to future emotional resilience. We pick up on their moods, their mannerisms, the way they view life. If their outlook is perpetually negative, it teaches a child to be overly vigilant because nowhere is safe. They learn from their caregiver's reactions which behaviours are rewarded and which are not. A child of a parent who is excessively cheerful, even in the face of significant hardship, might learn that it's not okay to show vulnerability. Poet Philip Larkin captured it perfectly in his poem 'This be the verse', which bluntly notes that your mum and dad fuck you up whether they mean to or not.

The messages we pick up on from an early age — behaviours our parents have learned through the lessons they inherited from their own parents — play a significant role in establishing our sense of safety and stability. Veronica explained that as very young children, when we're so vulnerable, in order for us to feel safe we need to believe there are capable strong adults around us who can 'fix' things when they go wrong. It's a survival instinct to want our parents to be invincible. When they turn out to be fallible and the child's emotional needs aren't met, it can cause major changes in the highly malleable young brain. Unhealthy patterns of behaviour begin to form, and those maladaptive neural pathways — the hikers' tracks through the forest — become deeper with reinforcement. By the time we're adults, the behaviour has been repeated so often we're not even conscious of the ways in which we habitually react. A neglected child who craved his mother's love may find himself as an adult in dysfunctional relationships with distant partners as his subconscious drives the need to be accepted. A child with an overbearing father who demanded academic perfection could grow up to be a workaholic, never finding enough success to reach fulfilment. Trauma, abuse, and neglect can have such a profound effect on the brain's wiring that people are often left with emotional scars that can derail their entire adult lives.

I grew up in Scotland in a home with parents who loved me and never held back on letting me know. They were supportive and generous in every way that mattered. They weren't wealthy but were financially comfortable, and, although they divorced after 38 years of marriage, when I was in my early thirties, their relationship throughout my childhood was strong and happy. I rarely heard them argue. Compared to some of my classmates, who struggled with family break-ups and worse, I felt lucky. My older brother Neil and I were raised in a stable home with a lot of love. And yet, I've been at war with my own brain since I was a kid.

Growing up, calamitous thoughts twisted in my head like shapes shifting inside a kaleidoscope. I had no idea what to do with them. So I talked. It was rare for me to have a thought I didn't verbalise. My endless chuntering earned me the nickname 'Grundig', after the German electronics company. Dad said I was like a television set with no off-button.

From an early age I worried about death. At some point, I determined it was down to me to keep my loved ones safe from calamity. I formed a habit of placing bets in my mind.

Running along the footpath and telling myself that if I didn't reach the nearest lamppost by the time the next car passed, my whole family would die. Counting steps as I climbed stairs, and if I landed on 13 I'd have to double back to make sure I ended on a safer number. When Mum went out for the night with friends, I'd stand by the window in my darkened bedroom for hours, waiting for her taxi to pull up and provide proof of life.

By the time I reached high school, the worrying had developed into something far more debilitating. At 16 I was diagnosed with depression, and by 18 I'd developed an anxiety disorder that made me long for the halcyon days of depression's numbness. Anxiety was a raging beast that never slept. My brain was so full it felt as if my skull would crack right open. Lying in bed one night, I felt a crushing tightness in my head. My heart pushed against my chest so hard I thought I'd break a rib. I was gripped by an overwhelming need to flee. I ran to the bathroom, threw open the door, and cowered in the corner, howling like a wounded animal. My mind had detached itself from the rest of my being, like a trailer unhooked from the back of a car and hurtling down a steep hill. It was my first panic attack, but I did not yet know it. I was sure I was dying.

My parents woke to my screaming. My memories of those hours are fuzzy. It would be two decades before Mum told me that when she found me I was banging my head against the bathroom wall, a tortured look on my face as I repeated the same four words: 'I want to die. I want to die. I want to die.' They called a doctor. He stuck a needle in me and I slept until lunchtime the next day.

In the weeks that followed, the anxiety became so bad I struggled to leave the house without having panic attacks. After a few months, I dropped out of university. It took nearly a year to find my way back to a world that I could recognise.

When I began seeing Veronica, I had no clue where my anxiety came from. If my family was loving and my childhood passed without major trauma, why had I turned out this way? And why had my brother—whose emotional constitution is so different to mine I often wonder if I was swapped at the hospital with another family's baby—not struggled with the same issues? Perhaps I was just pre-wired to be a worrier in a way that Neil was not.

We don't have to have experienced abuse to develop problems, Veronica said. It is part of the human condition that we all fall somewhere on the continuum of 'trauma'. The neuroses, addictions, relationship problems, and dysfunctional behaviours we struggle with as grown-ups almost always have their roots in childhood. 'In 20 years of practice, I haven't seen a client yet whose current-day issue is just about the present,' Veronica told me. 'Those first three years of life are critical.'

As I went through therapy, I retraced my family history during long Skype calls with my parents, and they filled in the gaps of stories I'd only known in fragments. It became apparent there had been a lot of pressures in our home when I was a young child. When Mum was pregnant with me, Dad became very ill. He was working as an accountant in a building firm and writing a book—the centenary history of the rugby club attached to his Edinburgh school. As the deadline approached, he grew increasingly stressed, working around the clock to get it finished. The night after the launch—attended by assorted Edinburgh dignitaries including former British prime minister Sir Alec Douglas-Home—things began to crumble. He suffered a complete nervous breakdown. For a time, he told me, he didn't know 'if it was night or day'.

He was granted extended sick leave and Mum took him and my two-year-old brother to stay with family friends in a picturesque village in Aberdeenshire, where the man my father called uncle had retired. Worn out and heavily medicated, Dad spent a lot of time in bed, only waking to be fed. It would be three months before he was back at work. He was offered no counselling. 'It wasn't the done thing back then. You just got on with it,' he told me. Almost 40 years later, Dad's eyes filled with tears as he recalled how hard those days were, emotions he hadn't allowed himself to feel suddenly brought to the surface by the proximity of my pain. I touched my hand to his face through the screen of my iPad and cursed the tyranny of distance. 'Funny that both our problems have been caused by writing books,' he said with a wry smile. I nodded and thought, *funny that your happy-ever-after turned out to be just as much of a mirage as mine was.*

During Mum's pregnancy, Dad became fixated on his unborn child. He was terrified I wouldn't survive the delivery, or would come into the world with a serious disability. Neil's birth had been traumatic: during labour, the umbilical cord became wrapped around his neck and they nearly lost him. Every one of the 15 days past my due date was torture for Dad.

I was born in March 1976 without complication, in a labour that was so quick Dad was still in the hospital lift when I shot into the world 'like a cork out of a bottle'. The years that followed were challenging for the whole family. Mum was trying to care for a recovering husband, a newborn, and my nearly three-year-old brother. Dad had returned to work and accepted a promotion, but his stress levels remained high. Our home in a recently built housing estate in Edinburgh's south-west was, he said, a 'hellhole'. It was like 'living in a goldfish bowl'. He felt that everybody knew their business. As his sense of suffocation grew, he became agitated and desperate to move. 'Those days were really rough,' Dad remembered, telling me that the stress of having a young family and buying a new home but not being able to sell the one they were in took its toll.

Finally, when I was six months old, they found a buyer and we moved to the southern outskirts of the city into a beautiful, double-storey Victorian terrace home that I would live in for the next 20 years. Those first few years were marked by extended periods of illness for my brother. I knew that Neil had been unwell but I hadn't realised he'd been sick practically from birth. When Mum recalled the times he spent entire days projectile vomiting, I suddenly flashed back to one of my earliest memories: handing her sheets and pillowcases as she moved my brother, limp and grey, from one bed to another. I must have been around three years old.

By the age of six, Neil had developed an acute pain in his lower back, caused by a kink in his urethral track. Waste was travelling back up into the kidney, which had lost almost all function. He needed surgery. There was a possibility he might require a transplant. Poor little guy spent his seventh birthday in hospital recovering from an operation that saved his life. Neil was in isolation and I wasn't allowed to visit—after such a complex procedure, the risk of infection from a germ-prone four-year-old was too high. Granny, my dad's mother, came to stay as Mum spent days and nights at the hospital.

The following year, Mum fell ill. Things became serious very quickly. I remember the paramedics wheeling her out of the house on a stretcher one night and thinking *where are these men taking her?* By some twisted quirk of fate, her kidneys were failing. An acute infection had taken hold and she was desperately ill. Granny moved in again as Dad stayed by Mum's bedside. The doctors told him at one point it was 'touch and go' whether she would make it.

My parents did a good job of shielding us from the worst of the situation because this was the first I'd heard of its seriousness. I had no idea how close we'd come to losing her.

Mum recovered and things settled down until the next year, 1982, when Neil fell ill again, this time with suspected meningitis. Again, he was fighting for his life in hospital. 'As you can see, we had a pretty awful few years,' Mum said, after recounting a history I'd only known in snippets.

In my sessions with Veronica, I hesitantly relayed this information. In some ways, it felt like a betrayal. I didn't want anyone to shoulder blame for the trouble I was having, least of all the people who had shown me nothing but love my entire life. And given it was Neil who had suffered all the health problems, shouldn't he be the one who ended up mad? Veronica stressed that it was not a matter of blame. Through the eyes of a young child whose family were distracted by crisis, those early years would have been a confusing, chaotic time. That sense of safety, so critical for an infant, would have been threatened. 'This is not about your parents not loving you,' she said. 'In those first few years of life, when children are pre-cognition and pre-verbal, they interpret what's going on by absorbing feelings. As an adult you can look back and see that your parents were doing the best they could and they were just preoccupied with the other stresses and demands on the family. But as a child what you would have experienced is a feeling of *there's no-one really here for me, nobody is connecting with me in the emotional manner that I need.*'

It was psychiatrist John Bowlby who made the most compelling link between parental–child bonding and emotional development with his 1950s work on attachment theory. During his time at the Child Guidance Clinic in London, where he treated emotionally disturbed children, Bowlby posited that this bonding process was critical to human development, and in an evolutionary context could be linked to continuation of the species. Attachment provides safety for the child, enhancing their chances of survival. It's why children instinctively crave their parents' love. Separation can trigger intense distress. Through a series of studies, he found that children who were neglected or whose mothers were absent for long periods of time in the first two years of life were more likely to have emotional problems. He theorised that infants have an innate need to bond with a caregiver, usually the mother, and when this doesn't happen it can lead to all sorts of problems, including depression, anxiety, aggression, and delinquency.

A seminal study in 1959 conducted by researchers Harry Harlow and Robert Zimmerman further boosted the case for attachment theory in an experiment that involved separating monkeys from their mothers. The monkeys were put in cages with two types of surrogate 'mother'. One was made from wire and was attached to a bottle filled with milk, while the other was covered in towelling cloth and had no bottle. The experiment found that the infant monkeys chose to cling to the cloth mother over the wire mother, despite the absence of food. The feel of the cloth on their skin, their need to be close to their mother, was more powerful than their desire to eat. Until that point, the prevailing wisdom was that a child's physical needs of food and water were the most critical to development. This research suggested that strong emotional bonds were at least as important.

In the late 1970s, this link was further strengthened with the now famous 'still face' experiments, first carried out by Ed Tronick, a professor of psychology at the University of Massachusetts in Boston, who investigated the effects of a mother's depression or stress on the emotional development of infants. He showed that babies connect with their mothers and caregivers through verbal cues and facial expressions, and as little as two or three minutes of expressionless contact can have a profound impact.

Watching the videos is an upsetting experience. You see a mother playing with her one-year-old daughter, wide-eyed and cooing as she uses her face and hands to convey emotion, clapping and pointing as the baby mirrors her responses. Then she turns her head, and when she looks back at the child, her face is completely blank. She does not move or communicate. At first, the child tries to recapture the mother's attention, smiling and pointing and repeating the games. But the mother remains blank-faced. Soon, the baby becomes agitated. She holds both hands up as if to say *what's going on here?* Then the infant begins to screech — a high-pitched call of confusion and distress as she holds her hands over her face and cries. Tronick observed that what was significant about the experiments was the child would repeatedly try to get the mother's attention back before eventually giving up, becoming sad and withdrawn.

When the child feels as though they're not getting that bonding experience — through a caregiver's abuse, neglect, absence, or distraction — it can shatter their sense of safety. The ancient part of the brain that's programmed to need that attention sends a signal of danger. On an unconscious level, the child feels they might perish. A study conducted during World War II comparing infants raised by their mothers in prison to children who were reared in an orphanage, where there was one nurse looking after seven children, found that the orphans suffered significant developmental problems. They grew unresponsive, rocking back and forth, emotionally dead to the world. The need for connection is so strong that without it, children can wither. Even when a caregiver is physically available to the child, if they are not fully present emotionally, it can lead to problems with attachment.

Without the cognitive functionality to understand that a mother or father is not attentive because they're tending to a sick child or juggling the demands of a busy job with raising a family, the child interprets a parent's distraction as a lack of care. Unconsciously, they believe that they have done something wrong—they have caused the chaos that is seeing their emotional needs go unmet. They internalise the confusion and, on a subconscious level, start to believe that if they weren't so 'bad', they would be lavished with the love and attention they crave. That unconscious belief can drive their behaviour throughout their life and impact on their emotional health and relationships. It's no coincidence, Veronica said, that the word I used to describe myself in our first session was 'defective'. It's also no coincidence that I've had attachment issues in many of my relationships and friendships. The need to cling to people for fear that they might leave has been a challenge not just for me but also for the ones I love. There has never been enough love to make me feel whole. Grasping for happiness through the affections of those closest to me only left me more distressed the tighter I gripped.

The tentacles of this intense need curl deep into my past and have shaped my life in many ways. On an unconscious level, my work as a journalist and a writer had become so tied up in my identity—a way to be seen and to get that love and approval—that when my book came out and it still wasn't enough, things inevitably fell apart. My sense of self was entirely focused on the external.

That acute sense of abandonment, of not being acknowledged, that comes at me in a split second and can erupt in panic or fury in the most inopportune places suddenly made more sense. When I've snapped at friends for talking over me in conversations or had stand-up fights with editors for spiking my copy or not listening to me in meetings, I've often felt that the emotion was coming from a place far beyond the present moment. It's an unspoken sense of neglect, of being ignored. As Veronica said, when the reaction is emotionally disproportionate to the situation, there is almost always a deeper issue at play.

I thought back to a moment as a teenager when I discovered, packed away in a hallway cupboard, two baby books. On the outside they looked identical, but when I opened them and saw that Neil's was filled with all his infant milestones—first steps, first words, favourite toy, birth weight and length—and mine was blank, I was bereft. A panicked grief churned in my stomach as I asked Mum why I didn't matter. 'Jilly, you have to understand how difficult it was back then,' she told me. 'I had a sick toddler and a new baby. I barely had a moment to myself. When Neil was born, it was just him. I had time to think.'

It made sense. But as Veronica explained, to an under-developed brain, there is no capacity for this logical reasoning. 'As a child, you couldn't acknowledge to yourself that Mum and Dad were not perfect because it was too much to handle emotionally, so in your subconscious you were the "defective" one, and that's why you didn't get the love you needed.' She stressed that she used the words 'defective' and 'love' in inverted commas. My parents' feelings for me were not in question. It was faulty wiring caused by misinterpreted messages. And if it could be learned, it could be unlearned.

Bringing to consciousness our unconscious emotional drivers is the challenge we all must conquer, Veronica said. And it was the key to understanding the true meaning of happiness and getting on top of the anxiety that had plagued me my entire life. Tapping into that confused and scared child part of me that felt unseen and unloved was the work we now had ahead of us. Reassuring her that she was not defective would be the cornerstone of therapy.

If you'd told me a few years ago that the way out of the unrelenting mental torment I was experiencing would be to make friends with my inner child, I would have told you to fuck right off with your woo-woo hippy bullshit and go seek immediate medical help. What Veronica was proposing felt ethereal. It was intangible at a time when I wanted to touch and feel the answer with my bare hands. I was still waiting for the magic bullet. This deep-dive approach was not part of the happy-ever-after narrative. And yet, as I began to do the work, I couldn't argue with the very real gains I began to make.

In those first few months off work, when I was desperately unwell, the twice-weekly visits to Veronica kept my head above water but left me physically and emotionally exhausted. My body was fatigued from the force of the anxiety coursing through me. The sensations were so debilitating that I was barely hanging on. In between sessions, Veronica would have me journal as an extension of our therapy. In those pages, so much was revealed. I could see how childhood attachment issues drove my distress and dysfunctional behaviour — both in my past and in my present. Recognising the patterns was one thing; having the skills and courage to change was an entirely different challenge. I worried that perhaps it just wasn't possible to turn around nearly four decades of problematic thought patterns.

Yet science held comforting answers. The centuries-old belief that the brain's patterns are fixed and can't be changed has been turned on its head in the past decade with the discovery of neuroplasticity — arguably one of medical history's greatest neuroscientific breakthroughs — which proves that the brain is plastic and can be rewired through the repetition of brain exercises. At the forefront of this movement is Canadian psychiatrist and researcher Dr Norman Doidge, whose international bestseller *The Brain That Changes Itself* tells the remarkable stories of people afflicted who had been written off as beyond help, only to transform their lives by changing their brain anatomy through mind-training exercises. The book is an extraordinary account of patients recovering from traumatic brain injuries, cerebral palsy, stroke, entrenched depression, anxiety, chronic pain, and learning disorders by harnessing the powers of their own brains.

While I was doubting that things could ever get better, Doidge's chapter on the mental-health applications of neuroplasticity provided me with compelling evidence that perhaps the work I was doing with Veronica was on the right track. In his chapter 'Turning Our Ghosts into Ancestors', he describes how 'talking cures' such as psychoanalysis were once dismissed as not being serious enough to tackle psychiatric conditions and acute emotional distress. Conventional science leant towards medical intervention and pharmaceutical drugs to address problems that had been thought to be largely due to genetics. But with the advent of neuroplasticity, it has become clear that early childhood experiences can greatly impact on the developing brain and cement dysfunctional beliefs and patterns of behaviour. Through psychoanalysis those early experiences can be brought to consciousness, acknowledged, and understood, honouring what the child experienced so that the process of rewiring the brain's neural pathways can begin.

Doidge describes how in the first three years of life, the left hemisphere of the child's brain — responsible for speech and conscious processing — has not yet experienced a growth spurt, and the right side of the brain dominates. This means that infants learn to understand emotions and receive reassurance through things like their mother's or caregiver's facial expressions, singing, and gestures. These non-verbal interactions between child and parent are essential to healthy emotional development. As Doidge points out: 'For children to know and regulate their emotions, and be socially connected, they need to experience this kind of interaction many hundreds of times in the critical period and then to have it reinforced later in life.'

When there are deficits in these interactions, it can lead to emotional problems. Just as was demonstrated in the still-face experiments, you don't necessarily have to have had major trauma or conscious memories of feeling deprived to run into cognitive difficulties. Indeed, Doidge maintains that it's likely there will be few memories from those first three years of life, but the child's pain will often be triggered seemingly 'out of the blue' when those individuals find themselves in situations that evoke similar feelings. These unresolved childhood issues go some way to explaining why people who seemingly 'have it all' never quite reach the happy-ever-after we're told that success will bring. Or why we can have explosive reactions to seemingly innocuous comments or events. Through psychoanalysis, these early emotions can be brought to consciousness and then the process of training the brain to react differently can begin.

Doidge cites the case of a man he treated, Mr L, who had been suffering from recurring depression for more than 40 years. When he was two, Mr L's mother died giving birth to his younger sister. A year later, his father fell ill and was too sick to look after the family, so at the age of four, Mr L and his seven siblings were sent to live with an aunt and uncle a thousand miles away from the farm where they grew up. It was during the Great Depression, and emotions were not discussed: there was no outlet for this little boy to talk about his grief. Mr L said he had never cried or felt any sadness for what happened to him, even as an adult. But he battled alcohol abuse and struggled in relationships, never able to commit and often cheating on the women he dated. Doidge describes how Mr L had learned to 'auto-regulate' by turning off his emotions, making it difficult for him to form intimate attachments. Through a long process of therapy, Mr L was able to get in touch with his sense of loss and separation from his mother and see how it was affecting almost every aspect of his adult life. He realised in an epiphany—which was the breakthrough for his depression—that whenever he met a woman, his first thought was that there was a better match somewhere out there. He was searching for his 'ideal' woman. Each time he cheated, it was just after he had become close to his partner. 'I just realized that that other woman seems to be some vague sense of my mother that I had as a child and it is she that I must be faithful to, but whom I never find. The woman I am with becomes my adoptive mother, and loving her is betraying my real mother,' Mr L told Doidge in therapy.

By bringing these unconscious associations into the light, Mr L was able to acknowledge his deep sense of loss for his mother and start working on changing the neural pathways that were driving his behaviour and fuelling his depression. He didn't see improvement immediately, but through hard work and repetition he was able to better regulate his emotions, understand his past and how it related to his present, and move from being a helpless child to an autonomous adult.

'Psychoanalysis is often about turning our ghosts into ancestors, even for patients who have not lost loved ones to death,' Doidge explained. 'We are often haunted by important relationships from the past that influence us unconsciously in the present. As we work them through, they go from haunting us to becoming simply part of our history.'

If a man now in his seventies could rewire his brain more than 60 years after the events that shaped its development, I was hopeful that I too could see change. It was therefore a serendipitous turn of events when Doidge's sequel, *The Brain's Way of Healing*, was released in early 2015, and I was invited to be Jon Faine's co-presenter on 'The Conversation Hour' on 774 ABC Melbourne to interview him about his findings. What I didn't tell Doidge, Faine, or the listening audience at home was that I had only been back at work a few weeks after nearly five months off with anxiety and depression, that I'd had a full-blown panic-stricken meltdown the night before this interview, and that my interest in Doidge's work extended well beyond journalistic enquiry.

In the studio, my chair turned towards his, I tried not to seem too eager during the hour-long conversation. But when I listen back now, I can hear in my voice how desperate I was to be reassured of my ability to exact permanent change in habits that had stretched over a lifetime. I brought up how in the book Doidge describes people with chronic pain, and what he calls the 'relentless' work they have to do to change the neural pathways in the brain, visualising the pain changing at countless times throughout the day, day after day.

'Do you believe that everyone has that capacity to change?' I asked him. 'Do some people have more of a capacity to change the brain's pathways than others?' Jason, listening in, later told me that when I asked that question he knew I was doubting myself. He had seen me break myself into pieces second-guessing my ability to change. Just the day before he'd listened to me sobbing down the phone as I catastrophised about my ability to even turn up for this interview. He knew it was not a question for the listeners at home so much as for my own reassurance.

Doidge's answer wasn't as definitive as I would have liked, but it offered hope. He said it wasn't yet clear if some people's brains were more adaptable than others, but you could put your brain into a more receptive state through regular physical exercise, which triggers neurotrophic growth factors, making it easier to consolidate neuroplastic change. I had been exercising religiously every day as part of my therapy, so this was comforting to hear.

What he was clear about was that advances in neuroplasticity would continue to revolutionise our lives and that the mind was being reintroduced to its 'rightful place' in medicine. He said that at the beginning of modern science a number of 'big mistakes' were made by treating consciousness and the mind as suspicious, 'something that wasn't real, ethereal', and focusing instead on the physical reality in the body. 'We are embodied minds, we have minds wherever we go. The idea of not using them is ridiculous,' he said. 'But because we didn't have ways of showing, for instance, brain change, because we didn't have certain kinds of scans, people just were suspect. Now, we can show them the brain changing through meditation and all these mental things I'm talking about, so suddenly mind is back in the game.'

Sitting in that studio with Doidge, an eminent scientist talking about the intersection between mind, body, and spirit, was comforting. With his neat beard, smart suit, and extensive back catalogue of peer-reviewed research, he was as far from a purveyor of woo-woo hippy bullshit as it was possible to be. It was the reassurance I needed that the pain I felt was real, and that there was the possibility it could be alleviated. For the scared little girl who felt she was beyond help, it was proof that she wasn't.

6

YOU CAN'T SIT WITH US

Some days I'm right back there. Legs pressed up against a cold cast-iron radiator. Her face flushed with fury, bearing down on me, snarling. I can smell her warm stale breath: 'Fucking slag.' She's pointing a finger in my face, stabbing at the air, her nail millimetres from my eyes. The other hand is bunched in a fist by her side. Her features are a contorted mask of anger and resentment. If I'm lucky I'll get away without a shove or a slap or a kick to the ankles.

She is by far the worst. But there are others. The girls hunt in packs. Every day they remind me how shit I am. I'm a bitch and a tart and a slut—which is ironic, given I'm terrified of boys and have not yet had my first kiss. The uniform Mum and Dad make me wear at a school where it's not compulsory means I'm also considered a snob and a swot. In my shirt, tie, and pencil skirt, I feel as if I'm being sent to school with a bomb strapped to my chest.

When finally my parents concede to my begging and let me wear casual clothes, things don't improve. My fashion choices are the source of endless ridicule. One day I have to go home and change at lunchtime because the taunts about my white skirt ('She looks like she's wearing a bandage') are unbearable. Nothing escapes their attention. They dissect the style of my hair and the way I speak ('posh bitch'), and spend an inordinate amount of time critiquing the size and shape of my breasts ('You're so flat the walls are jealous').

My house is a two-minute walk from the school gates—a disastrous parental property-purchasing decision that means every delinquent in the area knows where I live. On home economics days, getting out of class as quickly as possible is my goal. But sometimes I'm just not fast enough. The cheesecake they made that afternoon is gleefully hurled at me from multiple angles. It's in my hair and on my cheek and stuck to my back. The last of it lands with a wet splat on the brass knocker of our front door as I slam it shut behind me and collapse on the entrance porch tiles.

This was high school. It started in my second year (Grade Eight) and went on, to varying degrees, for three years. I learned to walk with my eyes fixed on the footpath. Over time I grew quiet and began to hunch my shoulders, trying to make myself smaller. There were times when I wondered if it would be easier if I didn't exist. By the end of those three years, I felt as if I'd evaporated. I'd come home and cry until I couldn't catch my breath. 'That's it!' Mum would say, her face awash with panic. 'We're moving you. This can't go on.' And I'd beg her not to make me do that. What if I moved to a new school and they hated me even more?

Ours was a tough school in a predominantly disadvantaged area. Academically, we were continuously towards the bottom of the Edinburgh City Schools Exam League Table. Few students went on to university. I lived in a big house in a good street and was top of our year in English; none of this helped me. But the resentment seemed deeper than that.

In science class, the girl whose stocky frame and indiscriminate rage had earned her a reputation as the toughest in school pulled me aside to ask a question. She handed me a copy of *Just Seventeen* magazine, opened at the agony aunt page. Smirking, she asked, 'Did you write this?' It was a question from a 13-year-old Edinburgh schoolgirl called Jill who loved the Scottish rock group Deacon Blue (I often wore the band's t-shirt to PE class) and was worried about being flat-chested, having no period, and what to do about the dark hair growing on her top lip. Across the room, the gang of girls erupted into laughter as my face registered what had happened. They had written to a national magazine. Actually sat down, handwritten a letter, bought a stamp and an envelope, and mailed it to London. For a bunch of girls who didn't give a fuck about anything and struggled to make it to school three days out of five, the effort they had put into my humiliation was staggering. It was as if on a cellular level they could sense that there was something not quite right. The way animals sense things they can't express. They just knew I was bad. They saw right through to my core. And my core was rotten.

The girls worked hard on my isolation. There were days when I'd come to school and find the small group of friends I'd managed to hold on to were no longer talking to me. They'd walk past me in the corridor, staring straight ahead like an army of teenage cyborgs, as I pleaded with them to tell me what I'd done wrong. They didn't answer. And so, in some ways, I got my wish: I ceased to exist. Later, I'd discover that my crime had been to give someone a 'dirty look' or say something 'bitchy' behind one of the bullies' backs. For my friends, choosing sides between me and the girls who ran the school was a no-brainer.

I'd eventually be allowed back inside the sanctuary of the group if I promised to repent my misdeeds. And even though I knew I hadn't done the things I stood accused of, I would do it because the isolation was suffocating. Each time felt like a death. The part of me that knew I was being tried for crimes I hadn't perpetrated grew smaller. Regina had turned You're Shit FM up so loud I couldn't hear anything else.

Still, there was a part of me that wanted to fight back. A small voice whispering, 'This is bullshit.' One day the whisper became a roar.

It was morning break and I was standing with friends at Door A—a sheltered entrance where we spent most of our free time between classes. They walked past the door—a sashay of shell suits and menace—and doubled back when they saw me. She was at the front, her dirty blonde hair pulled up so high on her head her eyes seemed to squint with the tension. My heart thumped faster. She was a big girl, tall and long-legged. She strode towards me and yelled into my face, 'I smell a tart,' which at the time was terrifying but in hindsight is somewhat comical. If only I could rewind time and ask her if she could be more specific. What flavour was it? Blueberry? Apple and cinnamon?

I looked at my feet. She repeated, 'I smell a tart,' adding a loud sniff for theatrical embellishment. The blood roared in my ears like ocean swell in a thunderstorm. I fought back tears. *Not this time.* Slowly, I drew my gaze up to meet hers. I did not blink. Then I saw it flicker across her face. A tiny flash of something I recognised so intimately: fear. She kept talking, 'Ya fucking tart ...' but I could see she was rattled. I just stared back, the faintest of smiles on my lips. I was at once petrified and invincible. Time stopped. But eventually she flinched,

71

dropping her eyes. And with a nod to her cronies she was off, pausing only to offer a defiant 'Smell ya later, slag' as she threw open the glass door with a bang.

After that, things were slightly better. The bear pit is not as much fun when the bear refuses to dance. When my tormenters turned 16 and left school, I was liberated. My friendships grew stronger. But the scars remained, even if I was reluctant to examine them. For years, I put them in the 'shit happens' basket and said to myself that the past is the past.

I told an ex-boyfriend some years ago of my experiences at high school and he said that I needed to toughen up. Lots of people were bullied. It wasn't like I'd suffered 'genuine trauma'. He was only saying out loud what I'd silently thought for a long time. I was ashamed that I could be so weak when others had faced far worse. But it didn't take much to transport me back there. I could be in a room full of strangers at a party and feel their eyes on me as if I was still wearing that pencil skirt and school tie. It was a conscious effort to remind myself that the gruff colleague who snapped at me was not reacting to my innate crapness but was simply hungover and grumpy. Even with my closest friends I could be doubtful. I worried that it was only a matter of time before they discovered I wasn't worth their energy. Sometimes, when there was a delayed reply to a message, that suffocating feeling gripped me from nowhere. Was it happening again?

The need for approval is incredibly powerful. It stretches all the way back to our ancient ancestors, when fitting in was literally the difference between life and death. If you were part of a tribe, you had food, shelter, and increased protection from human-eating predators. Being cast out meant a lonely scramble for survival in the wilderness.

We are hardwired to crave belonging. When American psychologist Abraham Maslow came up with his famous hierarchy of needs in a 1943 research paper, he put forward the theory that human behaviour is driven by five basic needs. Only once each tier of need is met are we able to move on to the next one. At the bottom of the pyramid are the physiological requirements we need to survive — food, water, warmth, and sleep. The second tier is safety. In the Western world, where having those first two groups of needs met is something so many of us take for granted, chasing the third tier on the pyramid becomes paramount. That is the need for belonging: love, friendship, acceptance, intimacy, affection — being part of something bigger than ourselves. According to Maslow, belonging is one of the most significant, primal requirements for humans to thrive. Perhaps it explains why so many of us chase the approval of friends we've outgrown or stay in jobs that bore us and relationships that slowly suffocate our spirit. We see it in the crushing fear of looking foolish at a party or being judged for dining alone. It probably accounts for the need to be constantly connected on social media and why FOMO (fear of missing out) has become such a crippling experience for many people today.

Only recently has science turned its attention to the effect that being ostracised might have — not only on the individual's psyche but also on communities as a whole. The world's leading researcher on ostracism is Kip Williams, professor of psychological sciences at Purdue University in Indiana, who has been studying its effects for more than 20 years. He calls ostracism an 'invisible form of bullying' that doesn't leave bruises, and therefore its impact is underestimated. But his research has found that the pain of exclusion is often deeper and can last longer than a physical injury. He has shown that ostracism threatens four basic human needs: belonging, self-esteem, control, and the sense of a meaningful existence. Long-term exposure depletes a person's coping skills and increases the chances of alienation, depression, helplessness, and feelings of unworthiness. Just as I felt that I was evaporating in high school, ostracism over a long period of time is a form of 'social death', Williams says.

In therapy, Veronica pointed out that the bullying itself had likely not caused my anxiety, but it would have further strengthened the part of me that felt unworthy, which had developed in those first few years of life when my parents were distracted with their own crises. At home, my relationship with my brother grew fraught, as he distanced himself—as teenage boys often do—from his 'annoying' younger sister, tolerating my presence on a good day, ignoring me completely on a bad day. The crucible of high school only amplified my sense of self-doubt, and that vulnerability was sniffed out like a drop of blood in shark-infested waters. Bullies can sense desperation. In some ways they're unconsciously drawn to it. My core belief was that I was broken and bad, which only served to heighten my need for approval. The more I craved acceptance from my peers, the further it slipped from my grasp. This, Veronica said, partly explained why I had placed so much stock in the success of my book. The validation and love I had strived for my whole life was going to finally be mine when I reached this goal. But when I got there, on an unconscious level there was the realisation, *Fuck. I'm still me.* Nothing external could satiate that longing to be liked. The book wasn't enough because underneath it all I was not enough. And being excluded from my peer group at school only cemented what I already felt about myself.

Williams' research shows that when it comes to feeling ostracised, it makes no difference who is casting you out. The psychological hurt is just as painful when people are ostracised by those they like as it is when it comes from those they think are mindless douchebags. The impact is also unaffected by the individual's personality and can be felt even with minimal exposure. More than 5,000 people have taken part in Williams' computerised 'Cyberball' experiment, in which participants in a ball-toss game experience the 'grief of exclusion' when a cartoon figure ignores them for two to three minutes. It evokes strong feelings of sadness and anger. MRI scans on Cyberball players reveal that ostracism activates the same area of the brain that is triggered when experiencing physical pain, suggesting we're predisposed to react negatively to ostracism on a basic physiological level.

Nowhere is the effect of being excluded more devastatingly apparent than within the lesbian, gay, bisexual, transgender, intersex, and queer community. LGBTIQ people aged 16 to 27 are five times more likely to attempt suicide and twice as likely to be diagnosed with a mental-health disorder. The National LGBTI Health Alliance points out that these outcomes are directly related to the experiences of stigma, prejudice, discrimination, and abuse individuals endure just for being who they are. Some are shunned by their own families or isolated from their peers. Sadly, I've interviewed many young people who have been ostracised as a result of their sexuality or gender identity, including a 15-year-old boy who attempted suicide after bullies terrorised him for two years, beating him with a skateboard and telling him to 'kill yourself, faggot'. Exclusion can be a life-threatening experience.

In hindsight, I can see that my passionate support for social inclusion and gay rights throughout my journalistic career was, in part, an attempt to rewrite the wrongs of my past—an unconscious kinship with those who know only too well what it feels like to live outside the safety of the group.

And it's not only childhood bullying that causes pain. In adulthood, workplace isolation, harassment, or exclusion from family or community can have devastating long-term effects on the individual, leaving them feeling helpless and despairing. Williams' research shows that the response to exclusion is often to strive harder to conform at all costs in a misguided attempt to be re-included and restore those basic human needs of belonging and self-esteem. He found that people who are ostracised are more likely to comply with requests, obey orders, mimic those who are isolating them, and be attracted to views and behaviours they would otherwise find abhorrent.

At school, I realised that if I was ever going to be liked, all the things that made me who I was had to go. Being respectful to my teachers had seen me labelled 'posh' and 'up herself'. So I tried to be more like the girls who despised me. I swore and smoked cigarettes and graffitied toilet doors. My love of words made me a target so I stopped doing homework, refused to answer questions in class, and went to war with my English teacher. She was a silver-haired sparrow of a woman in a twinset and pearls, just trying to survive in a zoo. The approval I gained when I tormented her was addictive. In those fleeting moments of acceptance, I was transcendent. I'd mimic her nasal tones and mock her clothes, picking imaginary head lice out of her hair as I stood at her desk, watching her examine the lines she'd made me write as punishment for swearing. When I locked her out of the classroom and she hammered her tiny fists on the glass, close to tears, the whole class fell about laughing. Not long after, one of the boys pulled her Harris Tweed skirt over her head, her bloomers exposed to the world. Then one day she was gone. The rumour was she'd had a nervous breakdown.

I also picked on a girl in my year. Short and overweight, she had a high-pitched voice and an awkward, mumsy manner. In the high-school hierarchy I was one rung up the social ladder. So I used that power to show my tormentors that, like them, I was tough. I ridiculed her relentlessly. It bought me some kudos. And when they were laughing at her, they weren't targeting me.

I wish I could go back and do things differently.

Williams' research has shown that this cycle of bullying is common, and sometimes the response to ostracism can be extreme. If they've given up on re-inclusion, some people may try to restore the other basic human needs threatened by exclusion—control and a sense of a meaningful existence—by becoming aggressive. Having abandoned all hope of being liked, they may simply want to be noticed. This can lead to violence. Williams points to a 2003 analysis of school shootings that found that 13 of the 15 perpetrators of American mass school shootings had been ostracised.

But often, the anger is turned inwards. By the time I was 16, I had no energy left to fight. I'd always been a high achiever, but as my exams loomed, I was floundering. My worries turned into a despair that felt bottomless. I lost weight I could scarcely afford to shed and slept through the days. After a doctor prescribed antidepressants and told my parents I would be hospitalised if my mood didn't improve within a few weeks, I was referred to the outpatient wing of a youth mental-health facility where I would undergo one-on-one sessions with a psychologist and also take part in group therapy with other teens, to talk about our problems.

I hated the place from the start. It was a dilapidated, single-storey offshoot of Edinburgh's only public psychiatric hospital. Sterile and unwelcoming, it smelled like bleach and school dinners. When I sat in the outpatient waiting room, I flicked through copies of the music magazine *NME* and tried to pretend I was waiting to get a vaccination for an exotic holiday. But the illusion was always shattered by the yelling and swearing coming from the locked inpatient ward on the other side of an adjoining glass door. I saw young people shuffling up and down the corridor like ghosts. Sometimes there was banging and non-descript, muffled shouting. I heard a girl screaming—elongated, howling sobs that left me in no doubt I could not end up on the other side of that door.

At home, at least, I felt safe. And the bullies couldn't reach me. Looking back, I'm grateful that I had the opportunity for escape. I can't even imagine what it would be like to go through high school in an age of social media and smartphones.

The relative safety of being behind a screen has given bullies a platform to behave in ways they might never consider face to face. And with no physical borders, the abuse can be unrelenting. For young people, that means there is no safe haven. It's the virtual equivalent of that cheesecake being lobbed into my lounge room night after night after night. Cyberbullying has become an unfortunate rite of passage. A recent report from the Office of the eSafety Commissioner found that children as young as 10 are being targeted by online bullies, with girls particularly at risk. Name-calling, violent threats, and revenge porn are all on the rise, according to the report, as kids are given their first mobile phone at ever-earlier ages.

The digital revolution has given bullies 24/7 access to their victims, sometimes with tragic results. Jessica Cleland was 18 when she took her life in 2014, the day after being bombarded with nasty Facebook messages telling her she was hated by those she considered friends. Her parents found 87 messages sent by two boys the night before her death. Jessica had begged them to stop. The Victorian teenager had shown no signs of mental illness prior to the incident. When I hear these stories, it brings me right back to my high-school days and those feelings of desperation and the sharp pain that exclusion brings. The idea that I wouldn't even have been safe from bullies in my own bedroom is terrifying.

The technology has far outpaced the education system's ability to respond. But there are people trying to turn the tide. My friend Lucy Thomas is co-founder of Project Rockit, a youth-led program, which has for the last decade run workshops in schools to empower young people to stand up to cyberbullying and to help build empathy and resilience. Lucy created the program with her sister Rosie after thinking that someone should really do something about bullying, then realising she was that someone. She told me the pressure for young people to be curating their image is constant. 'In the online world, your social media identity is basically an extension of yourself. When we're consciously curating ourselves it can seems like there's no excuse when our content isn't on point, or when we make mistakes. And when we are impulsively hateful to someone else, there's little room for forgiveness even with the most kind and conscientious teens.'

Lucy believes the public nature of social media has 'democratised popularity', allowing any young person to find a tribe online, but she said schools are struggling to keep up with the knowledge students need to navigate the digital world. When students face online hate and bullying, teachers advise them to ignore or block their trolls. But it's not always that simple. Unlike adults, who are more likely to have the rational capability to understand that their worth is not measured by the opinions of people on the internet, for teens, the intense need for belonging that characterises adolescence makes the quest for popularity a powerful driver. 'We often hear that while young people have access to all of the tools and the functional ways to shut down online hate, they're still vulnerable to that classic teenage driver—wanting to know what people think about you,' Lucy said. 'It's kind of that toxic spiral into welcoming people to share their opinions of you when those people don't *always* have your best interests at heart.'

For many young people, the digital world is a social lifeline, a place to find the connection, solidarity, and support they might not have in the real world. Tuning out is not always an option, even if it means being exposed to abuse. In that vast and diverse online landscape, everyone—even the terrified kid who feels like a freak—has a chance to find their people. I often wonder what imaginative methods my bullies might have used to torture me had they been living in the age of the smartphone. But I also think about the solace I could have found online from other teenagers who felt, like me, that they were broken and unlovable. The digital age has revolutionised the notion of belonging in as many good ways as bad. But while the technology may have advanced, the issues for today's young people remain the same as when I was at high school: how to fit in, how to be loved, how to ask for help when you're vulnerable. Adolescence is a critical stage of our emotional lives, and to dismiss as trivial the ostracism that so many teens experience, whether that's online or face to face, is to deny the very real impact it can have on the way we thrive—or don't—as adults.

In my sessions with Veronica, it became apparent that the bullying I experienced during those formative teenage years had shattered my sense of belonging and reinforced my unconscious childhood belief that I was defective. A part of me was perennially roaming those high-school corridors searching for a way to fit in. I was desperate to find my tribe. But as I would later discover, true belonging is not something that can be hunted or held captive. It is so much more complicated than that.

7

THE FAIRYTALE FILTER

In November 2014, during those first few weeks off work when the anxiety was overwhelming, I decided to get out of Melbourne. If my brain would not give me peace, I could at least go to a place where the external environment was peaceful. My friend Brigitte invited me to her in-laws' holiday house in a coastal town on the Bellarine Peninsula, about 100 kilometres south-west of Melbourne, to hunker down for a few days.

I had met Brigitte while working as a barmaid at a Fitzroy pub almost ten years earlier. We became good friends and have seen each other through some tough times. More than most, she knows what it's like to battle problems the naked eye can't see. Twice a survivor of breast cancer, she also has the debilitating chronic condition fibromyalgia, which forced her to quit her job as a primary-school teacher. She remains one of the most resilient, positive people I know. There was nobody better equipped to keep me company in those early days.

At the holiday house, we watched trashy television in our pyjamas, ate chocolate, and lay in the sun. Each evening, Brigitte's husband Simon came home from work, offering life-giving bear hugs and home-cooked meals. I tried to stay present, but my mind was speeding into the future. I felt wretched. Those days in between sessions with Veronica always seemed to drag. I took long walks by the water and sat on the sand, breathing in the salt air, hoping that nature's calm would seep into my cells and bring me respite. But anxiety was an extra limb. There was no leaving it at the front door while I took a vacation. I thought back to all the overseas holidays I'd taken, many of which I'd embarked upon with the sole purpose of switching off. They had rarely induced any meaningful sense of slowing down. When your brain is pre-wired to panic mode, the gentle tropical breeze could be whispering your name and playing panpipe lullabies and you'd still struggle to relax.

One morning, as we lay on the beach watching the waves gently rolling, I asked Brigitte to take a picture. I sat cross-legged in my bikini, facing the ocean, hugging my knees close to my chest, my back to the camera. Afterwards, I surveyed the result on my phone, filtered the image, making the sky bluer and the sand warmer, before posting it on Instagram, captioned with the word *therapy* and the praying hands emoji. What a tranquil sight. What a supremely chilled-out being. What an absolute crock of shit. I was as far from calm as it was possible to be and yet to the outside world I was projecting a picture of serenity.

This elaborately curated theatre had become a habit. It felt as though there was barely a thought that entered my head that I wouldn't immediately share with the world. Any moment of silence, stillness, or delay led me straight to my phone. Grundig the chattering child finally had an outlet for her thoughts.

The more anxious I became, the more I scrolled. Over the years, I had learned to share everything. An early morning start at the gym: must tell Twitter. The sunset that left me breathless: Insta-perfect. Dancing in my kitchen to a favourite song from my youth: straight to Facebook with the hashtag #lovinglife. The 90-second wait at the pedestrian lights was too long to just stand, doing nothing, when there was a world of stuff happening right there in my hand. The advent of Snapchat and Instagram 'stories' only heightened my compulsion. I could add endless images and videos to the narrative of my day, giving the world a front-row seat to the movie reel of my life. Nothing went undocumented. I'd find myself on the tram live-tweeting an eavesdropped conversation between a bunch of hysterical schoolgirls and wonder what had happened to my life.

I struggle to remember life before social media. A time when achievements existed without online approval. When we took a moment to enjoy the feelings of success or joy for ourselves instead of automatically sharing them with the world. I can't remember exactly what the tipping point was for me. It may have been that first tweet from the toilets at work. Or the day I felt a phantom phone vibration in my hip pocket. But by the time I started waking up in the middle of the night feeling the overwhelming urge to reach across and check my notifications, I knew something had gone awry.

I often wonder whether we'd have a cure for cancer or have found life on Mars by now were it not for the inordinate hours collectively spent online wading through '25 Celebrities Who Look Like Mattresses' listicles or taking BuzzFeed quizzes to figure out which Harry Potter character we are. So much of it is banal and yet somehow hypnotically alluring. All too often when I'm scrolling, I get stuck in a loop of mindless crap. Once I've caught up with my social-media notifications, I'm just flailing around in the dregs, passively consuming random detritus. Suddenly it's 1.00 am and I'm sickly enthralled by graphic earwax removal videos on YouTube, glued to a clip of an excessively chipper otter feeding itself a bowl of almonds, or transfixed by *Keeping Up With the Kattarshians*—a live stream of four adorable kittens cavorting in an Icelandic dollhouse.

But it's not only the addictive nature of social media that piques my anxiety. If my life is out of balance, Facebook can tip me further over the edge. When things were really bad, it wasn't just my performance art that was problematic, it was other people's. Every time I logged on, it felt like a punch to the solar plexus. Everyone was successful and content. Everyone belonged. Everyone had their shit together. By comparison, I was a sad, lonely outcast, too mad to work and utterly incapable of finding a way to be happy like all those shiny people kicking goals and #lovinglife in their pleasing autumnal tones. I couldn't bear all the grinning couples, faces squished together as they snapped a selfie in eveningwear at some glamorous event for glamorous people. Or the tight-knit circles of friends, their abundance of love engulfing a sunset dining extravaganza on a beach next to impossibly blue waters. Then there's always the family snaps—chubby, giggling babies, and groups of handsome relatives in pressed linen and boat shoes, gathered together in homes straight out of a Laura Ashley catalogue. Nobody was yelling at their partner for leaving pubic hair in the shower. There was no sign of a melancholy cousin in trackpants eating cereal straight from the box in the corners of these pictures. People definitely weren't weeping at Qantas ads or rolling home drunk at 4.00 am and making their cat slow-dance to Adele songs. Babies did not vomit or shit or cry. Life was perfect.

I had lost the capacity to contextualise. I couldn't see that the image I was viewing was a split-second in time. I couldn't see the effort that had gone into the framing and the filters and the carefully drafted captions. I couldn't see the backstory, or the events that unfolded before or after the picture was posted. I only saw evidence of my own failings. Everyone else was happy. They all belonged. What the fuck was wrong with me?

Social media has become one of the most ubiquitous and enslaving aspects of modern life. There is not yet consensus in the mental-health field about the psychological or neurological impact it's having, particularly on young and developing brains. Some experts believe we saw the same 'moral panic' over the gramophone and with the advent of radio and television. But there is no denying that many of us have developed an unhelpful, at times compulsive, relationship with our online personas.

As my friend Lucy has witnessed first-hand, for today's teen the bewildering period of emotional and physical change that is adolescence comes with the added pressure of navigating a digital space that can be as much a source of heartache as a path to belonging. She told me: 'We've got these ever-changing apps that often put into people's hands the capacity to craft a very vapid, surface appearance of a person … Now each teen has a tool in their hands that can craft a highlight reel—it's the editing suite of our lives.'

In 2016, the Australian Psychological Society's annual national Stress and Wellbeing in Australia survey found that more than half of teenagers polled felt worried, jealous, and anxious when they looked at social media and found they had been left out of an event. Sixty per cent were concerned when they discovered their friends were having fun without them, and 51 per cent felt anxious if they didn't know what their friends were doing.

The link between Facebook-envy and depression is well established. It's not that the social networking site necessarily causes mental-health problems, but a number of studies have shown that for those already struggling, it can exacerbate distress. In 2015, a University of Houston paper published in the *Journal of Social and Clinical Psychology* found that Facebook users felt depressed when comparing themselves to others. The study's author, Mai-Ly Steers, said that controlling the impulse to compare was difficult: 'Most of our Facebook friends tend to post about the good things that occur in their lives, while leaving out the bad. If we're comparing ourselves to our friends' "highlight reels" this may lead us to think their lives are better than they actually are and conversely, make us feel worse about our own lives.' She went on to say that the longer people with emotional problems spend on Facebook, the more intense those depressive symptoms can become, compounding feelings of loneliness and isolation. The act of socially comparing oneself to others was related to 'long-term destructive emotions'.

Researchers from Berlin found a similar trend in a 2013 study that showed that the fact our Facebook friends tend to come from similar backgrounds to our own means the negative effects of social comparison are heightened. I guess it's not as depressing to measure yourself against a Hollywood movie star as against the girl you went to primary school with.

The advent of social media has bolstered the notion that happiness is life's ultimate goal by selling us the myth that everyone else is living their bliss. But as one of my best friends, Nonie — a wise and thoughtful woman who has been by my side through some of the bleakest moments — frequently reminds me, if you're going to be jealous of someone's life, you have to be jealous of all of it, not just their top-ten greatest hits. In calmer times, I know that the online highlight reel of people's lives is a stage-managed performance. I'm aware of this because

I've often posted the happy, successful moments and airbrushed out the tough times. During my 2013 trip home to Scotland to launch *High Sobriety*, I uploaded a picture to Instagram of me at the top of a hill on the outskirts of Edinburgh. In the photo I'm in running gear, doing a star jump, an open-mouthed look of delight on my face, against the backdrop of my beautiful home city. The caption read: *Ran up Blackford Hill with @ckraine this afternoon. I was quite excited by the view. #edinburgh.* @ckraine is my friend Chris Raine, the founder of Hello Sunday Morning, the not-for-profit organisation challenging Australia's drinking culture that inspired my year off the booze. He was visiting from Sydney and I'd been showing him the sights. What wasn't pictured in this #inspo moment was the hour-long whinge I'd been having at him for making me exercise and the tears that had come when I'd explained how horribly anxious I was feeling ahead of my launch. In reality, I'd run only the final minute of the trek up that hill, having dragged my feet and sulked for most of the way like a child trailing after a parent in the supermarket.

Sometimes it feels as though we've become characters in a *Truman Show*–style version of our own lives. We know that the storyline is fake, the words are scripted, and the whole set so flimsy it could collapse in a light breeze, and yet we play along for fear of busting the fairytale.

Some people are starting to challenge the performance. Since launching her Facebook page in 2015, Constance Hall, a 33-year-old mother of four from Perth, has gathered more than a million fans with her brutally honest, expletive-ridden takes on motherhood, body image, postnatal depression, child rearing, and the paralysing guilt burdening modern women. Her posts are funny, poignant, stripped-to-the-bone confessionals, in which she reveals the truth about everything from her stretchmarks and period cramps to her mental health and marital sex life. In one post, Hall writes:

> To the woman at the park looking at her phone and yelling at her children, I salute you for not giving in to the public perception that you should be switched on 24 hours a day. For giving no fucks what the 'mothers group' thinks. To the woman with piles of dishes and washing who walks straight out the door for coffee with friends, I salute you. Being a good mum or wife or human does not mean spending eternity cleaning your house.

Australian model Essena O'Neill captured the world's attention in 2015 when she quit social media and announced to her one million followers on Instagram, Snapchat, and YouTube that her virtual persona was 'NOT REAL LIFE'. The then 19-year-old exposed the lie of 'candid' social media pics, recaptioning her Instagram posts to tell the true story behind the images. Under one shot of her lazing on a beach in her bikini, she wrote: *Took over 100 similar poses trying to make my stomach look good. Would have hardly eaten that day. Would have yelled at my little sister to keep taking them until I was somewhat proud of this. Yep so totally #goals.* Next to a picture of her in a yoga pose near the ocean, she added: *There is nothing zen about trying to look zen, taking a photo of you trying to be zen and proving your [sic] zen on Instagram.* Ironically, O'Neill's attempts to expose the contrived nature of social media led to claims she was a 'huge fake' who had orchestrated a publicity stunt to garner more attention. I thought it was refreshing to see someone who had been sucked into the fairytale filter call it out as bullshit.

The push to be more real is also being led by people who have historically been made to feel they had no right to occupy public space. Tired of being marginalised and fat-shamed, women with fuller figures have taken to social media to challenge the view of what 'healthy' looks like. Size 22 model Tess Holliday is at the forefront of the body positive, or 'BoPo', movement, inspiring her 1.4 million followers with her #EffYourBeautyStandards mindset. It's a stark contrast to the washboard stomachs, trout pouts, and thigh gaps so prevalent on Instagram, which was recently named by the UK's Royal Society for Public Health as the worst social media platform for young people's mental health, largely due to its negative effect on body image.

I'm a grown woman and I often feel deflated by the impossible beauty standards I see online. I worry for my nieces, Orla, aged 10, and Daisy, 13, who have been swiping and clicking since they were tiny. I hope they know that what they're seeing online is all too often not real. And I hope they don't get to the point I reached, where the sheer speed and volume of digital bombardment leaves them too wired to calm themselves. How does a 10-year-old separate the real from the fake, particularly when the market is now set up to increasingly blur the line between the two? The app store is full of picture-editing apps that can transform your everyday snaps into glamour shots. One of the most popular, Facetune, promises to give you 'perfect skin' and can reshape your nose, whiten your teeth, remove blemishes and wrinkles, and even make you thinner. I downloaded it and was mesmerised. Within seconds, I was younger, brighter, and prettier. I could contour my cheeks, reshape my eyebrows, and add a smile to a frowning face. At first, I was enthralled. I looked amazing. But when I looked in the mirror, the lines, shadows, and furrows were still there. And yet, if I posted a Facetuned snap of myself online, would anyone know? Or would people just be mad with envy at how hot I looked? We live in an age where we're jealous of people who literally don't exist.

As Maslow observed with his hierarchy of needs, approval from our peers is a basic human requisite. For our ancestors, being accepted by the group meant there was less chance of being eaten or succumbing to starvation or hypothermia. In order for the group to thrive, the weakest members of the tribe were often expelled. Conformity was crucial. Fast-forward some 300,000 years, to an age of convenience food, climate-controlled homes, and limited risk of being devoured by big cats, and pack living is no longer a human necessity. Yet, being accepted remains a primal instinct built on the evolutionary will to survive. Consciously or not, it's what we all crave. In the digital era, our social-media following is our tribe.

In therapy with Veronica, I started to unpack this further. Social media had become a crutch for me as I struggled with that core belief of not being enough. Reaching for my phone was a reflex action. When my anxiety was peaking, the child part of my brain that craved love and acceptance was unconsciously substituting online approval for parental nurturing. Every like and comment on Facebook fed that need for validation. But the satisfaction was short-lived, so I kept scrolling, refreshing, checking, looking for more, and the anxiety only ramped up.

After my beach *therapy* post, I could no longer lie to the world or to myself. I wasn't fine. There was no filter that would change that. The least I could do for my overstimulated brain was to switch off the noise for a few weeks. I deleted Facebook, Instagram, Twitter, and Snapchat from my phone, and for a while things were calmer. I tried to find a connection to myself rather than seeking comfort from the outside world. After the initial FOMO, I settled into a daily pattern that wasn't governed by screens. No longer was I losing hours hooked into Twitter mentions or falling down the rabbit hole of a friend of a friend's Facebook comment thread. My head was no longer cast downwards during tram journeys. I wasn't tuning out in the middle of a conversation with someone over lunch because I couldn't stop thinking about the events I was missing in my pocket.

I quickly realised that when I reached for the phone I often did it because of an underlying feeling of discomfort. Invariably my compulsions to check arose when I struggled with a difficult emotion or found myself paddling around in a pool of self-doubt. Jumping on to Facebook or checking my Twitter mentions was not only a way to find approval, it was my go-to method of avoidance. When that method was not available, I had to fight the urge to revert to other bad habits. It occurred to me that my apartment is never cleaner than when I am on deadline. Hamish, my cat, is at his most entertained when I have editors breathing down my neck. Looking at my phone or checking in to social media was a convenient way to avoid feelings I didn't want to face. Mindlessly scrolling through the internet served the same purpose as drinking to excess. It was a numbing agent—a distraction. A way to fill a void.

My challenge, once I gained this knowledge, was to find new ways to plug the gap.

8

CAUGHT IN THE CLICKSTREAM

My first mobile phone was the size of a small shoebox. An exciting accessory that came with my job as a junior reporter at *The Daily Record* — Scotland's highest-selling national newspaper — it was heavy as a rubber dive brick and had a battery life of approximately 23 minutes. If I stood at just the right angle on my tiptoes in a corner of a room, I could make and receive calls. Every incarnation of mobile phone I got from that point was smaller than the one before, until one day I had a flip phone so tiny I could barely read the messages on its screen without a magnifying glass. With expensive, metered phone plans it became an art form to condense everything you had to say into 160 characters or less, for fear of being charged an extra 25 cents for a superfluous exclamation mark.

Getting an iPhone changed everything. This wasn't just a phone; it was a computer, a stereo, a television, an infinitely resourced guide to the universe. It has revolutionised my life in myriad ways — equipped me with a sense of direction I do not naturally possess, allowed me to set fitness goals and track my exercise, and offered a way to share pictures, videos, and conversations instantly with my family on the other side of the world.

At first, it felt like liberation. For someone who is, to put it generously, technologically challenged, this device was both easy to use and breathtakingly brilliant. I was so amazed by its potential it was as if I was holding a magic wand in my hand. Nowadays, it feels less like magic and more like a hostage situation.

We are connected 24/7 and there's no pushing back the tide. A 2016 Ernst & Young report found that more than 80 per cent of Australians own a smartphone. Among 18- to 34-year-olds, the figure is 96 per cent. Some technology experts say that embeddable phones, which will literally be implanted into our bodies, could be commercially available by 2023. And our brains are evolving accordingly. We are always checking, checking, checking. The blue light from the screens in our hands has become mesmerising. Melbourne and Sydney recently joined many other cities in the world in installing lights on the footpath at busy intersections to stop 'mobile phone zombies' from stepping into traffic. The in-ground lights that flash red and green were introduced after a rise in the number of pedestrians distracted by their smartphones walking into incoming traffic and getting injured.

We live in a time where we are bombarded with information on our phones, tablets, laptops, televisions, and even internet-enabled watches and refrigerators. This glut of digital noise has become so all-pervasive it has earned its own name: Macmillan Dictionary describes 'infobesity' as 'the condition of continually consuming large amounts of information, especially when this has a negative effect on a person's well-being and ability to concentrate'.

The Ernst & Young report, which surveyed 1,500 Australians, found that 24 per cent of people felt overwhelmed by information overload when using their phones. Forty per cent said they were struggling to keep up with the rapid increase in digital device capabilities. And just like me, they took their phones everywhere. One in four used their mobile in the bathroom, one in five while driving, and more than half during meals at home. Seventy-seven per cent used their smartphones while watching television, and 64 per cent when in bed.

I often feel that my life would be simpler if there were fewer ways for me to keep in touch. There are texts and WhatsApp messages, emails from three separate accounts, instant messages, Facebook, Instagram, LinkedIn, and Twitter notifications and direct messages. Then there's voicemails and missed calls and Skype and FaceTime. Sometimes, I get to the end of the day and I have a nagging sense of having not responded to someone and I can't remember which platform it was on.

There are times when I'm so agitated I can barely sit through a 30-minute TV show without feeling the impulse to check emails, Facebook, my bank balance, the latest weather forecast, or any one of the other countless apps that light up my home screen like a poker machine. Sometimes the sense of fullness inside my skull is so intense I worry that my brain will blow a fuse, plunging me into darkness. Some days I wish for that.

I read those 'Why I Quit Facebook' articles and silently cheer the escapees who have found a way to flee the cult. So many of us seem to be hooked on a habit that has crept into our daily lives in ways so insidious we can't imagine ever breaking free. In some ways, there is comfort in knowing that this is a shared phenomenon, but it still feels pathological. The only way I could write this book was to download an app on my laptop that allows me to block my emails, social media, and news sites for long periods of time. Without it, this chapter might have been little more than a series of tweets. An entire industry has sprung up to help wean us off our addiction. There are multiple apps to choose from: SelfControl, Freedom, Cold Turkey, LeechBlock, RescueTime, Zero Willpower. I went with Freedom, which more than 350,000 people around the world are using, according to their site, to emancipate themselves from digital distraction.

Freedom's creators claim studies show that every time we check an email or social media notification, the mind requires 23 minutes to refocus on the task at hand. I'm certainly better able to concentrate when I don't have 16 windows open on my laptop at once. The compulsion to check goes away temporarily when my brain knows it's not even a possibility. If I try to click on a banned site, Freedom tells me *You are free from [insert site here]*, which always makes me feel rebellious, like a child who's run away and joined the circus. The app allows me to choose which sites I block and for how long, and I can synch all my devices to cut down the temptation to cheat. If I want to be hardcore, I can put it on 'lockdown' mode, which basically reverts my laptop to an old-school word processor and blocks the entire internet. Suck on that, Zuckerberg!

When I was quite unwell, Veronica suggested I try to limit my use of screens as it was clearly aggravating my anxiety. I decided to try a few days without using my phone at all. But I quickly realised that emancipation had its drawbacks. Leaving the house, I instinctively reached for my phone at the tram stop to check my tramTRACKER app and find out how far away my ride was. When I went for walks, I couldn't play music or record my route and steps on my fitness apps. I had to go back to hailing taxis rather than the cheaper and more convenient Uber service I preferred. Trying to find a carpark, I realised that many inner-city parking bays could only be paid for using a smartphone. When I left Veronica's office, I wrote our next appointment time on my hand because I didn't have a calendar. The receipt she gave me had to be physically taken to Medicare for a rebate, rather than sending a screen capture through the app on my phone. I couldn't order in food from my favourite takeaway place because they only offered delivery through an app. No emails were sent or received. No bank balances were checked. No photos were taken. I got lost—a lot. Luckily I wasn't in a hurry to be anywhere, as it occurred to me my phone had been my watch for the past several years. Opting out of using a smartphone seemed like a good idea, but in an environment entirely geared towards its use, it was like trying to navigate my horse and cart down a three-lane freeway.

This attachment to our devices isn't entirely our own fault. It's partly being driven by corporations whose bottom line depends on us always being plugged in. A fascinating investigation by news anchor Anderson Cooper on the US *60 Minutes* program in 2017 found that Silicon Valley is using clever forms of 'brain hacking' to keep us addicted. Cooper spoke to a former Google product manager, Tristan Harris, who wrote a 144-page manifesto about the pitfalls of the technological age and shared it with his colleagues at the tech giant. Harris argued that the bombardment of digital distraction in the modern world was 'weakening our relationships to each other' and 'destroying our kids' ability to focus'. He told the program: 'Never before in history have a handful of people at a handful of technology companies shaped how a billion people think and feel every day with the choices they make about these screens.'

Frustrated by a lack of change within Google, Harris quit after three years with the company. He said he didn't believe there were ill intentions in the technology sector, but grabbing the consumer's attention had become the sole focus, creating what he described as a 'race to the bottom of the brainstem', where products were being developed to drive behaviour that fuelled negative emotions, such as anxiety, loneliness, and fear. As an example, he cited Snapchat, which allows the user to send pictures, messages, and videos that disappear after a few seconds. The developers have invented a feature called 'streaks', showing the number of days in a row the user has exchanged a message with someone. Harris said the effect of this was to encourage young people to keep coming back to the app. 'The problem is that kids feel like, "Well, now I don't want to lose my streak,"' Harris said. 'And so you could ask, when these features are being designed, are they designed to most help people live their life? Or are they being designed because they're best at hooking people into using the product?'

Cooper also spoke to Ramsay Brown, the founder of a tech start-up, Dopamine Labs, that writes computer code for apps. The programs are designed to provoke a neurological response by pinpointing the best moment to give the user a reward, triggering the brain to want more. Based on the user's activity, likes or rewards are given at a time that is engineered to maximise their engagement with the app. I've often wondered why sometimes I'm on Instagram and I'll get a flood of likes all at once. Brown said these algorithms were being used by technology companies to record data every time we react. 'You're part of a controlled set of experiments that are happening in real time across you and millions of other people,' Brown said. 'You are guinea pigs in the box pushing the button and sometimes getting the likes. And they're doing this to keep you in there.'

One of the people interviewed on the program was Dr Larry Rosen, a Californian research psychologist and one of the world's leading experts on the effects of technology. I spoke with Rosen in 2012 for a story on digital overload, just after the publication of his book *iDisorder*—a term he coined to describe a modern affliction where our brains struggle to keep up with excessive use of technology. Diminished attention spans, impaired learning, sleep problems, and difficulties forming relationships in the real world were among the problems Rosen said he was seeing, particularly among young people, who tend to be heavier users of smartphones.

As I grappled with my anxiety and my own obsessive use of technology, I contacted him again to learn more. He had recently published, with a neuroscientist co-author, his latest book, *The Distracted Mind: ancient brains in a high-tech world*, which outlines why our brains are not built for multi-tasking and how the way we live is playing havoc with our ability to switch off. When I called him in his office at California State University Dominguez Hills, where he is a professor emeritus, I explained how my brain often feels overheated from the act of constantly checking and refreshing social media feeds. I didn't tell him that sometimes it feels like I can't physically stop myself from looking at my phone, or that I was actually checking my emails and Twitter mentions intermittently while we talked, but I suspect he knew.

'We are pleasure-seeking animals, and that means you're seeking the release of certain chemicals that we have identified with since we were little children as something that feels good,' he told me. 'Two of those chemicals are dopamine and serotonin—the good-mood, pleasure chemicals—and we strive to get those,' he said. 'So being able to watch a video might give us that pleasure, being able to see how our kids are doing on Facebook might give us that pleasure, so that drives our behaviour to go get more of that pleasure.'

The problems start, Rosen said, when our brains begin to habituate to the pleasure injection and we need more of it to feel the same high. 'Which means if we're getting pleasure out of Facebook, we need to spend more and more time to feel the same as we did just a week or two ago. And that eventually leads to an addiction.'

It sounded familiar. It was almost exactly the same process of habituation a very clever professor of addiction medicine had outlined to me during my year of sobriety. Only he wasn't talking about Facebook likes, he was talking about alcohol. Just as I had increased my tolerance to booze through repeated binge drinking, my compulsive online checking was becoming less satisfying the more I did it.

Rosen stressed that while it was a mistake to believe this is only a 'young person's problem', studies he has conducted with people in their mid-twenties showed that on average they checked their phone 60 times a day, for a total of 220 minutes. He found that when people were separated from their phones it provoked the fight-or-flight response, where the brain releases a burst of cortisol. In one experiment, people were brought into a lab and hooked up to devices that monitor stress levels. They were told they should read some material on a computer screen and answer a series of questions; they could keep their phones next to them. A few minutes into the task, participants were informed that their mobiles were interfering with the electronics and would have to be moved to the back of the room. A minute or so later, the researchers sent texts to the participants' phones. When participants heard their phones go off, immediately there were spikes in galvanic skin response, which measures the body's arousal and level of anxiety. The stress of knowing they had a message but weren't able to check it sent the body into overdrive. 'We've got this brain and we're constantly inundating it with chemicals that suggest that we are anxious or stressed, and it's just not good for your body to be under that fight-or-flight situation all the time,' Rosen said.

Essentially, our primitive brains are learning to view Facebook likes — or a lack of them — as a life-or-death situation. It's not necessarily our minds that have changed, but the environment to which they are being subjected. 'Cavemen didn't have smartphones. Cavemen had a simpler life, so their brains were wired to deal with that simpler life,' Rosen noted. 'You're taking a brain that was basically designed for food foraging and staying alive and making decisions about where your next meal was coming from, and now it's dealing with constant messages and texts and things like that. The brain is just not equipped to handle that nonstop.'

And what's driving our need to constantly check our phones? For Rosen, it all comes back to one thing: connection. 'As human beings, we crave connection; it's part of our humanness. But we live in a world where we have an ever-expanding number of people that we're connected to and we can never quite keep up with it all.' Rosen believes that the plethora of ways we now have to communicate means we're always on alert to make sure we don't miss those connections. More troubling, he maintains, is that the frenetic nature of those connections makes them briefer and less satisfying, and so we find ourselves in a spiral of diminishing returns, where the thing we seek slips further from grasp. 'Fifteen, twenty years ago, you'd sit and talk with someone for half an hour, an hour, you'd go home feeling great. Now, our conversations are very short, many of them are electronic, and they're even shorter because we use shortcuts and acronyms, so they're not as satisfying because they're not touching us as deeply,' Rosen explained.

I can count on one hand the people I regularly chat to on the phone. In high school, my best friend Fiona and I would spend all day together, come home, and chat on the landline for the rest of the afternoon, much to Dad's disbelief. These days, when my mobile rings I stare at it in horror, as though it's a grenade with the pin pulled out. I often let it go to voicemail while thinking, *Why can't they just text me?*

But while I agree with many of Rosen's sentiments, I don't believe that all online interactions can be dismissed as less nourishing than those that occur face to face. I've forged many strong connections on Twitter and Facebook with people in other states or even other countries whom I have never met but nonetheless I consider friends. Many interactions that began in cyberspace ended up with real-life meetings with people I would otherwise never have known. Powerful movements for social change have blossomed through social media—the 2011 Arab Spring uprising, the 2017 Women's March, or the hashtag #MeToo, which ignited a worldwide discussion about sexual harassment and gendered violence. Marginalised communities find strength in their shared experiences online. I have learned so much by listening to the diverse voices on the podcasts that fill up my phone. Meditation apps have helped me stick to a daily practice. For many people, collating pictures on platforms such as Instagram or Pinterest is a type of visual diary, a form of artistic expression that can bring great joy.

In his book *The Art of Belonging*, social researcher Hugh Mackay notes that online communities have provided an important emotional connection for some people, but he argues that the crucial difference between online and offline contact is the extent to which we make ourselves vulnerable to one another. 'As long as our contact is via a screen and keypad, we are able to maintain a certain distance. We have more control over the way we express ourselves and the amount of information we are prepared to reveal,' he writes. 'That ability to control the dataflow may be welcome in many circumstances—including online flirtations or other relationships that are never intended to move offline—but it is a radically different experience of "relationship" and "community" from the complexity and unpredictability of a personal encounter.'

When we go for speed and efficiency over face-to-face contact, Mackay says, we lose the nuanced messages that help us decode what is really being said. Without facial expressions, gestures, body language, and tone of voice, that sense of connection is diminished. 'Ever experienced relief when you've rung someone and encountered their voicemail service, where you can leave a simple message and not have to go to all the trouble of exchanging pleasantries? Then you already know how a revved-up life can actually begin to dehumanise us,' he wrote.

When my mental health was deteriorating, refreshing the page again and again wasn't just a hunt for that zap of dopamine; I think there was an underlying need to find something that would fill the chasm that had opened inside me. Yet the more time I spent online, the less fulfilled I felt. The interactions were always so fleeting and empty—one disposable, meaningless crumb of human contact before scrolling on to the next. At a time when we've never had more ways to connect, we are often profoundly disconnected.

I decided to take Larry Rosen's advice and attempt to break free from my captor. He said we have to stop behaving like 'Pavlov's dogs' and salivating every time our phone beeps. His instructions to turn off that automatic brain response start with switching the phone to silent or flight mode and setting an alarm to go off every 15 minutes. When the alarm sounds, you have exactly one minute to check any form of communication on any of your devices — emails, social media, texts, instant messages. Then, after that minute is up, close all the windows and turn your phone face-down in front of you. Repeat this process every 15 minutes. 'You'll know that your brain's getting it down when the alarm goes off and you say to yourself, "Just a minute, just a minute, I need to finish what I'm working on." Now you can jump it to 20 minutes, and then 25, and then 30,' he told me. 'Optimally, if you can get to 30 minutes, where you check in for a minute, go 30 minutes focusing and attending to whatever you're focusing on — this could be work in an office, studying, dinner with your family, watching a movie, talking to your spouse; anything where you can focus and attend for 30 minutes without getting distracted — that's a major miracle.'

I tried it, using 30-minute intervals for a few days, and it really did make a difference. At first, I found myself reaching for the phone instinctively and having to snatch my hand back like a child caught stealing from a cookie jar. Over time, that urge to check grew less intense and my work rate improved. The more time I spent away from social media, the calmer I became. Rosen explained that these exercises, if repeated often enough, change the way the brain handles its chemistry. 'It teaches your brain not to release chemicals that aren't good for you. So it literally gives you time to calm your brain down while you're working and not feel like you have to be constantly on edge and check in.'

I also tried to follow Rosen's advice to avoid looking at any screens for at least an hour before going to bed — the blue light from phones, laptops, and tablets can suppress the secretion of the sleep-inducing hormone melatonin, playing havoc with the body's circadian rhythms.

These days, I'm trying to be less reliant on my devices, even without setting reminders. I've already started to make inroads. Snapchat is gone forever, and I've deleted the Facebook and Twitter apps from my phone, which doesn't come with me to the toilet anymore. And I almost never check it when dining with friends. Yet, the urge to pick up that screen remains strong. These little computers in our hands are so much a part of our lives it's hard to go back to a simpler way. But I know that when I find myself in a spiral of obsessive checking, it's a red flag that things in my life are starting to unravel. I have to treat my overstimulated brain like a misbehaving child who needs boundaries. That little flush of pleasure when I click on that screen might feel good for a split second, but it's not what I need. What I need is to breathe, back away from the phone, and switch my brain to 'do not disturb'.

9

GENERATION ANXIETY

When I was deep into my therapy with Veronica, I picked up a book called *My Age of Anxiety*, hoping to bolster my road to recovery. This vivid memoir by Scott Stossel, a journalist and editor with *The Atlantic,* is an exhaustive exploration of the toll anxiety has taken on a man desperately trying to wrest back control from a condition that has haunted him since he was two years old. Seven pages in and after reading his list of all the ways he has tried to overcome it — including psychotherapy, role-playing, hypnosis, prayer, self-help books, yoga, drugs, alcohol, and a smorgasbord of pharmaceuticals — I got to this sentence: 'Here's what's worked: nothing.'

A tip for those playing at home: when you're in the midst of a breakdown and feel like you're going mad, reading a book about a man who suffers chronic and debilitating panic attacks, describes himself as a 'twitchy bundle of phobias, fears and neuroses', and believes nothing can help him is a terrible idea. After the first chapter triggered my own panic attack, I put the book down and promised to revisit it when I was stronger. What struck me when I picked it up again was Stossel's take on his predicament as a snapshot of a wider malaise. He says that anxiety has become a 'cultural condition of modernity', afflicting more than 40 million — or one in seven — Americans. And yet, he points out, as recently as 30 years ago anxiety did not exist as a clinical category. Stossel argues chronic stress is a hallmark of our times. 'We live, as has been said many times since the dawn of the atomic era, in an age of anxiety — and that, cliché though it may be, seems to only have become more true in recent years as America has been assaulted in short order by terrorism, economic calamity and disruption, and widespread social transformation,' he writes.

The same could be said of Australia. These are unstable, confusing times. And the people who seem to be the most on edge are younger generations. They have never known a life before screens and digital overload. They face a daily barrage of bad news and crushing social comparison, all in the palm of their hands. At the same time, they're bombarded with advertising and social media telling them that happiness is their ultimate goal.

But it's more than just a problem with their dependence on technology. They live in a vastly different world to the one in which their parents and grandparents grew up. There are no jobs for life. The workforce is increasingly casualised and unstable, the planet is broken, and thanks to tax incentives that favour older investors over young homeowners, they are all but locked out of the property market by the very people who often tell them to toughen up and get a job.

Writing in *The Guardian*, Australian journalist Simon Copland argued that anxiety had become a 'way of life' for Generation Y. 'Whether it is the commercialisation of public space or increasing working hours that reduce time for social activity, we live in a society in which we are all increasingly socially isolated and lonely, destroying one of the key mechanisms available to protect against mental anguish,' he writes. 'Anxiety disorders are not just medical problems. They are inherently social illnesses, ones that are becoming more of an issue as economic insecurity increases and social connections are destroyed.'

I've often heard baby boomers declare that younger generations have 'never had it so good'. Former Collingwood Football Club coach Mick Malthouse complained on the radio recently that rookie footballers were reluctant to move across the country to play for interstate clubs because they would get homesick. Calling them 'snowflakes', Malthouse said he applauded one father who told him he wasn't worried about his 18-year-old son getting homesick if he took up an offer with a club on the other side of this vast continent because 'at his age, I had a rifle on my back'. Military combat seems a pretty high benchmark for one of the acceptable causes of stress. But this is what older generations were taught: showing vulnerability is a sign of weakness. Children should be seen and not heard. Suck it up and be happy.

But happy they are not. Figures released in 2016 show that youth suicide rates are at their highest level in a decade. An Australian male aged between 15 and 29 dies by suicide every 18 hours; that's almost 500 lives lost each year—significantly more than the Victorian road toll. The number of teenage girls taking their own lives or self-harming has doubled since 2005. Among marginalised groups such as indigenous, LGBTIQ, and homeless youth, suicide rates are even more devastating. And yet, only 35 per cent of people with a mental-health condition are accessing services. Just 16 per cent of those with clinical depression receive adequate evidence-based care, despite it being one of the most significant risk factors for suicide. Many are caught in a system that tells them they're either too sick for treatment or not sick enough.

I think back to the genesis of my own childhood anxiety and it seems heartbreakingly apparent that without the right help at the right time, these kids—who face additional pressures I never did—are staring down the barrel of a mental-health crisis.

Over the years, I have often discussed these issues with my friend Michael Carr-Gregg, one of Australia's most high-profile adolescent psychologists. Like me, he is troubled by the rocketing stress levels among children and young adults.

In an open letter to Malcolm Turnbull, he recently urged the Prime Minister to act. Writing in *The Huffington Post*, he said youth suicide rates had reached 'catastrophic levels', and the number of young people with anxiety, depression, and substance abuse he was seeing in his clinical practice was so high it was the first time he had been compelled to write to a prime minister.

Carr-Gregg, or MCG as I call him, is a fierce youth mental-health advocate and a tireless campaigner against bullying who sits on the Project Rockit board. Our bond has been strengthened in recent years by a mutual love of the Hawthorn Football Club. Having a friend who is a psychologist is both a blessing and a burden when you're not at your best. There's no hiding the anguish from a man trained to see right through you. When things deteriorated for me, he immediately wanted to know what treatment I was receiving and was quick to offer suggestions for ways in which I could further enhance my chances of recovery. He dug up the latest research on anxiety and depression, and offered referrals to colleagues he thought might be able to help. I was grateful for his care and compassion.

When things were beginning to get a little better, I talked to him about that letter to the Australian prime minister. What prompted him to write it? And what could we do to prevent more young people ending up, as I had, saddled with chronic anxiety in the pursuit of a life that exists only through the fairytale filter?

'I actually reached the point where I thought, what the fuck can I do about this?' he told me in his inimitably direct way. 'The fact that we've now got the highest level of boys' suicide in ten years—that's just the tip of the iceberg. For every one of those kids there's hundreds that try. So let's go back and look at what's creating this problem in the first place.'

In his letter to Turnbull, he highlighted a Mission Australia report that surveyed more than 21,000 young people aged 15 to 19 from all backgrounds and areas and found that the top three issues concerning them were coping with stress, school or study problems, and body image. The survey has been carried out every year since 2002, and each year the proportion of young people saying that they don't have the strategies to cope with stress has increased.

In 30 years of practice as an adolescent psychologist, Carr-Gregg said the levels of stress he was seeing among young people had never been worse. He partly blamed 'developmental compression', where adolescents are developing faster than they once were, in an environment they're not psychologically equipped to handle. 'Physically, the kids are maturing earlier, so you've got these kids who look all grown-up but their brains, of course, aren't all grown-up. The boys won't be grown-up till the mid-twenties, minimum,' he said. 'Today's 11-year-old is yesterday's 15-year-old. That's causing a whole lot of pressures on young people. They're seeing porn, for example, at the average age of 11. Most of them are seeing this stuff before they have their first kiss. The divorce rate is 40 per cent—the average family now stays together for eight years—so you've got the pressures of divorce, separation, the blended family.'

An obsession with tests is also causing high levels of stress. The National Assessment Program—Literacy and Numeracy (NAPLAN) was brought into Australian schools in 2008, testing students in Years Three, Five, Seven, and Nine. There has been growing concern that it has not only created a 'teach to the test' culture in schools but has placed undue pressure on students to achieve high scores. Children are learning that their self-worth is tied up in a number. Some behavioural experts have warned that the constant testing has helped fuel an 'anxiety epidemic' in primary school–aged children. Perth paediatrician Dr Elizabeth Green told the ABC that every child she was seeing in Years Five, Seven, and Nine was scared about NAPLAN. Psychologists and counsellors around the country have reported an upswing in children seeking support for test anxiety.

Carr-Gregg believes that one of the other major drivers of mental-health problems among young people is disconnection from their local communities. He said many lack purpose and that boredom is a key risk factor for emotional stress. When kids are disengaged, they're more likely to self-medicate with drugs and alcohol, or turn to crime with other disaffected young people. The decline of religion, volunteering, and youth groups such as the Scouts and Girl Guides has left a void. 'I'm seeing more spiritual anorexics in my office than ever before—kids who believe in nothing. Kids who aren't part of anything that is bigger than themselves. One of the reasons why I'm an enthusiastic supporter of the Hawthorn Football Club is because I see there's an opportunity for the club, the family club, to actually provide young people with a sense of purpose, meaning, belonging, and maybe even some hope.'

He wants governments to fund programs that engage young people in art, music, dance, drama, and sport, particularly in rural and regional areas, where the risk of suicide is higher than in metropolitan hubs. And he says parents must have the courage to enforce rules, even if it causes them angst. 'There's been a fundamental shift in parenting. We've moved from authoritarian—which is the stuff that I got, where children should be seen and not heard and if you did something wrong you got belted and you basically learned to shut up—to authoritative, which is good parenting and you set limits and boundaries. You have consequences, but you have a developmental perspective. And now we've got the laissez-faire parenting, where we're not going to do anything to upset the little darlings.'

He said parents needed to go back to setting boundaries rather than trying to be their child's best friend, but conceded that this is a challenge in time-poor, stressed-out households, citing a 2010 Australian Childhood Foundation study which found that 80 cent of parents lacked confidence in their ability to parent. It comes back to that critical sense of safety children crave as they grow up. If the adults around them are strung-out and too busy to attend to their needs in a world where they feel disconnected and alone, more children are going to struggle with anxiety, just as I have.

Without change, Carr-Gregg believes the rates of mental-health problems and suicide in young people will only go up, and that intervention has to start young. He said 50 per cent of psychological problems that occur in adulthood start before the age of 15, and that this is where the focus should be, with no rationing of psychological services. 'Would it not make sense to at least provide adequate psychological services to that primary-school population and at transition, where we know a lot of the problems really consolidate, to have an unlimited amount of psychological help?'

When it comes to emotional distress, allowing people to talk and be seen and heard are vital pieces of the puzzle in figuring out what drives that pain. But there's little time for that in a quick-fix system that still treats a problem of the mind as the poor cousin to a physical ailment.

The lack of progress on fixing our mental-health system has been a source of endless frustration for me as I've reported on the failure of successive governments to address the problem. Every time I've told the story of a parent who's lost a child to suicide or listened to a mental-health nurse break down in tears describing the swollen waiting lists that force them to turn desperate people away, it leaves me reeling.

It's been seven years since the Gillard government committed a record $2.2 billion to mental health — the greatest investment in Australian history. It followed years of intensive lobbying by Professor Patrick McGorry, who in 2010 harnessed his Australian of the Year profile to shine a spotlight on the 'national emergency' of youth suicide. A quarter of the funding Gillard announced went to a national rollout of headspace centres — one-stop shops for young people with mild to moderate mental-health problems — and specialist youth early psychosis prevention centres, both services founded by McGorry. Yet still the death toll rises. The reasons for that are complex and varied, and I know it can't be solved with money alone, but there is no doubt there are major failings in the system.

The idea of headspace seemed sound — to intervene in the early stages of a young person's psychological distress, before a condition becomes debilitating or even life-threatening. Headspace's funky, bright-green drop-in centres, where 12- to 25-year-olds can receive counselling for a range of issues, from sexual health, anxiety, and drug and alcohol problems to bullying, relationship troubles, and exam stress, have proved popular with young people. Importantly, teens who might not want to share their troubles with their parents can turn up without a referral or medical records and be seen free of charge by a team of psychologists, social workers, doctors, and mental-health nurses; they can also receive counselling online. Internal surveys show 86 per cent of young people are satisfied with their experience at headspace, while 56 per cent reported a reduction in their psychological distress after three sessions.

When I first wrote about these centres, I was buoyed by the idea that young people would be given the time and space to be heard in a welcoming environment. It was a long way from the scary, white-walled outpatient wing of the psychiatric hospital I attended as a teen.

But like many noble ideas, a lot has been lost in the delivery. There have been concerns about how many young people headspace is actually reaching, and whether those with the most complex needs are falling through the cracks.

After I wrote a series of articles in which several former senior executives within the organisation raised concerns that it had become the 'McDonald's version of healthcare', the National Mental Health Commission released an independent report finding there was little evidence that headspace had increased access to treatment for young people, particularly those from disadvantaged communities or rural and regional areas. It said headspace's 'one-size-fits-all shopfront approach' was failing to meet the needs of young people from diverse backgrounds, including those with complex mental-health problems. Another major study found that less than a quarter of young people seen by headspace showed significant improvement, while the wellbeing of one in ten went backwards. Many in the sector felt that the headspace concept was good but the execution poor, and they were left to lament the fact that in a historically underfunded sector, precious funds had been squandered for little gain.

The troubles at headspace offer a neat snapshot of the wider problems within our woefully neglected mental-health system and the failure of politicians to adequately address the significant gaps in treatment, prevention, and research. There are few areas of health where the cost of inaction and underfunding is so deadly. All too often, young people pay the highest price.

A year after my own journey to the edge began, I was back at work and found myself covering a story that had become depressingly familiar. I turned up at a modest bungalow in Melbourne's northern suburbs to meet Hong Vo, a former refugee from Vietnam who came to Australia in 1982 and went on to raise two sons. Daniel, her eldest, was there with her when I turned up at their home. Her younger son, Martin, was not. Pictures of the cheeky 22-year-old were everywhere. His high-school swimming bag still hung on a door handle in the hallway. But Martin's absence was palpable. It had been a year since his suicide, and Hong's grief was still so raw she occasionally slipped into talking about him in the present tense. She told me they were telling Martin's story because, 'We want to remember his life and also how we lost him. We want to eliminate this loss for other families.'

Martin was a high-achieving, popular young man who had recently graduated from university and was completing an internship in radiology at a hospital a few hours out of Melbourne. During a four-week placement he became convinced he was failing in his new job, and struggled with feelings of inadequacy and isolation. His family were unsure how long he'd been suffering, but his condition deteriorated rapidly. Towards the end of his placement, Martin's girlfriend told the family they should intervene because he was talking about ending his life.

'That was a huge shock for Mum and me,' Daniel told me. 'When he got home he was sitting down with his back against the couch and it took him ages to respond; he was really down. We later found out that he wasn't eating. He had been depressed throughout that week, but he didn't reach out.'

Hong took Martin to a doctor, who, despite hearing of his suicidal thoughts, told him he should hang in there and that 'life will move on'. The GP referred him to Orygen Youth Health—a public mental-health service for 15- to 25-year-olds in Melbourne's north—and he was assessed over the phone. They told him the earliest appointment he could have in person was in a month's time. Martin took his life two days later.

Pat McGorry, executive director of Orygen, told me he had 'enormous sympathy' for the family and that sadly stories like this were common. Orygen wasn't resourced to cope with the rising demand for treatment and had been forced to turn away more than 1,100 young people in 2015 alone. 'These people simply cannot wait, and the risk of dying is significant,' he said. 'Imagine if this were happening for people with chest pain, at risk of possible heart attack.'

On the day Martin died, Hong, a social worker who had been vigilant about her son's condition since discovering he was suffering from depression, checked on him around 3.00 am. 'He was sound asleep and snoring gently. In the morning I went to wake him up, but he wasn't in the bed. I looked around the house; no sign. So I rang him but the phone was at home. I looked out in the driveway and no car.'

She called Daniel, and Martin's girlfriend. Neither had heard from him. Her next call was to the police. Soon, two uniformed officers were at her door. 'They came in and asked me to take a seat and that's how they said to me, "We found him."'

Martin had left the family home in the early hours of the morning in his mother's car, driven to a bridge on a nearby freeway, and parked on the side of the road. The car was found abandoned with its hazard lights on.

After Hong and Daniel told me this story, while an *Age* photographer took their portrait in the lounge room I excused myself, stood in their front yard, and cried. The loss of this bright young man was so pointless and most likely avoidable. It was almost exactly a year ago that I too had nearly lost the will to live. Only through good fortune and life's financial lottery was I able to get immediate help when I needed it by paying to see a psychologist in the private sector. Martin was just one of 2,864 Australians who died by suicide that year.

These are complex problems. I don't pretend to have the answers. But when I think back to my primary-school days and how much I worried, even as a young child, I wonder if the trajectory that ultimately led to an anxiety disorder could have been changed if I'd had a teacher or a psychologist who had taught me how to manage my catastrophic thinking. Perhaps if I'd learned from an early age that what I was feeling was valid, that failure was okay, and that living in a permanent state of unbridled happiness was an unrealistic life goal, I'd have been saved a lot of heartache.

The pressures today's young people face are unlike those we've seen before. They live in a true age of anxiety, confronting a bewildering set of political, economic, and social challenges as they come of age. Cyberbullying and the pressure to project the perfect image on social media pose unique challenges at a time when family and community structures that used to provide support are splintering. Young people are taught that test results are everything, and failure is not an option. They live in a culture that insists they be happy but makes the quest for calm and contentment increasingly difficult. It's hardly surprising their mental-health outcomes are so poor.

Something has to change. No system will prevent every person from falling through the cracks, but when those cracks are cavernous, the risks are higher. Young people such as Martin Vo shouldn't be told they're not sick enough for help. They should be given help when they need it. They should still be here.

10

HOW TO BUILD A BETTER CHILD

Intensive therapy is a marathon, not a sprint. There is no express lane to clarity. Making sense of the anxiety I'd dealt with since childhood was like scattering a 1,000-piece jigsaw puzzle on the floor and getting down on my hands and knees to put it back together, piece by tiny piece. With every fragment I slotted into place, the picture began to take shape. But it was painstaking work. In my sessions with Veronica, whenever I'd worry I wasn't making progress quickly enough, she'd remind me it had taken nearly 40 years to develop the problematic thought patterns that caused so much of my discomfort. I couldn't expect to turn it around in a few months.

I began to wonder how different things could have been if I had learned to understand my emotions from an early age. What if we didn't have to wait until we reached breaking point as adults before we unlocked the unconscious drivers of our reactions and destructive habits? Could we reduce the burden of mental distress on young people and build more resilient generations if we helped children lift the veil on their inner lives?

After every session with Veronica, more layers were revealed. I still experienced doubt and anxiety, but by beginning to understand some of what was driving it, I started to feel a comfort I had never before known. Whenever I freaked out about the future, catastrophised over friendships, or found myself furious about an inconsequential infraction, I learned to pause, breathe, and connect to what the fear was really about. Over time it became an automatic response, and instead of rushing straight to the worst possible conclusion, I was able to offer calm, rational reassurance to the part of me that felt she was somehow defective or not deserving of love.

The more I learned about myself, the more I also started to understand the foibles of those around me. When people behaved in ways that were emotionally disproportionate to the situation before them, I remembered what Veronica had said—it's almost never about what's going on in that moment. It helped me to view those who had caused me pain with a little more empathy. The girls who bullied me were most likely suffering themselves. Many came from disadvantaged backgrounds and fractured families, and our teachers struggled to deal with their complex needs and behavioural problems. How much of the aggression was misdirected frustration or a desire to be heard?

My school wasn't short of compassionate teachers, but leaving aside their lack of time and resources, they worked in an institutional culture that saw problematic behaviour as something to be punished, not explored. When announcing a new 'tough on crime' approach to juvenile offenders, UK prime minister John Major said in 1993, 'Society needs to condemn a little more and understand a little less.' As a 16-year-old with a fledgling social conscience, the statement outraged me so much I cut it out of the newspaper and stuck it on my wall next to my Kurt Cobain pictures and Jack Kerouac quotes. Yet I still didn't have the emotional insight to join the dots between the behaviour of the girls who tormented me daily and the baggage they might be carrying. I just thought they hated me and that I deserved it.

It is heartening to see things are starting to change. Emotional intelligence teaching is now being taken more seriously in classrooms, helping to equip kids with the skills they need to understand their feelings and articulate them. In the past few years, there has been exponential growth in social and emotional learning in Australian schools. Children are being taught how to be mindful and resilient—lessons previously learnt, or not, through the hard knocks of life. What has been a major educational trend in the United States for more than a decade is starting to take off here as emerging research shows that aggression, anxiety, and stress can be reduced through emotional-literacy programs. In part, the push is in response to the concerns voiced by Michael Carr-Gregg and others about alarming rates of mental-health problems, bullying, and youth suicide. But there is also evidence that children who are in touch with their feelings perform better academically. By learning to be aware of their emotional triggers and how these affect their day-to-day existence, their inner landscapes are becoming a little less opaque to them.

In a teaching environment, it makes sense that a calm, well-supported child is better equipped to learn than one who feels agitated or socially isolated and is unable to express it. Calming exercises, such as deep breathing, taking a six-second pause, or even laughing, trigger physiological changes in the body that help alter mood. Stress hormones dissipate, the heart rate slows, and the blood is oxygenated. When a child is asked to verbalise their emotion, they immediately access the brain's prefrontal cortex (the part used for language and processing). It takes them out of their amygdala—the lower region of the brain, which is responsible for strong emotional reactions—helping them to calm down and control their impulses. Practised regularly, these exercises cause changes in the brain, establishing new neural pathways that can boost traits such as patience, optimism, and even empathy. They're the skills I've only recently learned from Veronica to combat problems I've experienced since I was a child.

The hope is that with this teaching, the children of today will go on to be the calmer, more resilient, and more compassionate adults of tomorrow. But it's not about coddling kids. Emotional intelligence is the antithesis of the self-esteem juggernaut—a movement that hands out medals for taking part, and encourages parents to shower their children with praise regardless of talent. When every child is taught they're 'special' and that if they want it enough they can have anything, it's no wonder so many people grow up to be profoundly disappointed with the real world. Pumping up children's tyres to the point that they think they're uniquely gifted, unbreakable miracles does not foster resilience. It creates emotionally fragile narcissists.

In a seminal 2011 *Atlantic* article entitled 'How to Land Your Kid in Therapy', US psychotherapist Lori Gottlieb shone a spotlight on this phenomenon, reporting that many of the young adults she saw—largely from stable, loving, advantaged homes—were feeling confused, anxious, and empty due to overprotective parenting that focused too much on feeling happy and shielded children from adversity. When these kids were thrust into the real world, even minor obstacles became catastrophic. It was a trend being witnessed by others in the mental-health field. Clinical psychologist Wendy Mogel, an adviser to schools all over America, told Gottlieb that college deans were reporting growing numbers of freshmen they dubbed 'teacups' because 'they're so fragile that they break ... anytime things don't go their way'.

This tallied with what I heard a few years ago when talking to experts at a Melbourne conference called Happiness and Its Causes. Carol Dweck, professor of psychology at Stanford University, told me: 'More and more, parents are unwilling to let their children struggle. They want them to feel good at all times so they're telling them how smart they are, they're really showering with what we call "person praise" — "You're talented, you're smart, you're special." My research shows it backfires. It makes kids worried and tells them that the name of the game is to be smart.' This leads to kids lying about their performance when they're given more difficult problems because their identity and sense of worth get wrapped up in doing well. Dweck urged parents to talk to their children about their struggles as much as their victories, and to give them 'process praise', focusing on the effort and strategies they employed. Teaching them to accept setbacks and shortcomings rather than blocking them out was, she said, the key to resilience.

Looking back, these were the messages I received as a child: *You can be anything you want. Just be happy. Follow your dreams. You are special. The only limitation is your imagination.* It was hard to reconcile these ideals with my growing disdain for the person I was becoming. As a desperately self-conscious adolescent, the opinions of others meant everything to me. With every year the worrying grew worse, until it evolved into a desperate, visceral need to be liked.

When I told Mum about my worries, her response was always the same: 'People are far more interested in themselves than they are in you. Don't be so big-headed.' Technically, she was correct. But as a child who felt as far from conceited as it was possible to be, what I took from that was that my anxieties were frivolous, self-indulgent, and inconsequential.

In the months prior to my 2014 breakdown, I got a glimpse into how different things could have been. I visited Girton Grammar in Bendigo, a regional town 150 kilometres north-west of Melbourne, for a feature on the rise of emotional-intelligence teaching in Australian classrooms.

I arrived on a hot, dry Tuesday afternoon, sitting down on a small grey plastic chair, my knees uncomfortably close to my chest. The teacher asked the class to greet their guest, Miss Stark, and the children of 4D stood up as one and addressed me in a sing-song chant. It had the simultaneous effect of making me feel welcome and 100 years old.

As they did every day, the students began to talk about their feelings. Nine-year-old Evie was feeling confident and enthusiastic. Her teacher, Paul Flanagan, 'Mr F'—a tall, engaging man in a tailored suit who wouldn't look out of place in a bank or a real-estate office—asked her to plot where she was on her 'mood meter'. She tugged the ends of a raggedy blonde ponytail, pulled high over to one side by a red-baubled band, and gauged she was a +3 for energy and a +2 for feelings. On the chart, divided into red, yellow, blue, and green quadrants, she placed a small 3D figure of herself in the yellow. But not every day was like today. If school had been tough or someone was mean to her, she might find herself in the blue. If she was feeling particularly chilled out, she could be in the green. Sometimes, she was in the land of the red. 'On the weekend, I was in the red because my sister was trying to fight with me and I had to stop and go to my room and think about my best self. Then I came out and I said sorry, to be the bigger person, even though she's bigger than me,' she said with a giggle.

When classmate Isabelle felt a tingling in the fingers or a twisting in the tummy that put her in the red, she explained how she had learnt to take a 'meta moment': a short pause of emotional recognition. Visualising how she would react if she was her 'best self'—a concept defined by a collection of words, such as *patient, kind, caring, sincere,* and *considerate,* that she feels describe her at her best—helped her calm down. And then she would take action. 'I just breathe and try to think of a suggestion to get me into the yellow or the green. My main strategies are to drink more water or have something to eat, because I can get angry when I'm hungry.'

I sat down with Evie after the class finished. I wanted to know if she had times when she felt difficult emotions. Surely it was okay to be in the red sometimes? Evie smiled knowingly, like a tiny, golden-haired Buddha, and said: 'You've got a right to feel angry, but you shouldn't react to it. You should apply some strategies.'

I looked at her, open-mouthed. It's hard to imagine nine-year-old Jill being able to articulate her feelings, much less regulate them when things weren't going well. When I started school, kids were still getting the belt for acting up in class. The cause of behavioural problems was rarely explored. But Evie and Isabelle, like their Year Four classmates, were at an advantage. They were being taught that understanding their emotions has a profound effect on their behaviour and that of those around them. They're among a new wave of children with arguably a greater grasp of the full human experience than their parents. They're the early adopters in what will hopefully become an emotionally literate generation. One that won't be sucked in by the happiness fairytale or beaten down by the demands of modern life. This is the start of a movement to build a better child.

During my time in the Girton classroom, it was clear that this was not a box-ticking exercise. The children were not simply reeling off a list of feelings like they would their times tables. They were able to identify and articulate complex emotions—what it feels like to be 'overwhelmed' or 'unacknowledged'—and were learning the nuanced differences between assertiveness and aggression, between envy and jealousy, between sadness and depression. Importantly, they understood that everyone has an inner critic, and while negative thoughts are unpleasant, they are not facts. Ball-breaking Regina George-Ratchett might make an appearance inside the heads of these kids, but in the face of their emotional insight her power would be greatly diminished.

What I found so impressive about Girton's program was the emphasis on there being no wrong emotions. Unlike my generation—who grew up believing that happiness and success were the ultimate goals, while mental-health problems were stigmatised to the point of virtual silence—these students were being taught that feeling sad or frustrated or disappointed is normal. They learned that a bad day may be just that, and dark moods do not define you. It's what they do with those emotions that counts. It means that when life knocks them down, they'll be better equipped to get back up.

Mr F told me that in his 18 years of teaching, nothing has had such a positive effect on classroom management and student wellbeing as emotional-intelligence teaching. 'A lot of us grew up in a society where you didn't talk about your emotions; they weren't important. I can't remember someone ever asking me how I felt or if I'd had a good morning and what might have affected my mood on a particular day,' he said. 'What we're actually giving these students, with the skills, the vocabulary, the social and emotional training — we're equipping them for when they head out into society. It just sets them up for a world that at times can be ruthless. If we can develop students who are socially and emotionally aware of themselves and others, then they're set for big things.'

Girton, an independent school, is the first in Australia to use a program designed at Yale University's Center for Emotional Intelligence—a world leader in the field. Headmaster Matthew Maruff, a passionate advocate who maintains that 'emotions are the gatekeepers to the intellect', sent three teachers to the United States in 2011 to be trained in the RULER program, which teaches how to recognise, understand, label, express, and regulate feelings. As we walked around the Girton campus, its red-brick buildings sprawling over two blocks in downtown Bendigo, he told me how the program is now the foundation for every part of school life. All teachers and staff have been RULER trained.

Chatting with him, I was struck by how he was unlike any teacher I've ever known. In an education system obsessed with tests and academic performance, it's rare to hear a school leader put 'feelings' at the top of their list of teaching priorities. But during our stroll through the blistering heat from the senior campus to the junior school, Mr Maruff, with a smile as wide as the brim of his floppy sunhat, greeted every student by name and told me that, 'When you ask the kids, they say they just want to be listened to and valued.'

He was remarkably open with his own feelings and said he encouraged his staff members to check in with a mood meter daily, for their students and themselves. He told me that the greatest challenges for his pupils when they leave school will be emotional, not cognitive. In the future, he said, the traditional pillars of learning, the three Rs (reading, writing, and arithmetic), will be replaced with the four Cs: creativity, collaboration, communication, and intellectual curiosity. He acknowledged that success in these areas is hard to measure, but noted that they've seen a marked reduction in bullying and a modest improvement in academic performance since introducing the RULER program.

The experiences at Girton are being replicated in the public system. The federal health department's Kids Matter program, which started in 2006, is now being taught in more than 2,600 urban, rural, and regional primary schools across Australia. Designed primarily as a mental-health and wellbeing program, it's a flexible teaching framework that can be tailored to an individual school's needs and focuses on social and emotional learning, respectful relationships, and fostering belonging and inclusion. Similar programs, Response Ability and Mind Matters, are among the emotional-learning programs being taught in secondary schools.

Mr F said that behavioural problems in class had also improved. 'We had an incident with a child who was displaying a lot of anger and aggression, but we did some work with them and identified that what they were actually feeling was left out in their peer group. We were able to give them skills to manage those emotions, and that child has moved on to be a great success. If they didn't have those skills, they could easily have taken the wrong path,' he said.

But was it possible to see these types of results in schools where the children's needs are complex? What could emotional intelligence teaching achieve in a school more like the one I attended? And so I visited Coolaroo South Primary School in Melbourne's northern suburbs — a low socio-economic area with a large migrant and refugee population — and discovered that at this school, at least, there is evidence that emotional learning can have benefits for children from all backgrounds.

It was a Wednesday afternoon, and Year One students were learning about resilience — or, as they know it, bouncing back.

'Do bad feelings last forever?' teacher Stephanie Clarke asked the five-year-olds sitting in a circle on the floor.

'Nooooooooooooo,' they hollered, grinning. Taking turns to bounce 'Bruce' the bouncy ball, they were reminded that, 'We may go all the way to the ground and feel really, really sad, but very shortly we will bounce back.'

In Jenny Bartlett's Year Five classroom, the walls were papered with life advice: *Keep things in perspective. It's only part of your life*, and *Catastrophising exaggerates your worries. Don't believe the worst possible picture*. Another read, *Everybody experiences sadness, hurt, failure, rejection and setbacks sometimes, not just you. They are a normal part of life.*

I was so impressed with this wisdom I took pictures on my phone, partly to prove to myself that what I was seeing was actually real. I wondered about the impact it might have had on my developing, over-analysing brain as a child to discover that what I was experiencing was normal and that life wasn't meant to be all sunshine and rainbows and baskets full of puppies. For these students, growing up in a digital age where social media airbrushes out life's tough times, the lessons are a critical reality check. They're an inoculation against the happiness fairytale's most dangerous pitfalls.

The kids were discussing body language and how the way you hold yourself can change your mood and demeanour, which in turn changes the way others respond to you. I got the sense that just by giving them permission to voice their feelings, it diminished the power of their darker thoughts and provided a sense of autonomy. Ms Bartlett asked them what happened to their bodies when they went into the 'red zone'. Slumped shoulders, clenched fists, and a furrowed brow were among the replies. 'When your body is tense it takes a long time for your mood to change. So if you can relax your body, put a smile on your face, and do the self-talk and go to your happy place, that will help your mood to change,' she told them. For some, their happy place was imagining a day out at the beach with the family. Others said it was on the footy field, or floating on a pink fluffy cloud with Katy Perry.

She then asked the students how they coped with anger or sadness or loneliness. Dilara said that playing guitar or singing a song made her feel better. Raven liked to take a moment and relax her shoulders and face. 'I just tell myself that there's no point being angry at this person and I take a deep breath,' she explained. For Erkam, it was about counting to ten: 'Then I say to myself that bad things never last.'

Since introducing Kids Matter in 2010, principal Karen Nicholls said that playground conflicts have dropped, attendance and behavioural issues have improved, and children are generally more caring and compassionate. She also noted a 'small but definite improvement' in academic performance, which she put down to the children being more engaged in school and therefore happier to attend. 'We're not psychologists, but as teachers we need to be aware of the issues children are grappling with outside of school. One child may have experienced significant trauma, but for another child it may be that they've got a new baby brother in the household who's getting all the attention, and for that child that's really significant.'

It's these little things that in an adult world defined by hectic work schedules, financial pressures, and family demands can seem trivial. But to a child, feeling like they're going unnoticed can seem like the end of the world. Left unaddressed, it can lead to significant emotional problems. All it might take to turn that around is for someone to listen.

At the end of the school day, the kids in Bartlett's classroom filed out. I asked her if this level of emotional engagement with students is a burden on her time. She laughed and shook her head. 'These lessons are a gift,' she said. 'It's about knowing that they can offload their negative emotions here in a safe space. A lot of them think that it's bad or wrong to be crying or sad, and so I say to them it's okay to be down low as long as you can work towards getting back up. It's a proactive way for them to deal with all the issues that are increasing in our world, and the challenges they have to deal with. Some of these children come from very stressful, heartbreaking backgrounds. They need these skills to survive. What do they do with that anger if they can't learn to regulate their emotions?'

The answer is not an easy one to confront. Child protection experts warn that children exposed to prolonged trauma, violence, and hardship may face a lifetime of problems. They have flagged an emerging phenomenon of 'toxic stress'—a state of constant alert in which the child's fight-or-flight response goes into overdrive, causing physiological changes to the architecture of the brain. The results can have a catastrophic effect on their ability to regulate emotions, impairing cell growth and disrupting the formation of healthy neural circuits. These changes in the hippocampus—the part of the brain responsible for memory and emotional control—cause shrinkage, which in turn can trigger learning and behavioural problems, difficulty with impulse control, and a heightened sense of rage and self-loathing. Long-term, the concern is that kids who grow up experiencing issues such as family violence, sexual abuse, neglect, economic hardship, and parental mental illness or drug and alcohol dependency become trapped in an emotional spin cycle that impairs their social skills, makes it difficult for them to form relationships, and can lead them down a path of aggression and anti-social behaviour.

Stress in itself is not damaging. The increase in heart rate or hormone levels a child might experience on the first day of school or when getting an immunisation can be a healthy and essential part of childhood development that will promote resilience. Even traumatic events, such as the death of a close relative, parental divorce, or a natural disaster can be overcome if the stress activation is time-limited and the effects are buffered by loving, supportive relationships. But the evidence suggests that stress turns toxic when the trauma is prolonged and when both parents are emotionally unavailable.

The mother's psychological state during pregnancy can also significantly impact on the baby's brain development in the womb, leading to an increased risk of physical and emotional problems, including anxiety. As our society becomes increasingly strung out with the pressures of twenty-first-century life, children can quite literally be stressed before they're even born. Viewed through this lens, it's hard to dismiss social and emotional learning as a trendy feel-good fad. Some educators believe it's so important to child development and the future cohesiveness of our communities that they're pushing for an educational and parental paradigm shift from teaching 'a life of tests' to 'the tests of life'.

Linda Lantieri is at the forefront of that movement. After meeting her at the Happiness and Its Causes conference in Melbourne, I became convinced that this diminutive native

New Yorker with the style of Nana Mouskouri and the accent of Barbra Streisand might well be able to change the world. A Fulbright scholar and an international expert in social and emotional learning and conflict resolution, she has worked as an educator for 40 years, both as a teacher and as a director of a middle school in Harlem. Her vision is for schools that 'educate the heart along with the mind'. But it was her work after the September 11 terrorist attacks that fascinated me most. She was commissioned by New York authorities to help counsel 8,000 traumatised children who had been forced to evacuate schools when the planes hit the World Trade Center's twin towers. She told me that through the inner-resilience program she set up in the aftermath of the attacks, she learned that children can recover from even the most unimaginable trauma if given the skills to make sense of their experiences.

Lantieri said that helping these young people to feel their emotions rather than encouraging them to forget or block out the traumatic event is key to how they respond:

> If we help them reframe what happened to them, if we help them to interpret those events, to give them meaning, then that becomes more powerful than what actually happened. It's giving kids the ability and the openness of communication to be able to talk about their fears. [The September 11 attacks] taught us that we can't protect kids from an uncertain world any more. We can't say bad things won't happen, but we can say they could get better, and we can learn from those things and we can teach kids that talking about it is helpful, that knowing how to calm yourself is helpful. It's about giving kids skills, not false optimism.

Meditation, mindfulness, and breathing skills were among the tools taught in the resilience program, as well as encouraging teachers and parents to set up 'peace corners' at home and in schools to give children safe spaces to centre themselves. These calm areas, decorated by the students, were cooling-off places where kids could listen to music, engage in artwork, or just sit quietly with their emotions. Lantieri believes that with increasing pressure on children at home and at school, it's crucial that emotional and social wellbeing skills are given as much priority as English or maths, to protect children from the risk of toxic stress.

The idea of teaching kids to get in touch with their emotions might not gain much support from the shock jocks and conservative commentators who dominate Australia's media and believe that violent youth offending is fuelled by bleeding-heart lefties taking a 'softly-softly' approach to education and parenting. But the evidence doesn't lie. A Flinders University evaluation of Kids Matter found that it not only significantly improved mental health and behavioural problems in schools but also boosted NAPLAN results. Children who had taken part in the program were up to six months ahead in academic achievement. These schools are seeing firsthand the change that can come from letting children make room for their feelings. It's the same shift that is prompting schools around the world to introduce meditation practice for students, with a growing body of research suggesting it can play a role in calming children, boosting learning, and managing behavioural issues. A randomised clinical trial with 300 fifth- to eighth-graders in two disadvantaged Baltimore city schools found that students who received mindfulness meditation instruction for 12 weeks saw improvement in mood, anxiety levels, self-hostility, coping ability, and post-traumatic symptoms.

Teaching children to block out their feelings and 'just be happy' has clearly not worked. In a time when kids are dealing with pressures previous generations didn't face, we need a fundamental shift in how we deliver teaching, and in the skills and abilities we value as a community. I'm pretty sure that in the real world I have never used the knowledge I gained (and then promptly forgot) about algebraic formulas or the structure and formation of cumulonimbus clouds. But a lesson on how to manage my temper, deal with isolation, or refrain from getting caught up in negative thought spirals would have been super-helpful for me in pretty much every aspect of my life to date. No doubt it would have helped the girls who bullied me, too.

It's encouraging to see more schools recognise that we can't keep doing what we've always done. But that change has to be sustained and widespread. Today's kids are navigating an increasingly complex world, and if we want them to grow up to be functioning adults, they need to be equipped with the skills for life in the modern world. They need tools to make sense of their emotions and the permission to give those feelings a voice. In our age of anxiety, children deserve to be seen *and* heard.

11

MIND THE GAP

Sometimes I worry that my anxiety is making my cat anxious. His resting face is a mask of alarmed alertness. It's the exact same expression my brain would wear if it had a face. Dilated pupils as large and glassy as marbles, ears forever pricked up to anticipate the impending apocalypse, Hamish is a wreck. If the animal behaviourists are right and pets can pick up on their owners' moods, I have a lot to answer for. He is restless and fragile and jumps at the slightest noise. When I go to the bathroom, he looks at me as if I've just dumped him in a cardboard box by the side of the road. He simply will not countenance a closed door. Once, he hissed at the air-conditioning condenser on my balcony, staring intently at its invisible internal demons for so long I was convinced I would require an exorcist. I described his behaviour to the vet, and she asked gently if there was 'any stress in the home environment?'

'Not really,' I lied, omitting to mention all the times Hamish has quizzically sniffed my limp body as I lie in the foetal position, wailing into the hallway carpet. She suggested I buy a Feliway diffuser—a wall-mounted air freshener that, instead of releasing pleasant aromas from the Everglades, emits synthesised feline pheromones into the atmosphere to stop my domestic short-hair moggy from clawing my lounge suite to shreds and yowling at the split-system. She also sent me home with a packet of cat Valium, which I later discovered is just human Valium with a paw print on the box—a fact that would come in handy for those times when I needed to calm down quickly and couldn't get to the pharmacy until the morning. You can't truly call yourself a crazy cat lady until you've necked your psychologically disturbed cat's anti-anxiety medication in a fit of panic.

Maybe it's not my fault he's mad. Perhaps it's just that the universe has naturally paired two troubled souls. I picked him out from a pet rescue adoption website where you flick through cat profiles the way you might look for a partner online, and there was something about those searching green eyes that spoke to my heart. Like most cats, he is aloof, demands affection only on his terms, and can often be a complete arsehole. But there have been times when this eccentric bag of fur has been my anchor. There is something innately calming about his presence when he's resting. If my brain is racing, I breathe deeply and just observe the rusted tip of his nose; the signature tabby v-shape on his forehead; his gentle vulnerability as he sleeps, wedged between my legs in a cocoon of his own making. I find myself mesmerised by the way he spends an inordinate amount of his day cleaning himself, even though he's an indoor cat and not even remotely dirty. It's meditative to observe the care he takes making sure no patch of fur goes unlicked. The way he pays particular attention to his paws, splaying his claws wide as he gnaws deep into the bone, chewing each nail vigorously with a *num num num*, always makes me chuckle.

And there are moments where he has given me the strength to keep breathing. On one particularly awful carpet-dwelling evening I was curled up in a ball, listening to Tracy Chapman, and dreaming of escape. My tears merged into a primal groan that came from another place. It was one of those evenings where my insides were cramped with a knot of pain that stretched far beyond the current moment. I was grieving for the parts of me I'd lost, the parts of me I might never find again. In the midst of my anguish, there he was, lying down next to me, mirroring my pose. I swear he was trying to spoon me. Burrowing into my back, he butted his head against me again and again. It was as if he was saying, *You can do this. You will survive this.* In that moment, I felt hopeful. Awake to the possibility of life.

These times with Hamish are about as close as I have come to mastering the art of mindfulness. I have all the books on the topic, and I wholeheartedly agree with the concept that living in the moment is the key to a calmer existence. Mindfulness is the act of quietening the mind by staying in the present, paying careful attention to the sights, sounds, and sensations around you. It's a simple yet effective concept, when it works. But putting it into practice has proved more of a challenge. Anxiety, by its very nature, is the act of projecting into the future or fixating on the past. I am constantly scanning the horizon for the crest of the tsunami about to hit me, or gazing into the rear-view mirror at the reflection of my mistakes. After a lot of hard work and repetition, I have retrained my brain not to believe the worst-case scenarios. But my mind still wanders. Actually, it's more like it straps on hiking boots and sets off to circumnavigate the globe. Trying to tame it has often left me frustrated. Why can't I be like all those lithe, ponytailed goddesses in activewear on Instagram, mindfully dispersing their troubles with their obediently quiet brains? Being mindful shouldn't be that hard. You're just sitting still, being aware of your surroundings, focusing on the body and the breath. It's basically just being alive. And I suck at it.

In an attempt to change this, I decided to join the millions of people around the world who have hopped on board the adult-colouring craze. It's proved so popular that the world's biggest pencil manufacturer, Faber-Castell, had to put on extra shifts in its Bavarian factory to keep up with demand. I bought the bestselling *The Mindfulness Colouring Book,* which told me that one of the best ways to soothe anxiety and eliminate stress was to work with your hands. *Take a few minutes out of your day, wherever you are, and colour your way to peace and calm,* the blurb read. I coloured religiously for days and waited for the peace I'd been promised. But all I ended up with was a sore hand and Regina screaming in my head, 'You can't even colour right, you fucking crazy woman!'

It's not surprising I felt like a failure. If you listen to the hype on mindfulness, you'd think it was the panacea for the troubles of our time. Just stare at the intricate grooves of a raisin for ten minutes, eat a square of chocolate one millimetre at a time, or wash the dishes with an observant mind, and you'll be on the fast track to emotional clarity. We have mindful workplaces, mindful schools, mindful eating, mindful parenting, mindful healthcare, and even mindful military action, where army troops are being trained in meditation exercises to help prepare them for combat. I'm not quite sure this is what Buddha had in mind when he first came up with the practice as a path to enlightenment.

There is solid research to show that mindfulness can have a positive effect on mental health. The UK's National Health Service funds mindfulness sessions as an alternative to medication for some patients, and there is evidence it may be as effective as a treatment for recurrent depression. But its reputation as a cure-all for life's challenges has been overplayed. Everywhere I look—in bookshops, in podcast charts, on the app store, and in online advertising—I'm promised that mindfulness will set me free. Maybe it will, in time. But it requires continued hard work and commitment to tame the mind, a muscle that needs to be flexed regularly. Once again, we are being sold a quick fix for our emotional and spiritual malnourishment. Happiness can be yours for the price of a 99c mindfulness meditation app.

While mindfulness has its roots in Buddhist traditions, American scientist and author Jon Kabat-Zinn is widely credited with bringing the practice into the mainstream through the Mindfulness-Based Stress Reduction Clinic he founded in 1979, followed by a series of bestselling books that helped people learn the technique in their own homes. A number of these books sit on the shelves in my apartment. They have titles like *Full Catastrophe Living*—which sounds like my autobiography—and *Wherever You Go There You Are*, which is all about 'using the wisdom of your body and mind to face stress, pain and illness'. I have found some of the readings helpful. But non-judgementally staying in the present is no small feat for someone prone to catastrophic thinking and who has an inner monologue that sounds like a caffeine-frenzied sports commentator calling a horserace. On some days, with all the will in the world, I am unable to find stillness.

I am gradually getting better at it. I've found mindful breathing exercises and guided meditations to be calming, when used regularly. The effect is cumulative, so dedicated practice produces the best results. But diligence is a virtue I possess only in radical spurts. It's hard to be fully present when you're down the social-media rabbit hole; mindfulness only works when I take my head out of my phone. I've found that I am at my most still when there are no distractions. In the shower, I have learned to mindfully observe the warmth of the water, enjoying each drop hitting my skin and treating it as an indulgent experience rather than as a daily chore.

I've also gained a lot from the writings and audiobooks of modern-day Buddhist teachers such as Pema Chödrön and Tara Brach, who have helped me learn to embrace whatever I'm experiencing—good or bad. Observing the full depth of any given moment can make the happy times more fulfilling and the difficult times easier to bear. When I practise mindfulness meditation consistently, it does make a difference to my levels of anxiety. My brain might still be racing, but I'm able to witness the procession of negative thoughts as if I were a bystander watching a passing circus parade: I can take in all the rich colour and detail, but I don't get involved. My experience does not define me.

Yet ultimately, while mindfulness may help me slow down and alleviate some of the more debilitating symptoms of anxiety, it will not 'cure' it. I will have to continue to address the underlying emotional drivers of my distress if I want to live a calmer, more meaningful life. The same can be said of our culture's sickness. There are no shortcuts. Critics argue the Western corporatisation of Buddhist mindfulness practice has led to a 'McMindfulness' approach to mental suffering that commodifies 'wellness' while ignoring the underlying societal issues causing so much of our stress.

Writing in *The New York Times*, Ruth Whippman, author of *America the Anxious: how our pursuit of happiness is creating a nation of nervous wrecks*, argues that mindfulness is the new 'think positive' movement, with a focus on self-improvement that blames unhappiness on the individual's inability to live in the moment rather than societal disadvantage. 'The problem is not your sky-high rent or meagre paycheck, your cheating spouse or unfair boss or teetering pile of dirty dishes. The problem is you,' she writes. Giving disadvantaged schoolchildren mindfulness classes rather than tackling education inequality, or teaching office workers mindful breathing instead of offering better conditions, is part of a systemic culture of overwork, Whippmann claims. Ideally, we'd do both. But that's not what's happening.

In 2014, an analysis by accounting firm Pricewaterhouse-Coopers estimated that undiagnosed mental-health problems were costing Australian businesses up to $11 billion a year in absenteeism, compensation claims, and lost productivity. Many companies are responding by giving employees 'wellbeing' leave or offering mindfulness courses. ANZ, Wesfarmers, and Bupa are among the organisations providing colouring books for their workers as a way to declutter their minds. But wouldn't it be more effective to actually declutter their lives?

I have 2,301 unread emails in my inbox. I try to get through them — respond to the ones that matter, cull the ones that don't — but there's always more. A journalist friend told me recently that he spent his summer holiday deleting 200 emails a day just to avoid an overwhelming backlog when he returned to work. In November 2016, to promote national Go Home On Time Day, The Australia Institute released a study which found that the average full-time worker does 5.1 hours of unpaid overtime each week — or 264 hours per year. More than half of those with access to annual leave don't take their full entitlements. 'Live to work' has become a national state of mind.

Similarly, a survey carried out by Microsoft in the United Kingdom found that almost 60 per cent of respondents thought about work as soon as they woke up in the morning. Forty-five per cent felt obliged to respond to a work email instantly, no matter where they were or what they were doing. This cult of busyness is unlikely to be fixed by token 'wellbeing' days, while businesses continue to flog their staff to death for the rest of the year.

Writing in *The Conversation*, psychotherapist Zoë Krupka said that the booming 'stress reduction industry' was a bandaid for a deeper problem—many of us simply work too much to be well. 'Nothing can alleviate the stress of overwork except working less. Like the road signs say, only sleep cures fatigue … For the madly overworked, we need reminding that the only cure for working too much is to stop.' Krupka said the wellness industry and corporate stress-management programs traded on a culture of overwork and that the answer had to be political, not personal.

In France, the government has tried to restore some semblance of work–life balance with legislation that came in on 1 January 2017, requiring companies to provide their staff with a 'right to disconnect' from technology outside working hours. Organisations with more than 50 staff must negotiate deals with their employees, setting out their rights not to reply to emails or take phone calls during their personal time. It could be tricky to enforce, but at least it sets a clear message about the kind of society citizens should be entitled to live in. If we don't shift our mindset from this 'always on' culture, we're setting up the next generation—already over-burdened with stress before they even reach the workforce—for a lifetime of unnecessary pressure and mental exhaustion. And if parents are so distracted by overflowing inboxes and excessive workloads, what does that do to their levels of distraction in those critical early years of a child's life, when bonding is so important to brain development?

One of my childhood friends, Lisa, who I grew up with in Edinburgh, shared her own experiences of feeling overwhelmed by the demands of the modern age. A primary-school principal, she'd been chatting with an older teacher who said she felt the pressures today were far greater than when she first started working and raising a family. The conversation made Lisa, a working mother of three, reflect on just how hectic her life had become. She shared her daily schedule, and it floored me:

> I say to my teachers all the time to switch off and take time with family but I don't do it myself. I start at 7.30am (actually I start at 6.00 in the house before I even get out of bed) then I work until 5.30–6pm at school on a good day, sometimes up to 9pm if we have something on. I don't get a lunch or tea break because I'm on duty all day long.
>
> I go home, open the door, collect a child/children and take them to whichever club/activity/school thing or work that they are going to and I work whilst I wait for them to finish. I get home late evening, make dinner, do housework, help with homework then when they go to bed after 10 I prepare my own bag/get lunches ready for next day and sit down around 11pm for the first time to do my work emails. I go to bed around 1am then start all over again.

She loved her life, but had recently realised it was out of balance and entirely unsustainable. There was no time to exercise, socialise, relax, or often even go to the toilet on an average day. The pattern was being repeated with her children, where they were on a treadmill of school, study, and work with no downtime. 'We have created a society of young to middle-aged adults who work with no balance. We are all heading for complete mental and physical burnout,' she wrote.

When did life get so hectic? We used to say 'good, thanks' when someone asked how we were. Now, the standard response is 'crazy busy'. I saw a meme recently that said, 'Adulthood is emailing "Sorry for the delayed response!" back and forth until one of you dies.' Racing towards burnout shouldn't be a competitive sport, but exhaustion has become a badge of honour. A commentator I follow on Instagram recently posted a picture at 1.30 am of a screenshot of her alarm, which was set for 3.00 am, with the hashtag #90minutessleep.

It used to be that the more money you earned, the less you worked. Leisure time was a marker of wealth. Now, the opposite is true. A Columbia Business School, Georgetown University, and Harvard Business School study found that in America, a busy person was seen by others as possessing 'desired human capital characteristics (competence and ambition) and is scarce and in demand on the job market'. Essentially, the busier the person, the higher up the social ladder they must be. Conversely, in Europe, where many shops are closed at the weekends, workers have more legally protected paid holidays, and leisure time is prioritised, a higher social status was bestowed upon those who worked less.

In Australia, I suspect we'd find similar results to those in the States. Social-media feeds are filled with people humblebragging about their demanding schedules and hectic social commitments. It often makes me wonder if by 'crazy busy' they actually mean 'completely overwhelmed and heading for a nervous breakdown'.

This race to oblivion is yet another footnote in the same old script. Happiness will come once we reach the finish line. That promotion, that pay rise, that pat on the back from our boss. But really, we're just pounding the treadmill and going nowhere. In therapy with Veronica, she pointed out that when we're pushing ourselves to extremes—whether in our professional or personal lives—it's worth examining what's driving that need to please. What validation are we seeking from making ourselves indispensable? What void are we trying to fill? If you truly believe the world will crumble if you don't send that midnight email or take that work phone call during a family reunion, perhaps it's time to pause and ask what really lies beneath.

In German, the word *Stark* means strong. I didn't know this until Jason started dating a beautiful, soulful man from Hamburg called Marco, who told me he believed I was the living embodiment of my name. It was a nice change from the 'Winter is coming' jokes that I usually got when people heard my surname. The *Game of Thrones* references had become so common I decided to wear my name with pride and bought myself a bright blue hoodie with the words *I CAN'T KEEP CALM I'M A STARK* printed on the front.

By the time I met Marco, the joke had become a self-fulfilling prophecy. I'd reached a point where I was fantasising about the peace death would bring. My brain was so heavy with ceaseless, catastrophic thoughts I wanted to wring it out like a sodden sponge. The longer I was off work, the more I worried I'd never go back, and the more defective I felt. Round and round the anxiety hamster wheel spun. I was scared every second I was awake. It was like I was balancing with one foot on a landmine; one false step could see me blown to smithereens. If I managed one meal a day I was doing well. Sleep came an hour or so at a time, and only with the help of tranquilisers. I developed an angry, full-body rash that clung to me for weeks. When I looked in the mirror, my brokenness stared back at me and I wept.

On the way back from the doctor one day, I found myself standing at the pedestrian lights, watching cars speed past, drawn to the intoxicating freedom that would come from taking one simple step into the traffic. That month, I drafted suicide notes and then ripped them up in despair when I realised my hell could not be escaped by passing it on to those I loved. I looked for solace in this small concession. Despite the pain, I at least had the lucidity to know the people closest to me would not necessarily be better off without me. But that knowledge was its own prison. I felt trapped by this thing, this beast. It brought an endless grief as I mourned for my disappearing self and the lost concept of hope.

My friends stepped in, taking responsibility for a life I no longer recognised or wanted. One morning, after I'd swallowed just enough Valium to turn me into a zombie but not quite enough to kill me, Chris let himself into my apartment and found me there in bed, the blinds on every window closed. Lying down next to me, he stroked my hair as I cried. He gently urged me to get up and opened the blinds, presenting me with a toasted sandwich and a bottle of Gatorade—his go-to morning-after cure, which he hoped might have a similar effect on my Val-over. Wrapping me in a blanket on the couch, he turned on the television and I stared at it blankly. We watched *Teen Wolf* and through my fog, I remember thinking how odd it was that a werewolf was playing high-school basketball and nobody found this peculiar.

Chris messaged Nonie and she left work, bringing her laptop to my place. She worked at the kitchen table as I lay on the couch under a doona, crying and sleeping and crying and sleeping. Later, my friends fed Hamish and stood in my kitchen, speaking in whispers as I sought counsel on the phone from Veronica. Then they drove me to the doctor and waited as Dr Fiona called Veronica and they discussed the next steps. Knocking myself out with Valium was not a sustainable plan. My family were on the other side of the world and my friends couldn't keep putting their lives on hold to watch over me. Fiona suggested hospitalisation as an option. But I was scared. I thought back to my teens and that locked ward with the screaming behind metal doors. I didn't want to go. Not yet.

Nonie brought me home and asked me what I could manage to eat, but decisions were beyond me. She went out and came back with tacos, quietly laying the food out, coaxing me to eat, as if I were a scared animal. I took a few bites and we sat under doonas, watching Jimmy Fallon's *Lip Synch Battle*. When she left, Jason tag-teamed, having jumped in the car and driven across the city in his pyjamas. Standing in my hallway, he held me, and I remember thinking if he let go I might die, shattering into a thousand pieces right there on the carpet. We got into bed and he wrapped his arms around my waist and told me I was safe. I was not alone.

The next day, Chris picked me up and took me for a drive. I was disconnected, staring through the windscreen at a world that was muted and out of focus. He talked, telling me silly stories about people we knew as he drove me around, destination nowhere. We stopped at a hipster burger bar and I lay my head on his shoulder as we shared a vanilla milkshake with two straws. Back in the car, Bobby McFerrin's 'Don't Worry Be Happy' came on the radio and I cried as I wondered if I'd ever again be able to laugh at irony.

In those difficult days, weeks, and months, my loved ones held me up. Not just Chris, Nonie, and Jason, but so many loving, compassionate friends and colleagues who visited, walked with me, held my hand, or just sat patiently while I cried. It was a village of helpers, and I'm grateful to every single one of them. There were times when I was so depleted, the strength of their love pushed me through moments that felt infinitely hopeless. Family sent cards and letters from different parts of the world. Flowers from my brother and his girls appeared on the doorstep. Food parcels and care packages were brought round with hugs. I couldn't see a path to the future but when Nonie sat on my couch, her voice breaking as she imagined a world without me in it, the heartbroken look in her eye made me promise to hold on.

I was also lucky to have an incredibly empathetic editor at *The Age,* Duska Sulicich, who backed me all the way and persuaded management to keep paying me throughout my absence. I was so grateful for that gesture of faith. It eased the pressure and allowed me the space to recover my strength and do the emotionally gruelling work in therapy. She kept in touch with Fiona and Veronica, and together we formulated a plan to get me back to work gradually, building up my days over a period of months until I was able to return full-time.

But not everyone has this experience. A 2013 study of 1,000 Australian workers found that four out of ten people who take sick leave for depression hide it from their employer, with almost half fearing they would lose their job if they revealed their illness. I suspect that figure would be even higher for more stigmatised conditions such as bipolar disorder or schizophrenia.

While workplace mindfulness programs and yoga classes might provide organisations with a cheap way to be seen to be doing something about the overwhelming demands on employees, they also obscure the structural problems that make it so difficult for people to speak up when they are struggling to cope.

Around the time I was making tentative steps back into the newsroom after nearly five months off work, beyondblue CEO Georgie Harman hit the headlines when she stated publicly that employees who disclose mental-health problems are risking their careers. She said she couldn't in good conscience encourage full and open disclosure because discrimination remained rife in many industries. Her advice was simple: 'Don't, because you might not get that promotion, you might get the sack, there might be repercussions.'

It was an extraordinary statement from the head of a mental-health organisation that has been an awareness-raising juggernaut, searing the prevalence of depression into the national consciousness. For 17 years, beyondblue, founded by former Victorian premier Jeff Kennett, had been urging people to speak up and get help; now here was its CEO saying, actually, don't, it's too risky. It was the same advice I was given just a few months later, when I was asked to appear on a panel discussing mental health in my capacity as a journalist who had covered the issue for many years. Prior to the event, I confessed to a contact who heads up a major mental-health organisation that I was considering disclosing my own struggles with anxiety. The advice was brutally honest: 'Don't. It might be used against you. I wish it wasn't true, but you will be judged.'

It made me realise how fortunate I'd been to keep my job. When I spoke to Harman some months later, she agreed that this was a sad reality and stood by her previous comments:

> As a society we are at that really interesting point of social change where organisations like beyondblue have been banging the drum and encouraging people to talk about it [mental illness] and educate themselves and come out

and be open and seek help and at the same time we haven't quite got the structures, the systems or the case law. We haven't got the kind of markers as a society that say, 'If you do this, it will be okay, you'll be protected.'

The culture has shifted in as much as we're having conversations about mental health we've never had before, and for that I'm grateful. My teenage self would have been spared a lot of angst had I known other people faced similar problems. But Harman's comments serve as a stark reminder that we have a long way to go. Raised awareness can only be considered a success if that awareness translates into meaningful change.

It's become almost fashionable to show support for people with mental-health problems. Wear a wristband for depression. Start a hashtag for suicide prevention. Get a beaming celebrity to post an Instagram endorsement of your fun run for anxiety. But when services are stretched beyond capacity, cheap slacktivism is not enough. I don't want to read another passive-aggressive, copy-and-paste (MUST COPY, NO SHARING!) suicide awareness post on Facebook. Soulless and manipulative, they're little more than modern-day chain letters. There's always the kicker: *I know 99% of you won't share, but if even one of you does it will make a difference to people in need.* Subtext: you can join me up here on the moral high ground or you can be a heartless monster who wants to see people die. Your choice.

One I saw recently read:

Many people think that a suicide attempt is a selfish move because the person just does not care about the people left behind. I can tell you that when a person gets to that point, they truly believe that their loved ones will be much better off with them gone. This is mental illness not selfishness. TRUTH: Depression is a terrible disease and seems relentless. A lot of us have been close to that edge, or dealt with family members in a crisis, and some have lost friends and loved ones. Let's look out for each other and stop sweeping mental illness under the rug.

It went on at some length before imploring people to cut and paste the status for one hour to give a moment of support for people who were struggling. One hour. One whole hour of allowing a paragraph written by a stranger to occupy your tiny corner of cyberspace. In your face, suicide! Cop that, depression! I'm sure it's well-intentioned and maybe it even gives some comfort to those who have lost loved ones to suicide, but when I was struggling it just made me angry. People living with mental illness or emotional distress need more than hashtags, wristbands, and platitudes. They need supportive workplaces, well-trained GPs, investment in research, and a system that doesn't cast them adrift if they don't recover in the socially accepted timeframe. More often than not, they need cold hard cash.

My psychologist costs almost $200 a session. Some cost even more. With the Medicare rebate, I get $125 back each time. When things were really bad, I was seeing Veronica twice a week just to survive. I tore through my ten Medicare-subsidised sessions in five weeks. After that, I had to raise almost $400 every week — more than $1,700 per calendar month — to pay for treatment. Finding Dr Fiona was a welcome relief from the quick-turnaround GPs I'd had in the past, but it came at a cost. Her extended consultations were billed at $250 a session, and the out-of-pocket gap I had to cover was substantial. When she referred me to a psychiatrist for a medication review, it cost a staggering $430 for a 45-minute consultation. My private health insurance gave me $300 a year in psychological services, which covered fewer than two sessions with Veronica. And when Dr Fiona suggested the possibility of a short-term hospital stay, I was shocked to discover that despite being covered for inpatient care for a range of physical health problems, there was no cover for psychiatric admissions. I could no more separate my mind from my body than I could grow a third arm, but as far as the system was concerned, they were completely different entities. More than half of all health insurance policies don't provide adequate cover for a stay in a private psychiatric hospital.

In a landmark 2015 case, 21-year-old University of Melbourne student Ella Ingram won a David and Goliath battle against industry giant QBE when the Victorian Civil and Administrative Tribunal awarded her $20,000 after ruling the company had breached the *Equal Opportunity Act* by denying her travel-insurance claim. She'd taken out the cover as a Year 12 student before a school trip to New York. But soon after she became depressed and suicidal, requiring hospital treatment for a fortnight. Her doctor advised her to cancel the trip while she recovered. QBE refused to pay her cancellation costs, despite her condition developing after she had taken out the cover. Taking them to court was a huge gamble that nobody before had taken and won.

When things were really rough for me, I managed to stay out of hospital by being lucky enough to have a generous support network and continuing with weekly intensive therapy. But as it cost a small fortune, I dipped into my savings and Dad stepped in to help. He drew down on his mortgage and sent me money so I could pay for sessions with Veronica in advance. Without his assistance I honestly don't think I'd be alive. Sometimes I lie awake at night wondering what will happen if I find myself back in a place of despair. I never for a moment forget how fortunate I was to be in the position of having financial support. I think of people who are unemployed, on minimum wage, from vulnerable communities with families to feed. How do they keep going? Often they can't. It's impossible to ignore the very clear link between mental illness and poverty. Disadvantage, income inequality, and a lack of emotional support and connection to community are major drivers of mental ill health. And if people can't afford to be sick, it's not surprising they deteriorate. A mindfulness colouring book and corporate 'well washing' programs are no substitute for proper investment in treatment or the social structures that provide a protective barrier from psychological problems. People need the right help at the right time. If it's not there, things can go wrong very quickly. Martin Vo's family can attest to that.

Of course, we should keep working to reduce stigma and have open and frank discussions about mental health, but awareness-raising is not enough. We desperately need more money for treatment and scientific research. There is still so much we don't know about the brain and the intricately complex realm of emotional health. The treatment options available are not as advanced or evidence-based as in other areas of healthcare. I know none of this is easy. But surely we can do better? Surely we can do more than update our status on Facebook? We need our leaders to stop paying lip service to change and take real action. When we ask 'R U OK?' there needs to be somewhere to go when the answer is no. The chances of surviving our emotional pain should not be determined by the balance of our bank accounts.

12

THE NEW NORMAL

We all have labels. There are the ones that make us part of something bigger than ourselves: daughter, aunty, sister, friend, ally, godmother. There are those that put us into tribes: Scot, Aussie, journo, leftie, Hawks fan, Gen X. Then there are the ones that only we can see. They're usually the labels that constrain us: crazy person, procrastinator, depressive, fuck-up, defective, fraud.

There is one label I can't seem to peel off: problem child. Its adhesive is watertight. I don't know exactly when the term first came into my mind, but I remember feeling that I'd been marked from the day I was born. Wednesday's child is full of woe, and there was nothing I could do about it.

There's a story my family tells about an incident in my childhood. On holiday in France when I was about six years old, we visited a park with a map of the world carved into turf in the middle of a lake, allowing visitors to hop from country to country. Neil and Dad had gone back to the grassy bank by the side of the lake, while Mum and I were still navigating our way through the nations of South America. At the southern tip of the continent I attempted to make the leap across to Antarctica, but misjudged the gap and plunged into the murky depths off the coast of Argentina, thrashing around in what was only knee-deep water but to me might as well have been the bottom of the ocean. My brother and Dad burst into laughter, while Mum helped fish me out, dripping wet as I cried in abject mortification at the public spectacle I'd become. Every time Dad retells the story he sings 'Don't Cry for Me Argentina', and we all laugh at the hilarious scene I caused. But I can remember even in that moment thinking, *Why do I always stuff things up?*

When my adolescent angst stretched on for longer than it should have, the problem-child label really took hold. It was a bewildering time, and I remember feeling ashamed of the way I couldn't get over what Dad discreetly called my 'troubles'. I felt guilty for the distress I was causing my parents. Every family has an oddball, and I was it. A red wine stain on a crisp white tablecloth. I visited a succession of GPs, psychiatrists, and psychologists, who made diagnoses and predictions that served to confirm what I had thought for so long: I was not normal. One doctor told me I might have to take antidepressants for the rest of my life. Just as my brother needed medication to manage his epilepsy, I would require pills to keep me sane. They said I had a chemical imbalance that needed correcting.

I remember my psychiatrist—an elegant, grey-haired man in a three-piece suit who practised from a grand Victorian house with huge bay windows and antique wooden furniture in Edinburgh's southside—offering me, at 19, an interesting take on my future. 'You're going to have a very successful life. You will achieve anything you put your mind to. The challenge for you will be whether you can overcome your anxiety enough to enjoy it.'

As *carpe diem*s go, it was a bit shit. But the words stayed with me. Anxiety was going to be my meal ticket or the ball and chain around my ankle. In some ways it was both. He was right that my life, by any objective measure, has been a success thus far. I've enjoyed a great professional life and have reached many of the life goals that make up the formulaic equation for happiness. I've jumped out of planes (twice), swum with sharks, appeared on live radio and television, and passionately spoken my mind on more occasions than has probably been good for my career. But it hasn't made the worrying go away. And through it all, I struggled to shake the belief that I was abnormal. My fate had been sealed by the prognosis I'd been given.

Labels can be informative and necessary. The skull and crossbones on a bottle of bleach warns kids it's not for drinking. But they can also pose their own risk: they can be limiting and self-defeating. I often wonder what would have happened if I hadn't been told at an early age that anxiety and depression would be with me for life. Would I have still viewed myself as damaged goods? Or perceived every bad day as the start of an impending breakdown? Maybe, like so many teenagers struggling with a developing mind, a changing body, peer pressure, and the desperate need to belong, given time, with the right professional who would offer the space to really listen, I would have been okay. Instead, I came to believe the narrative that I was an abnormality to be fixed.

My struggles evolved during a dramatic period of change in the way society perceives and responds to our emotional health and the vagaries of the mind. Stigma is slowly being reduced, encouraging more people to seek help. But the rising prevalence of psychological disorders has coincided with a broadening definition of mental illness. Experiences that might once have been considered transient, normal facets of the human condition can now be classified as disorders. The figures say that one in five of us will experience a mental disorder in any given year, and almost half will be afflicted in our lifetimes. It's hard to know if mental illness is more prevalent than it once was, or if medicine has simply blurred the boundaries between normality and disease. One person's *eccentric* is another's *senile*. There's a fine line between *creative visionary* and *deranged heretic*.

Over the last decade in particular, there has been a growing unease within mental-health circles about the medicalisation of the human experience. This shift, according to some experts, has sparked false epidemics of psychiatric disorders and led to more people being unnecessarily medicated. They believe the diagnostic bar has been set so low that everyday sadness and personality quirks are being pathologised. In a culture that places such a premium on happiness, any deviation from this expected default emotional position is viewed as aberrant.

At the heart of the debate is the changing definition of mental illness and the contentious document used globally to diagnose disorders. *The Diagnostic and Statistical Manual of Mental Disorders* (DSM), produced by the American Psychiatric Association, has grown from a 130-page booklet of around 60 broad illnesses in its first edition in 1952 to a 947-page tome listing almost 300 disorders. Its fifth and most recent edition, published in 2013, dropped the threshold for many existing conditions and introduced a range of new disorders, including 'disruptive mood dysregulation disorder', which critics say essentially turns children's tantrums into an illness, and 'mild neurocognitive disorder', which some say makes the natural forgetfulness of age a treatable disease. It's also now easier for a boisterous child to meet the diagnosis for attention-deficit/ hyperactivity disorder (ADHD), as the number of symptoms required for a diagnosis has been halved. There's already been a global epidemic of the condition and a subsequent spike in kids being medicated since it was added to the DSM in 1987.

These revisions to the manual's fifth edition caused an international outcry, with 51 health groups, including the American Counselling Association, the American Psychological Association, and the British Psychological Society, calling for an independent review. It also sparked a bitter divide within the psychiatric community, with the debate as much about the ideological future of the profession as about the nature of mental illness. Perhaps the most controversial decision was the removal of the bereavement exclusion when diagnosing major depression. Previously, doctors had been urged to refrain from giving a diagnosis of clinical depression within the first few months of a patient experiencing grief. While the symptoms may be similar to a major depressive disorder, bereavement is not a sickness, they argued. But under the new DSM, a person can be classified as having a depressive illness after just two weeks of grieving. Two weeks. We have medicalised a normal, albeit intensely painful, part of the human experience. Anyone who has experienced grief knows all too well that no pill can ease the heartache of losing a loved one.

When I was diagnosed with depression in my teens, it coincided not only with several years of bullying but also the death of four people who were close to me. I lost my gran, my great-aunt (who was like a grandmother to me), my uncle, and, finally, the five-year-old daughter of one of my mum's oldest and closest friends. By the time I was 18, I'd been to more funerals than most people twice my age. As a pessimistic individual with a natural propensity to catastrophise and obsess about death, it heightened my angst at the fragility of the world. I struggled to make sense of my loss. And yet, when my parents sent me for help, the professionals showed little interest in discussing the bereavements that had taken such a toll on our family. Their silence on the subject indicated that they thought this wasn't enough to explain my mood. I don't know if they were wrong. I was definitely terribly unhappy and I needed help. But there was something about the label *depressive* that cemented my problem-child status. It was a self-fulfilling prophecy as I came to believe that I was helpless, that being mentally defective was an integral part of my identity.

I didn't want to be crazy. It wasn't that long ago people displaying signs of mental ill-health were locked up in austere, high-walled asylums, as governments attempted to shield polite society from their madness. In Victoria, suicide was considered a crime until 1958. Sixty years later, and we still routinely talk about people 'committing' suicide. For many years I was an advisory group member of the Australian government's Mindframe National Media Initiative—set up in 2002 to promote responsible, accurate, and sensitive representation of mental illness and suicide in the media. Our job was to educate journalists about the stigma created by using words such as *psycho*, *lunatic*, or *maniac*. We helped foster shifts in editorial policies such as the now-standard practice of including links to Lifeline at the ends of stories dealing with suicide, and avoiding reporting on the details or method in order to avoid a suicide contagion effect. We also tried to bust the inaccurate stereotype that people with mental illness are dangerous, pointing out that they're more likely to be a victim of crime than a perpetrator. It might have changed some of the reporting in *The Age* newsroom, but as I was trying to return to work, I learned that we still have a long way to go to shift cultural attitudes. The management executive who liaised with my boss, my GP, and psychologist on my 'transition plan' was well-meaning and kind, but when we met, she looked at me as if I was a live bomb that could blow up in her face at any moment. Some of the paperwork I was made to fill out did not inspire confidence. One form—which asked a series of questions including which duties I could and could not carry out—stated that this was to secure a 'safe working environment' for me and my colleagues. I can't be sure what risk they thought I posed, but I couldn't help but think this paperwork was less about looking after my wellbeing and more an arse-covering exercise to protect the company from litigation should I turn out to have homicidal tendencies and shoot up the newsroom.

Much of the shame and fear that remains around mental illness stems from the labels we use to describe people who are different, unconventional, or just having a bad day. I'll hear a friend joke about someone being 'completely mental' and think, *Yeah, but that could equally apply to me.* How mental do you have to be to be 'completely mental'? Does believing your loved ones are dead if they don't reply to an email get you there? Or not being able to drive a car because the panic makes you feel like the steering wheel's dissolving and your limbs are turning to liquid nitrogen?

Sometimes I'll self-identify as 'a total crazy person' after an episode that has seen me behave in a way that seemed entirely rational at the time but through clarity's rear-view mirror reveals itself to be comical. Like the occasion I was sitting in the forecourt of a service station in Jason's car, waiting for him to pay for petrol, and he took longer than expected—but because I wasn't wearing my glasses I couldn't see there was a long queue and only one attendant, so naturally I assumed he was lying on the floor having a seizure as fellow drivers delivered mouth-to-mouth, and life seeped from his limp body. Or the time that Dr Fiona's receptionist unexpectedly brought my pap smear follow-up appointment forward by a day and for three agonising hours I sat rigid at work, utterly convinced I had end-stage cervical cancer. Or the fact that despite my period being an event I have lived with for more than 25 years, every month without fail it takes two days of spontaneously weeping at videos of soldiers being welcomed home from combat by their dogs before I remember I'm not on the verge of a breakdown but am just premenstrual.

Finding humour in the absurd things my brain tricks me into believing allows me to view the anxiety as something that is happening to me rather than a condition that defines who I am. But the mockery is still a judgement. There's an element of self-criticism in quantifying my emotional state. People undergoing chemotherapy don't describe themselves as 'totally cancer-ridden' when things are bad. And yet the way I talk about my emotional health can often be disparaging. It has a history that goes all the way back to adolescence, when I was given a label and began to view myself as damaged. And, of course, this was a script that the child part of me that already felt broken and bad was only too willing to recite.

In some ways, I'm a product of the psychiatric trends of my time. The diagnostic categories of mental illness have expanded with every edition of the DSM, and the threshold for being diagnosed with a depressive illness has gradually dropped. While once depression was broadly divided into two types — melancholic depression, which was seen as a disease and had no obvious cause, and reactive depression, sparked by stressful life events — DSM-3, released in 1980, four years after I was born, essentially created one condition that varies by severity. Mild or moderate sadness was lumped into the same category as what was once considered clinical depression.

GPs now grade patients against a checklist of symptoms—the Kessler 'exactly how fucked up are you' scale I have come to dread so much—to arrive at a diagnosis of mild, moderate, or severe depression. It's a blunt instrument that doesn't take into consideration life circumstances or underlying drivers. It's a snapshot of a person's emotional state at a specific moment in time. It is little more than a number on a chart. A number that can assign a label that sticks for life.

In a system set up to deliver the magic bullet, GPs—who prescribe 85 per cent of all psychiatric drugs in Australia—simply don't have time to investigate the many potential causes of psychological distress. And when people are at their lowest point, a 'happy' pill is often welcomed as a short, sharp salve for their pain. It's been a boon for the pharmaceutical industry. The most recent figures on the global psychiatric-drug market value the sector at around $88 billion. It's a long way from the 1950s, when the world's first antidepressant, imipramine, was invented, and manufacturer Geigy worried there weren't enough depressed people for it to generate a profit.

In Australia, the market is flourishing. A 2013 report providing a health overview of the 33 Organisation for Economic Co-operation and Development nations found that Australia was the second-highest prescriber of antidepressant medications, with the rate of use doubling in a decade. It showed that 89 Australians in every 1,000 were taking antidepressants, compared to 45 in 2000. The following year, researchers from the University of Sydney discovered that the number of children aged 10 to 14 being prescribed the drugs had jumped by more than a third between 2009 and 2012.

When antidepressants first hit the market, the thinking was that they helped correct malfunctioning neurotransmitters in the brain by strengthening the serotonin signal between nerve cells. I've lost count of how many doctors told me that depleted levels of serotonin—one of the mind's 'happy' chemicals—was the reason I was so sad. This chemical imbalance theory became firmly rooted in the public consciousness from 1987 when Prozac—one of the first of a new generation of antidepressants known as selective serotonin reuptake inhibitors (SSRIs)—went on sale. It became the most widely prescribed antidepressant in history, a potent symbol of our culture's quest for the happiness quick-fix. By 2007, 54 million people worldwide were taking it.

I've been on and off various antidepressant medications since I was 16. I took them because the doctors told me if I didn't, my 'imbalanced' brain would continue to malfunction. If I wanted my happy-ever-after, it would come in a little white pill taken every morning with breakfast.

There have been times when I've felt the drugs have helped me function again. Other times, they've barely touched the sides of my pain. Most recently, I took them, reluctantly, because I'd reached the point where each day was a slow dance with suicide. I couldn't expect my friends to keep putting their life on hold to watch over me. I either tried medication or I went to hospital.

Things slowly improved, but the improvement coincided with profound breakthroughs in therapy with Veronica that untangled so much of my past and helped me rely on myself more. I can't know for sure whether it was the medication, the therapy, or a combination of both. But the weeks of debilitating physical and psychological withdrawal symptoms I've suffered every time I've come off these drugs leave me in no doubt that they are incredibly powerful chemicals I'd rather not take unless left with no other options.

And I'm not the only one having doubts. An increasing number of clinicians and researchers now argue that the case for antidepressants as an effective and widespread treatment option for depression and anxiety has been based on a lie. The debate was blown open in 2012 when Harvard Medical School scientist and psychologist Irving Kirsch told the US *60 Minutes* program that his extensive research revealed the difference between drug and placebo is very small, and in half the studies non-existent. While he didn't deny many people improved after taking antidepressants, he concluded, 'It's not the chemical ingredients of the drug that's making them better. It is largely the placebo effect.'

Around the same time, in a series of articles in *The Age* looking at the pathologising of the human condition—which in hindsight was perhaps an attempt to untangle my own emotional problems—I spoke to Professor Michael Baigent, a psychiatrist and a director of beyondblue, who echoed Kirsch's views. He stressed that for those with severe and otherwise untreated depression, not taking antidepressants could be life-threatening, but people with more moderate symptoms are far less responsive to medication. 'The chemical imbalance explanation is an oversimplification of a very complex picture,' he said. 'There's a tendency to want to dumb it down and say people are depressed and all depression needs an antidepressant, but when you look at the research you see that their effect is really greatest with the more severe forms of depression. With the less severe forms they're often no better than a placebo.'

Kirsch's findings were backed up by two studies co-authored by Dr Walter Brown, clinical professor of psychiatry at Brown University's Warren Alpert Medical School. He said that it was the mildly depressed who largely accounted for the huge increase in antidepressant prescriptions over the previous decade and yet they were the ones least likely to benefit from them.

This is not something you hear very often when you visit a doctor to discuss your emotional health. I can't remember a GP ever telling me that the chemical imbalance theory was flawed or that taking antidepressants might be no more useful than swallowing a sugar pill. Perhaps when I've felt they worked for me it was the placebo effect. Maybe it doesn't matter. If the end result was me feeling better, why should I care? But looking back, I can't help wondering what effect these pills may have had on my developing teenage brain. According to a 2016 *Lancet* study, the majority of antidepressants given to children and teenagers are ineffective, and some are potentially dangerous, increasing the risk of suicidal thoughts. Of the 14 types of antidepressant taken by 5,000 children in the study aged nine to 18, only Prozac was found to be statistically more effective than a placebo. Among those shown to be ineffective were the two drugs I was prescribed at 16 and at 18.

Millions of people across the globe continue to take antidepressants. For some, there is no doubt they can be life-saving. Medication is an important part of the treatment regimen for many conditions, and people should have access without judgment or shame. But how many millions of people are taking pills in an attempt to 'correct' a brain imbalance that simply doesn't exist for them? Their suffering is real, but the way out of it might not come in a blister pack of daily tablets. Perhaps we don't really want to hear that the drugs don't work—we just want the magic pill that will take the pain away.

The broadening of categories in the DSM is in some ways a reflection of our culture's inability to sit with our discomfort. We are so focused on the expectation of happiness we don't want to feel loss or anger or the myriad shades of profound sadness life can throw at us, so we label it as sickness. If there's a malady, there must be a remedy. We want the fairytale ending, however we can get it.

The most strident critic of the pathologising of the human condition has been American psychiatrist Allen Frances, who chaired the expert committee that developed the DSM-4 in 1994. He has labelled DSM-5 a 'dangerous public health experiment' that will inappropriately inflict the 'mental disorder' label on millions of people previously considered normal.

Frances believes the system is now set up to misdiagnose or unnecessarily medicate people who are not mentally ill, while at the other end of the spectrum, people are told they're not sick enough for support and only receive care when they reach crisis point. His critics paint him as a disgruntled malcontent seeking relevance after his moment in the spotlight has passed. I disagree. We've spoken many times and I've always found him to be informed, considered, and congenial. During a trip to Australia as part of a speaking tour, we met in person and it was clear that he finds the explosion of psychiatric diagnoses genuinely troubling. Permanently tanned, with a full head of thick white hair, the 75-year-old told me there has been an 'imperial, wholesale takeover of normality' and that the 'pool of normal has shrunk to a puddle'.

In 2013, he documented these concerns in *Saving Normal: an insider's revolt against out-of-control psychiatric diagnosis, DSM-5, Big Pharma, and the medicalization of ordinary life*, which became an international bestseller. We reconnected as I was writing this book, and while previously I'd interviewed him for his views on over-diagnosis, this time I laid bare my own history of mental-health problems.

He has retired from practice, but remains Professor Emeritus of Psychiatry and Behavioral Sciences at Duke University. Speaking from his home in California, he'd lost none of his passion for the cause. There was an audible gasp when I mentioned I'd been told as a teenager I might need to take antidepressants for the rest of my life. 'That's terrible misinformation. Very often the symptoms that present in youngsters are transitory and related to adolescence,' he said. 'There's no evidence that antidepressants work very well for teenagers, and they have considerable risk for that age group. Similarly, ADHD drugs and antipsychotics are widely overused. We're conducting a population-wide experiment in bathing immature brains in powerful neurotransmitters, not knowing what the long-term impact is, and there's very little evidence that for most kids they're helpful.'

For teenagers, Frances said, a 'watchful waiting' approach was best. Family stress, developmental issues, peer pressure, exams, and relationship problems can cause acute distress for a short period of time, but that distress doesn't necessarily constitute a mental disorder, much less one that will last a lifetime. Given what was going on in my life at the time, he said it was possible my distress would have been short-lived if I'd had access to the appropriate counselling. Just because I'd been a chronic worrier since I was a child didn't necessarily mean I had a psychiatric disorder.

'Lots of people have anxiety; it can either be crippling or it's something that you can manage very well, that much is true,' he told me. 'The part I object to is the prediction that it looms over your future as a haunting black cloud. We can make prognostic guesses, but there's tremendous variability, even without treatment, especially in young people, and to make these magisterial comments as if we know exactly how things are going to turn out is just unsupported by facts. It's arrogant and it can be very harmful.'

When I asked him about Australia's rising youth suicide rate and how he can reconcile this with the idea that there is a false epidemic of psychiatric diagnoses, he pointed out that not everyone who takes their own life has a mental disorder, particularly impulsive teenagers who can pursue drastically permanent solutions to temporary problems. 'Often they're experiencing bullying or have stress at school or they lose a romantic relationship and that can be the trigger. Part of why we haven't had that much effect on suicide rates is because not all suicides are related to the conditions we treat.'

Frances believes adolescents should be given more time with GPs and access to psychotherapy before drugs are considered. He stresses that he does not doubt that many people—including some children and teenagers—suffer from diagnosable mental disorders that can be incredibly debilitating and may require medication. But the threshold for emotional distress to be considered a disorder should be if the symptoms are 'classic, severe, persistent, and cause considerable distress and impairment'. This means monitoring patients to ensure their emotional state is not transient. 'People coming in during the worst day of their life often will feel much better in a very short period of time. If they get medicine during their first visit, they'll be convinced it was the medicine that made them better and maybe feel compelled to stay on it for a long duration when it's really just placebo.'

He partly blames flawed epidemiology for over-inflating the prevalence of psychiatric disorders, but saves his greatest ire for pharmaceutical companies, which he claims are only slightly higher up the moral food chain than illegal drug cartels. It's been in their interests, he says, to turn every facet of the human condition into a problem requiring a pill. If people aren't really sick, it works to their advantage.

'People with very severe conditions have a placebo response rate under 10 per cent. People with mild conditions have a placebo response rate of over 50 per cent,' he said. 'The person taking the pill doesn't know whether they're a placebo responder or not, but the most satisfied customers will be those people who are taking a pill they don't need. The drug companies could not have gotten as rich as they did treating severe disorders because it's a small market.'

Given what we now know about neuroplasticity and the ability to change our brains through psychotherapy rather than psychotropic drugs, it seems clear the chemical imbalance theory is an unhelpful, catch-all notion for many of the people who have been medicated and given labels that can impact on their whole lives. As Norman Doidge, the psychiatrist and author, discovered, our brains are not fixed. A tough time doesn't necessarily mean we will be sick forever. We might not be sick at all. When we view our suffering solely through the prism of a biological malfunction, we ignore the underlying drivers of that pain. Feeling the full depth of life's low points is not something you often see depicted in the neat Hollywood ending, but it does not make you mad or weird or broken. Frances points out that the capacity to experience suffering and pain is a necessary part of the human condition. 'Evolution doesn't have sadness and grief built into us for no reason—these are normal, useful emotions. People who don't feel anxiety get into terrible trouble. The essence of being a mammal is being able to love and attach, and the price of that is a sense of loss.'

I am by no means anti-medication. But what would have happened if I'd been offered more of a choice when I was young and at a crossroads? Perhaps I still would have struggled with anxiety throughout adulthood. Perhaps I wouldn't. I just wish there was better research on the therapeutic responses to the emotional distress so many of us experience. I wish we had a system that provides the time and space for people to have those conversations—for their life stories to be heard. A system that doesn't cap therapy at ten hours a year, and that offers solutions beyond the prescription pad. Most of all, I wish we had a system that sees the person, not the label. As Frances told me, it's easy to give a diagnosis, but it's very hard to take it away.

The work I've done in therapy has helped me see that I am much more than a label. It's also allowed me to start accepting that the challenges I've faced—as tough as they've been—do not necessarily make me abnormal. In a culture that puts happiness and perfection on a pedestal, everyone has issues they secretly worry make them a bit weird. So many of us view ourselves as damaged, defective, not quite right. And yet, clearly, most of us are not living out the happiness fairytale that we've been sold as the norm. It's time to flip the script. If everyone struggles, we can't all be mad. Or if we are, maybe that's okay. As Veronica pointed out one day in a statement I found strangely comforting, 'We're all fucked up. Every single one of us.' Perhaps, in these challenging times, 'not quite right' is the new normal.

As I look back, I realise that in some ways the problem-child label stuck because part of me needed to believe it. Being defective had become my identity. Who would I be without it? I'm reminded of the episode of *The Simpsons* where Homer gets his hand stuck in a vending machine. Waiting for firefighters to rescue him after being trapped for hours, he is eventually asked by a co-worker, 'Homer, are you just holding on to the can?' He sheepishly lets go, removes his arm, and walks free.

Flipping
The Script

—★

13

IT'S ALWAYS DARKEST
BEFORE THE DAWN

When the ground beneath me crumbled, it was my dark night of the soul—a sort of spiritual reckoning in which everything I'd known to be true had collapsed. For so long I had chased the external fix to bring me happiness. I had always looked outside myself for reassurance. In my child's mind I'd come to believe that being sick and helpless was how I would be noticed and loved.

Some of my most vivid childhood memories revolve around times when I was in need. When I was knocked off my bike during my early morning paper round and was scooped up off the road by a lovely couple in a passing car who had swerved to avoid running me over. They brought me home, and I tearfully showed Mum my buckled bike and bloodied knees, revelling in her attention. When I was home from school with a cold or a stomach-ache, and Mum would wrap me in her fluffy black-and-white sheepskin coat and lay me on the couch. We called it the 'sick coat', and wearing it was always a treat. Even now, when I return home, just running my hands across its soft down makes me feel safe.

As desperate as I felt in those days when I had lost all will to live, it was perhaps an unconscious attempt to go back to that familiar childhood state that brought the ones I loved rallying to my side, just as they had for my brother. But it was a narrative that no longer served me. I was not the problem child. It was time to stop viewing myself as broken. Veronica put it to me: 'It's a cocoon. It's warm and cosy and you don't want to leave, but you have to ask yourself, what is the cost of remaining here?'

My parents, 17,000 kilometres away and feeling helpless, were frantic. Mum's instinct was to get on the first plane. But she was sick herself, struggling with a blood-pressure problem that left her exhausted, anaemic, and prone to passing out. Her doctor strongly advised her not to fly. We shared a distraught Skype conversation and she was adamant she was coming anyway. I wanted nothing more than to feel Mum's arms wrapped around me. But I couldn't let her risk her own health. And what would she do when she got here? The sick coat wasn't going to fix me. I needed to start looking after myself. I told her to stay home and get better.

This was a turning point. I fought for myself harder than I've ever fought for anything in my life. I began to claw my way to the surface of a deep well, my nails cracked and bloodied with the effort of dragging myself up, inch by inch, to a place where I could finally snatch a few breaths of clean air.

A huge part of building my resilience came from journalling. It allowed me to wade through the murky soup of anxiety and shame that took up so much space in my head. Committing my thoughts to the page was like opening a pressure valve. I was completely uncensored. Nothing was off limits. I wrote about my deepest fears and my most irrational out-of-touch-with-reality beliefs. It was all recorded in a stream-of-consciousness brain dump that often made little sense. But in the hours or days that followed, something would shift. At a time when I was trying to move away from helplessness, just writing down my thoughts was a form of self-care that allowed me to strengthen the part that had for too long sought reassurance from the outside.

During those tough times, when a good week was one in which I managed a whole morning without crying, I went full *Rain Man* and started documenting my wins in a colour-coded sticker system on a large wall calendar. It was a visual reminder that I still had choices. Green was for when I'd exercised, blue was for meditation, yellow was for when I'd managed to get out of bed before 9.00 am, red was for eating, and pink was for when I'd practised being a good parent to the child part of myself by not acting on the irrational thoughts she so regularly conjured up. It allowed me to note correlations between my mood and the actions—or lack of them—I took, to give myself the best chance of getting through the week. Invariably, when my calendar was a riot of colour I did much better than when there was a whole lot of white space. The colour reminded me I was not powerless.

The sticker system has since been retired, but I still keep a journal. The collection of prettily patterned, brightly coloured notebooks takes up a whole shelf in my coffee table. Despite external appearances, those pages are predominantly filled with pain. The journals are, by design, a safe space for unadulterated grief and angst. I rarely read back on what I've written. If I did, it would give the impression that my life is one long purgatory of abject misery. It's not.

For this reason, I also keep a gratitude journal as a counterweight. Every night before bed I make a note of three things I'm grateful for or which went well that day. Sometimes it's easy. The morning walk that left me feeling energised. An intimate dinner with dear friends. Meeting a deadline for a complex piece of work. But it's on the tough days I have to look a bit harder. And yet the more I practise, the more I find that even on the shittiest day, when life kicks you in the crotch, spits in your face, and steals your lunch money, if you keep your eyes clear and your heart open, there is always something to be grateful for.

When I'm consciously looking for positives, they start to present themselves. As I clawed my way out of the well, it was a small comfort to commit to paper something good I had achieved that day. Of course, there's a clear difference between being grateful and the 'think positive' movement, which wants us to grin our way out of the blues. When I was really struggling, I'd read those 'inspirational' memes on Instagram and want to put my fist through the wall. *Happiness is a choice. Live in the moment—it's all there is.* Go fuck yourself. What if the moment is an excruciating purgatory that feels like being slowly stabbed to death by your own brain? I was more drawn to the growing 'demotivational' counterculture, which cheekily takes aim at the motivational quotes blanketing the internet in a sickly sweet hue of positivity and offers a different view. I started following Unspirational, an account that, instead of offering peppy life lessons set against images of tranquil beaches and rolling meadows, appealed to my dark sense of humour by providing advice such as, *Don't cry because it's over. Cry because eventually everything will be over too.* Or, *Success is just failure that hasn't happened yet.* Giving thanks privately, in a confessional space such as a journal, is not the same as plastering a smile on your face and repeating affirmations in the mirror that 'all is well' as your life blows up around you. Gratitude is about accepting the hard times but realising all is not lost.

Some days, when I'm doing it really tough, my gratitude journal entries are as basic as they come:

- Lady in the pharmacy was kind when I was sad.
- Made it to the gym even though I didn't want to get out of bed.
- It was nice being cosy in my apartment with the rain lashing down outside.

On other days, my list can spread over two pages. This nightly ritual has helped me appreciate the simple things. My friendships are richer as a result. Recording the moments when I'm grateful for the love and support of those around me allows me not only to feel lucky but also to remember to convey that to my friends and family, which in turn deepens our connection. It makes me realise how fortunate I am to have the basics. At home, I find myself sometimes just happy to have a warm bed or an apartment that feels inviting and mine. When my knees creak at the gym, I'm reminded that I'm still healthy enough to work out and financially stable enough to afford the membership.

Science is starting to catch up with what some religions and philosophies have extolled for centuries — that counting your blessings is an integral part of health, wholeness, and contentment. University of California at Davis psychologists Robert Emmons and Michael McCullough — the world's pre-eminent experts on gratitude — have conducted experiments which showed that people who kept gratitude journals reported fewer health complaints and felt more optimistic and more motivated than those who recorded their daily troubles or neutral life events. Their research also shows that gratitude practice can be beneficial for people managing chronic conditions. In a group of adults with neuromuscular disease, they discovered a 21-day intervention resulted in boosted energy, engendered positive moods, and led to better sleep quality and a greater sense of connection to others.

Being thankful can change the way your mind processes events. A 2009 National Institutes of Health study found that gratitude triggers changes in the hypothalamus—the region of the brain that controls functions such as eating, drinking, and sleeping—and has an impact on stress and metabolism. It also activates dopamine, the brain's 'feel-good' chemical. Actively seeking out the good just makes you feel better. This is the theory behind Grateful in April, a global campaign to help people focus on the good in their lives. Founded by Melbourne social entrepreneur and former crime reporter Melina Schamroth, it encourages people to spend the 30 days of April counting their blessings in order to cultivate an 'attitude of gratitude' that will help create a more positive world outlook. Schamroth told me that when people are having a run of bad luck, they often seem to attract more of it no matter what they do. But when they're on a run of good luck, the opposite can happen because they're focusing on the positives around them instead of the misery:

> It's like when you decide you're going to buy a particular type of car, that's all you see everywhere. It's very easy to find something to complain about, but most of us, when we're hungry, we have access to food; we have shelter; we have the basics. That's not to say that bad things don't happen and you shouldn't acknowledge them. But it's about refocusing your attention to realise that there are positive things you can take out of those situations.

Schamroth has seen the change that can come when people are able to unearth hope in the midst of adversity. She started the campaign after supporting communities affected by Victoria's devastating 2009 Black Saturday bushfires. She realised that those people who had lost everything took strength from shifting their perspective and focusing on the things of value that still existed in their lives. This is a common theme for many who sign up to the gratitude challenge. 'We've had people facing very dire situations, health problems, relationship breakdowns, who have reported back that at the end of the month they've been able to turn their thinking around, turn their actions around, and in some cases turn their lives around,' Schamroth said.

When I reached my rock bottom, I had to make a choice. I could continue to believe I was helpless and broken, or I could rewrite the script. It was a daily, at times minute-by-minute, battle. But there was always hope, if I actively sought it out. And it started with me. Marco was right. Stark was strong. I just had to believe it.

I've lived a fortunate life as a middle-class, straight white woman in prosperous, developed countries. I'm acutely aware of how privileged I've been in ways in which so many are not. It's undeniably easier for me to find gratitude in my daily life than it is for those not born into such advantage. Not long after I was back on my feet, I met someone who brought that reality into sharp focus. Chido Govera taught me a valuable lesson about the power of looking for hope and gratitude even when life makes that seem impossible. She was in Melbourne as part of a series of talks with The School of Life, an organisation founded by British philosopher and author Alain de Botton that is committed to developing people's emotional intelligence and fostering social change. I was honoured to be asked to host her at an in-conversation event.

More than most, Chido could be forgiven for feeling angry and defeated by the obstacles life has put in her way. Growing up in Zimbabwe, she was orphaned as a child when she lost her mother to AIDS. At the age of seven, she became a parent to her younger brother and carer for her nearly blind grandmother. It meant waking up at 4.00 am to gather firewood, walking at least a mile to fetch water, working in the field, and somehow finding a way to attend school. She would often go to bed hungry. At eight, she was sexually abused by an uncle, and by her ninth birthday, the struggle of caring for her family and trying to put food on the table forced her to drop out of school. At 11, a family member offered her what they said was her only way to escape the poverty trap — she would marry a 40-year-old man and he would become her provider. But Chido refused. She chose another way, making a promise to herself that she would grow up and protect other orphans. Instead of giving in to anger and hopelessness, she channelled her suffering into a powerful movement for change. She learned to farm mushrooms, and through this most unlikely of escape routes transformed her life and those of more than a thousand women in Zimbabwe, Congo, Ghana, Cameroon, Tanzania, South Africa, India, and even in Aboriginal communities in Australia, teaching them to be self-sufficient through her Future of Hope foundation.

Meeting Chido was intimidating. Nothing makes you examine your contribution to the world quite like taking a look at what this woman has achieved, and all by the age of just 31. When we met at St Kilda's White House — a classically beautiful

160-year-old former home to Victoria's solicitor-general—she had only arrived in Australia the previous day, accompanied by two of her seven foster children, who range in age from 12 to 20. It was the first time either of these teenagers had left Zimbabwe. In the green room, as they tapped away on their phones, I told Chido that so much of what she taught resonated with me. She held my gaze and I felt energised by her strength and compassion.

It's rare to watch a room of 100 people completely captivated for an hour and a half. There was none of the usual fidgeting or shifting in seats. The audience sat forward, transfixed by Chido's warmth and openness. We had all come looking for hope, and she offered it freely, sharing the lessons she had learned from living through the greatest pain. When I asked Chido, whose name means passion, how she dealt with the abuse she had suffered and the loss of her mother, she told us that the anger had propelled her forward. She refused to give in to helplessness. 'We are not what happened to us,' she said, as she described how she encourages the young women she mentors not to view themselves as victims. When a doctor diagnosed her with post-traumatic stress disorder and said there was nothing he could do to help, it was a turning point. 'I realised that I had to tap into the internal. I could not wait for others to make me happy or to relieve my anger. The power was within me.'

As I heard her utter those words, something gave way inside me. I felt a surge of strength and gratitude. I was reminded of that deep reserve of resilience that allowed me to keep going. And although our lives could not have been more different, I felt a profound connection to this woman. We shared the most fundamental of human qualities—the capacity for hope and perseverance. I must stress that I'm not suggesting people who find themselves struggling with ongoing trauma or emotional distress are somehow not trying hard enough. But meeting Chido helped me see that it is often when we are in a place of hopelessness that the power of hope reveals itself. As Holocaust survivor Victor Frankl observed in his memoir, *Man's Search for Meaning*, those who survived longest in Auschwitz had often found a way to have hope and purpose; they comforted others or gave away their last piece of bread, and these active choices sustained them. 'Everything can be taken from a man but one thing: the last of the human freedoms — to choose one's attitude in any given set of circumstances, to choose one's own way,' he wrote.

For Chido, having an open heart helps her find the strength to keep going. 'A lot of hard things, if we allow ourselves to get stuck in that, and not be open enough to learn from new experiences and to have new experiences ourselves, then we will not survive.'

Without an open heart, she told me, we don't see opportunities when they cross our paths. While anger can be a painful and challenging emotion, she believes it is one we cannot avoid. We can also learn from it. 'It has to generate some kind of forgiveness and lessons that allow us to go forward with a light heart.'

I wondered how, in a world that can often feel bleak, with problems that seem insurmountable, she maintained this outlook and discovered to my surprise that it was her traumatic childhood experiences that shaped her sense of optimism. Instead of saying, 'There's nothing I can do, I'm just a child,' Chido recognised that although she was only one person, she was someone who could drive change every day through her actions.

Chido can't possibly reach all of the orphans in Zimbabwe, where almost 10 per cent of the population have lost their parents. But she's making a significant difference with the girls she supports and, in turn, she hopes they'll have a similar impact on future generations. 'I hope to set an example — if not for the girls themselves, then for other people. If not for the people in that community, for other leaders in the world. And gradually the change I want to see in the world will be there.'

Chido pointed out that if she looked at the situation in Zimbabwe as a whole and waited for people in power to enact change, she would feel depressed and helpless. But by tackling problems in which she can make a difference, she has dropped a pebble in a pond, and the ripples are being felt far from home. The two teenage daughters she'd brought with her, bright and full of youthful possibility, face a very different future to the one they might have had if Chido had not intervened. She is not blind to the enormous challenges the world faces but finds hope in her strength, her convictions, and the belief that by taking responsibility for her future she can make a difference. The answer, she believes, almost always comes from within. 'It's important not to think that change will come from the outside, especially in relation to different kinds of hardship. My world changed when the doctors finally told me what I was suffering from, but they couldn't help me. It was one of the most difficult things to hear, but when I look back it was one of the most empowering things because it enabled me to turn my life around to the way it is today.'

For me, the realisation that nobody could come to my rescue was also a pivotal moment. Helplessness was an appealing, familiar place that would have allowed me to abdicate all control and give up, railing against the hand I'd been dealt. But as Chido learned, handing the reins to despair and anger only entrenches our suffering. Finding hope and gratitude in that dark night of the soul allowed me to tap into a part of myself I didn't know was there but I now suspect had always existed. I discovered that it is not our greatest joys that have the power to transform but our deepest pain. The things we think will destroy us are so often the pathways to growth and healing.

14

CLEARING SPACE

Every single piece of clothing I owned was strewn across my lounge-room floor. Every handbag, every scarf, every pair of shoes. It looked as if my apartment had vomited up a garage sale. I tiptoed through the debris and marvelled at the geometry. How had it all fit? I live alone in a one-bedroom apartment and yet somehow I'd been hoarding enough clothing to kit out an army. A petite Japanese woman with a sweet smile had brought me here—Marie Kondo, queen of decluttering. I was starting to wish I'd never read her stupid book.

I usually avoid fads. Any author, fitness freak, or self-help guru described as having a 'cult-like following' is one I do my best to ignore. I've never tried 'clean eating' or been persuaded by Pete Evans' paleo diet crusade. I'm yet to read *Fifty Shades of Grey*, and I'd rather be incarcerated in a tiny room with no windows, being barked at all day by prison wardens, than sign up to Michelle Bridges' 12-week body transformation (although I suspect there may not be a lot to separate the two experiences).

And yet something drew me to the Kondo fad. As I grew stronger and unpacked my life with Veronica in therapy, there was a growing sense of wanting to offload not only my spiritual baggage but also the excess debris that filled my home. Kondo's book *The Life-Changing Magic of Tidying Up* has sold more than three million copies and been translated into 30 languages. A self-made 'cleaning consultant' and 'tidiness guru', she has turned her passion for decluttering into a global business. The runaway success of her book forms part of a wider trend that has seen people all over the world downsize their lives as an antidote to the rampant march of consumerism. With environmental catastrophe and materialistic excess at the forefront of our collective consciousness, minimalism has become the Western world's hottest social craze. On Buy Nothing Day participants are encouraged to reflect on the impact of overconsumption by buying nothing for 24 hours. Others are going one step further and purging their homes, getting rid of surplus clothes and other material possessions, and even selling up and moving into smaller, more environmentally sustainable properties.

Leading the charge are Joshua Fields Millburn and Ryan Nicodemus, who started the blog *The Minimalists* in 2010, as they approached 30 and realised that their six-figure corporate jobs and luxury lifestyles were not making them happy. 'There was a gaping void, and working 70–80 hours a week just to buy more stuff didn't fill it: it only brought more debt, stress, anxiety, fear, loneliness, guilt, overwhelm and depression,' they wrote. The pair quit the corporate rat-race, published their first book, *Minimalism: live a meaningful life*, and now have a global audience of more than 20 million people. They made a hit documentary and tour the world spreading their 'less is more' message. Minimalism, as they describe it, is a 'tool to rid yourself of life's excess in favour of focusing on what's important—so you can find happiness, fulfilment and freedom'. Their homes have been stripped back to the bare essentials; just a handful of clothes hang in their closets. Fields Millburn took inventory of every possession he owned and found he had 288 items. The average American household has more than 300,000.

I didn't imagine I would end up with an apartment as sparse as his, but I was definitely starting to feel burdened by the clutter in my life. The cupboard in my hallway — a cavernous space that I used to be able to walk into — had become so crammed with crap that when I opened the sliding doors the contents burst out at me like the parasitic beast in the *Alien* movies. I had no idea what was in there anymore. My wardrobes were overflowing with clothes, and every drawer, shelf, and corner was jam-packed with trinkets and random detritus. On the surface, I was pretty neat. But open a door or a drawer and the truth revealed itself.

I started Kondo's book and raced through it in an afternoon.

Using her KonMari Method, she promises to revolutionise your life with an emotionally aware approach that means you tidy by choosing what you want to keep, not what needs to go. Her number-one rule is the items you keep must 'spark joy'. I borrowed the book from Nonie, who had recently KonMari-ed her bedroom and was loving her newfound minimalist lifestyle. But she is by nature an ordered and tidy person, so I wasn't sure the method would have the same effect on me, with my propensity for hoarding. And I just couldn't imagine how my sweaty gym socks were ever going to spark joy. But I imagined the sense of lightness I'd feel by shedding the stuff that no longer served me, and couldn't wait to get started.

Now that I was standing in the detritus of my exploded apartment, I was wishing I'd never begun.

Kondo insists that you must not take a room-by-room or little-by-little approach. You tidy by category. And you go at it in one massive cull. She recommends clothing first. The secret to success is gathering clothing from every cupboard, drawer, and hook in the house. Then you pile them all in one spot, divided by sub-category: tops, bottoms, jackets, socks, underwear, and so on. But one wardrobe in and I was already feeling the weight. I was crushed by a sense of shame and Western guilt. At one point I stood in a mountain of tops and dresses that reached nearly to my knees and screamed, 'THIS IS APPALLING!' I felt like I was personally responsible for the global sweatshop trade.

Kondo writes that if something brought you joy in the past but no longer serves that purpose, you should thank it for the memory, for its service, and let it go: 'By handling each sentimental item and deciding what to discard, you process your past.'

I was sceptical. This is the same woman who says that decluttering your home can make you richer and more beautiful and even act as a detox, leading to spontaneous bouts of diarrhoea. One hour in and I was yet to find fortune or get the runs, but slowly, something began to happen. As I felt each piece of clothing, I was flooded with memories. I picked up a delicate black-lace dress. How I loved this when I bought it ten years ago. I hadn't worn it in years, but I'd been unable to get rid of it. My eyes travelled down the neat pleats in the skirt and across the fine detail of the neckline. I slipped it on and remembered wearing it to my thirtieth birthday party. It was one of the last happy memories I have of being with my former partner. I took a deep breath and placed it in the discard pile.

There was one dress I loved so much I held it up and thought, *How can I throw this out?* But I couldn't fit into it. When I last wore it, I was tiny. And I was tiny because I was so anxious I wasn't eating. As I ran the fabric through my fingers, it wasn't joy that I felt; it was deep sadness. So it went.

Each pile gave way to questionable justifications. I found myself wanting to keep things because they were expensive. I was checking the label rather than checking for joy. Did I really want this G-string simply because Elle Macpherson's name was on it, even though it looked like it would fit a pre-schooler and cut into my arsecrack like razor wire? Bin. Was I actually going to keep these boots that had been stuffed under my bed for five years because I told myself I would get round to re-heeling them one day? Bin.

Four hours in and I was exhausted. And then, just as I felt like throwing in the towel, there it was. Twisted up into a ball inside a jumble of black stockings and leggings: my favourite black top, which I hadn't seen for more than a year. With its soft cotton finish and flattering neckline, it matched everything, and I loved wearing it. But one day it had just disappeared. I turned it over in my hands, wondering at its beauty like an archaeologist excavating a lost relic. I thanked it for returning and promised to appreciate it more.

By the end, I had ten full bin bags of clothes, shoes, and accessories. Then I began the process of putting everything back. I turned to the chapter Kondo entitles 'Storing Your Things to Make Your Life Shine'. She says that every item must be designated a home. Without everything having its allocated space, you increase the chances of your home becoming cluttered again, or accumulating stuff you don't need. She describes how every time she unlocks her front door she announces to her house, 'I'm home,' before taking off her shoes, thanking them for their hard work, and putting them in their rightful place in the shoe cupboard. She also empties the entire contents of her handbag, removing all receipts and putting her wallet in a designated box in a drawer under the bed, next to her train pass and business-card holder. Her wristwatch, jewellery, and empty handbag also receive her thanks before being stashed. I already had one-sided conversations with my cat. I didn't need to start talking to my accessories. But I did like the idea of effective storage that might make my life more efficient.

Slowly, it started to come together. I followed her KonMari folding method and organised my clothes standing up on their side, in a way that allowed me to actually see what I owned every time I opened a drawer. I started with my underwear, and when it was finished I felt genuine joy at seeing those little packets of colour-coordinated neatness in clean rows. My dresses were no longer packed in so tightly nothing could move. They could breathe. When I looked at my wardrobe, I flicked through the wooden hangers as if I were picking out items in a clothing store. And everything I saw was something I wanted to wear. The more progress I made, the more excited I became at this newfound order. At one point I clapped my hands like an overstimulated child and shouted, 'WHO EVEN AM I???'

By the time I was done it was 11.20 pm and I'd been going for 12 hours. My Fitbit told me I had walked 27,060 steps — 18.44 kilometres — without leaving my apartment. My legs were stiff. My back ached from all the bending and folding and trying things on. My fingernails were thick with grime. I was sneezing and wheezing from all the dust. But I lay in bed smiling, knowing I'd completed a task that seemed impossible.

A fortnight later, after enjoying the newfound order of my wardrobe, I committed to starting on the rest of the apartment. It took a full week. I deviated from Kondo's rules and tackled things by location, not category. First up, the hallway cupboard. This was a monster. Things were piled high, floor to ceiling — boxes, appliances, bags, brooms, mops, a set of plastic drawers, more boxes. Anything I didn't know what to do with had been thrown into this abyss. It had inhaled the surplus debris of my life. I started pulling things out. Good God, there was some crap. I found a small television, a printer with no cables, three laptops (one that was so heavy it was like a relic from the land time forgot), two rugs, offcuts of carpet, plastic bags, canvas bags, Ikea bags, a backpack stuffed with sweaty boxing gloves, picture frames, coat hangers, two hairy pet beds that my fickle cat slept in twice then rejected, several ugly blankets, a magazine rack, paint pots and congealed brushes, and three boxes and two expandable file folders crammed with bank statements and utility bills dating back to 2003. What was I planning to do with them? It kept coming. Warranties for appliances I no longer owned; a wicker basket full of leads, adaptors, and cables that must have connected to something, but I had no way of knowing what; several packets of square floppy disks; an old rice cooker, which, when presented to me as a Christmas present by my former partner, caused a festive meltdown that nearly ended the relationship; more boxes. So. Much. Stuff.

When I looked at the evidence of my mass spending orgy, I realised it had not brought fulfilment. Each purchase may have engendered a burst of happiness, but the satisfaction was temporary. And yet, for so long I had continued chasing the notion that contentment was just one more acquisition or milestone away. My friend and *Age* colleague Cam, a hard-nosed investigative crime reporter known for his dry wit and laconic take on life's twists and turns, offered me a piece of wisdom some years ago that sums it up: 'Starkers, nothing is ever as good or as bad as it seems.' It was classic Cam, by turns pragmatic and hopeful. And he was spot on. When I think back to the stuff that

I thought would bring me my happy-ever-after — the success of a debut book and the recognition of my professional worth — I can see that those milestones weren't what they seemed, at least not in the context of the value I'd placed on them. And then, when I was struggling to keep my head above water after it all fell apart, I found a way to stay afloat. It was bad, but it wasn't as bad as it could have been. As humans, we have a capacity to adapt to our environment and the circumstances life hurls at us.

This is the theory of the 'happiness set point', which posits that whatever is happening in our external world, we all have a base level of happiness. It's the emotional status we return to no matter how terrible or wonderful life becomes. The concept came from a 1978 study which found that lottery winners were not significantly happier than those in a control group, while conversely, people with spinal-cord injuries were much happier than might have been expected. We quickly adapt to these life-changing events and return to the level of happiness hardwired into our DNA. It goes some way to explaining why so many rich people are miserable. Once you get that mansion and discover you're not fulfilled, you have to buy the yacht. When that doesn't do it, you need a jet, then an island, then a luxury hotel chain, a network of golf courses, your own global beauty pageant, and before you know it you're the leader of the free world and even that's not enough so you have to antagonise North Korea, ban the press corps from the White House, and create fake wrestling videos so you can punch a television station in the face.

This ability to return to a set point of happiness no matter what positive or negative events occur is also known as hedonic adaptation or the hedonic treadmill. We have to constantly keep moving towards the thing we think will bring us satisfaction. But the more we strive, the further from reach the goal becomes. When mining magnate Andrew 'Twiggy' Forrest gave $400 million of his personal fortune to cancer research and various other charities, it became the single biggest private donation in Australian history. He said he'd lived a fortunate life and wanted to share that with others. But as economics editor Peter Martin observed in *The Sydney Morning Herald*, perhaps Forrest had simply discovered that giving feels good. He cited a Harvard Business School study in which a happiness questionnaire was given to staff at a large Boston firm one month before and two months after they each received bonuses of around $6,800. Many were no happier after the windfall than before, but those who were had given some of the money away to charity or as gifts to loved ones. On average, the more they'd given away, the happier they were.

While the saying 'money can't buy you happiness' holds weight, there is no denying that for those living in poverty or disadvantage, extra cash could provide the basics of shelter, security, and three square meals a day, which contribute significantly to physical and emotional wellbeing. But once you earn enough to reach a comfortable standard of living, more money won't actually make you happier. A 2010 Princeton University study of 500,000 American households found that the amount of money an individual needed to achieve a standard that brings happiness was an annual income of around US$75,000. After that, there is no measurable positive effect on daily mood. And yet, in our aspirational culture, where the pursuit of wealth and material goods has become a national obsession, we continue to believe that bigger, better, richer is the key to happiness.

When I looked at all the stuff I'd accumulated, it was clear that while it may have cluttered every corner of my small apartment, it had not plugged the gap.

Resigning myself to the fact that this was going to be a process that stretched out over several days, I sat cross-legged in the middle of the lounge-room floor, among the scattered papers, bin bags, and half-empty boxes, and started combing through my past. I found a box full of journals and notepads going back 15 years. And a pile of papers held together with a bulldog clip: email correspondence between my ex and I when we were trying to hold together our romance across several continents.

I read every single journal entry, every card and letter, each university assignment and email printout. I studied every photograph and relived the memories and emotions. It was a difficult experience. On one hand I was struck by how much love I've been fortunate to receive from family and friends, and the rich experiences I've enjoyed. But the flipside was the pain and angst so apparent in my correspondence and journal entries. It filled enough pages to stock a bookshelf. The self-loathing and insecurity of my twenties jumped from the page as I described how even the simple task of walking into a shop filled me with dread. I assumed the retail assistants were judging me, as if my skin was translucent and they could see right through to my core badness. I couldn't even order food in a takeaway shop without being incapacitated by paranoia and the fear of looking stupid.

The back of the cupboard also produced an old video camera—the kind that in 2001 would have been described as 'compact' but in the era of smartphones was comically bulky. I spent hours watching tapes of myself with my ex, and my friends and family, both in Australia and back home in Edinburgh. I was smiling in these home movies, but as I watched I was struck by the way I carried myself. I was awkward and self-conscious, shrinking from sight, almost apologetic about taking up space in the world. My clothes were mismatched, my hair limp. I remember how much I used to agonise over what to wear and whether I was wearing it right. The scars of high school were still so raw it made me second-guess every fashion choice. As I picked out clothes, I'd hear the voices of the girls who yelled out a running commentary on my outfit as I walked home from school. Every time I put on makeup, I'd think of the time a classmate on a school field trip stole my fire-engine-red lipstick and hid it, telling me she did it for my own good because I looked like a cartoon clown.

The girl I saw in these movies was distinctly uncomfortable in her own skin, and it made me ache to watch. But also, I was proud. I was learning to accept myself, embracing my foibles and celebrating all that I was. I was growing into myself in every possible way. Holding on to all this stuff no longer felt necessary. I kept journals from the recent past, but I was ready to farewell the rest. One diary I tore up, page by page, thanking it for its job in getting me here, and reassuring the girl who wrote in it that she no longer needs to carry this shame. She is not defective.

By the end of the week I had tackled every space in my apartment. Superfluous crockery, glasses, and utensils were removed from my kitchen cupboards. The bathroom was cleared of all expired toiletries and old hair and makeup samples. Even my bookshelves got a going-over, with any title that didn't spark joy taken to the op shop. Goodbye, Hawthorn goofball Shane Crawford's autobiography. Farewell, *The Da Vinci Code*. Two full car-loads of excess junk—front and back seat and boot—were taken to the tip. What was left was an apartment that felt cleansed. I'd brought every single part of me out into the light; every crevice and dark corner had been mined, the contents spilled out on the floor. When I'd wanted to give up I kept going. I couldn't live in the mess. Wading through all my shit, I'd made the tough calls on what parts worked and what parts I could let go. I felt lighter. Everything was starting to fit.

15

FREEDOM FROM CHOICE

Have you tried buying a new bed lately? I have, and it was terrifying. A Sunday-afternoon trip to a furniture store became a dizzying navigation of 'ergonomic sleep technology', 'pillow science', and 'revolutionary pressure-relieving' mattress choices. There were hybrid mattresses, gel mattresses, pillow-top mattresses, memory foam, latex. I could find out what my 'sleep number' was—somewhere between 0 and 100, ranging from extra firm to feather soft—to ensure that my bed was uniquely designed for my body. There was also the option to seek the advice of an in-store sleep consultant, or lie on a computerised bed that could take my measurements and analyse my body mass before spitting out my 'sleep profile'. And I would need this assistance because, as the marketing continuously stressed, 'Buying the right mattress is one of the most important decisions you will make.' During my pre-purchase research, one website warned that the risks of choosing the wrong mattress included drowsiness, back pain, obesity, lung and throat irritation, weakened immune system, heart conditions, memory problems, reduced libido, and premature ageing. If I didn't get this right I would be exhausted, sore, fat, forgetful, unfuckable, and destined for an early grave. No pressure.

When I finally made my decision—after several months of research and nearly two hours in the bedding department of a major retailer, lying on countless beds and interrogating the salesman as if he was a tight-lipped prisoner-of-war—I can't say I was satisfied. A fortnight later the bed was delivered, and although it was perfectly comfortable, it took weeks of crippling buyers' remorse before I could accept that the one I had chosen was probably just as good as any I had left behind.

In his book *The Paradox of Choice*, American psychologist Barry Schwartz put forward the theory that the free-market economy has led to paralysis, not liberation. In a TED talk discussing his research, Schwartz maintained that even if we managed to conquer our overwhelm and make a choice, we ended up less satisfied than we would be if we had fewer options to choose from. Using the example of the 175 different salad dressings on offer at his local supermarket, he said it was easy to imagine that a different choice would have been better. The imagined perfection of the alternative leads to buyer's remorse, even if it was a good decision.

I can't count how many hours of my life have been lost to a troubling sense that the decision I've just made was probably the wrong one. When my new bed was delivered, the old mattress was still lying on my lounge-room floor, waiting to be picked up by a friend. For a full afternoon I leapt from the floor mattress to the new bed, jumping and sitting and lying as I compared comfort, bounce, and support, agonising over whether my new purchase was any better than the bed I was discarding.

Schwartz talked about the 'escalation of expectations' and how the wider the choice, the more we expect from the product. In the days when there were fewer options, our bar was set lower. He described how disappointed he was after he went to a shop to replace his worn-out jeans. It had been so long since he'd bought a new pair he was dazzled by the choice: slim fit, easy fit, relaxed fit, button fly or zipper fly, bootcut, tapered, distressed. He walked away with jeans that were arguably better than he'd ever had, but he felt worse because they weren't perfect. 'Adding options to people's lives can't help but increase the expectations people have about how good those options will be,' he wrote. 'And what that's going to produce is less satisfaction with results, even when they're good results.'

The burden of choice can be a trigger point for the overly anxious. When I was quite unwell, I found myself in my local supermarket one day shuffling up and down the aisles trying to think of something I could eat. I had no appetite, but even on the very worst days, the least I could do for myself was put food in my body. It was a sensory overload. When did supermarkets get so bright? Is it to keep the staff awake? Does lighting up the store like a Vegas casino trick the brain into spending more? Tuna. I'd grab a can of tuna and make a pasta bake. Comfort food. I found the tuna aisle, and that's when things fell apart. There were approximately 64 varieties of tuna. Tuna in brine, tuna in oil, tuna in spring water, tuna with rice, tuna slices. Then there were all the flavours: lemon and cracked pepper; street Asian, Korean barbeque, fiery chipotle, roasted capsicum, and three beans. My eyes darted from one flavour to another. *I JUST WANT A FUCKING NORMAL CAN OF TUNA.* I dropped my empty basket on the floor and ran from the store, silently weeping over an abundance of canned fish.

A psychiatrist back home in Edinburgh once told me that the most common place for his patients to have panic attacks was in the basement of the Marks & Spencer food hall on the city's main shopping thoroughfare, Princes Street. He said that the glaring strip lighting, low ceilings, and crammed aisles, combined with an exit that could only be reached via two sets of escalators, provided the ideal breeding ground for acute anxiety. But I suspect it was also the bewildering array of options that drove people to lose their shit.

We are spoilt for choice in every aspect of our lives. A digital smorgasbord of movies and television shows are available at the click of a button. Streaming services have turned me into a glutton as I binge watch the latest Netflix series, promising myself 'just one more episode', before I discover it's 3.00 am, I haven't left the couch in seven hours, and I've lost all feeling in my legs. Every song ever written can be accessed in an instant, and we can source practically anything we want from an infinitely stocked online marketplace. But have all these options made us any happier?

In a famous experiment conducted by Columbia University, researchers set up a table offering six samples of jam in a supermarket. Every few hours the table was swapped for one displaying 24 varieties of jam. On average, shoppers sampled no more than two jams, regardless of how many were displayed. What was interesting was that while 60 per cent of customers stopped at the table with the larger assortment, compared to 40 per cent at the smaller one, a third of those who stopped at the table with only six choices went on to buy jam. Only 3 per cent of the shoppers who stopped at the larger assortment bought a jar.

A survey by insurance comparison service Choosi found almost 90 per cent of Australians feel that too much choice is making consumer decision-making harder and leading to buyer's remorse. In Australia, supermarket chains Coles and Woolworths are scaling back on the number of products they offer to compete with discount store Aldi and its limited range of brands. In 2015, British supermarket chain Tesco announced it was scrapping a third of its 90,000 products to make the weekly shop easier for customers. Tesco stocked a whopping 224 types of air freshener compared to Aldi's 12. It's this same tyranny of choice that can lead us to stay wedded to power companies, phone providers, and banks that at best don't serve us well, and at worst are robbing us blind. We may be sick of the huge bills, crappy service, and excessive fees, but the prospect of scouring the market to compare the competitors' small print is just too overwhelming. It's like trying to extricate yourself from a dysfunctional but comfortingly familiar relationship.

Making the 'right' choice is not just about getting value for money or making sure we're not being ripped off. When I drill down into where my decision-making angst comes from, it's deeper than that. My choices are a reflection of me. What is the perfect floor rug, kitchen appliance, or house plant to say, 'Here is a well-adjusted, sophisticated adult woman with her shit together who would never dream of eating doughnuts for breakfast and wearing her pyjamas like a uniform'? It's often more an exercise in trying to control the things I can't — particularly other people's opinions of me. And I'm not the only one. A few years ago, Nonie was flying to Queensland to meet her then boyfriend's family for the first time. She was nervous, which was natural, but the reasons for her anxiety went beyond that. She told me that her biggest fear was looking silly on the beach. He came from a beach-going family, whose lives revolved around sand and surf. She was vampire-pale and had grown up in the country, lathering herself in the strongest sunscreen on the rare occasions when she might be exposed to prolonged periods of sunshine. 'I just don't know what to do with myself at the beach. I feel like I don't belong and everyone can tell,' she said as

I drove her to the airport. In an attempt to appear as effortlessly beach chic as she imagined her boyfriend and his family would be, she went on a last-minute shopping spree, looking for a little black skirt she'd seen a beach-dwelling friend wear recently. She'd convinced herself that an exact replica of this skirt was the only thing that could transform her into a laidback goddess and thus save the holiday with the in-laws from certain disaster.

She didn't find it. The trip turned out just fine.

Nowhere is the burden of choice more apparent than in the world of online dating. I'm starting to believe that option overload has ruined romance. You swipe and click and swipe, making split-second decisions based on the scantest, most superficial snippets of information. It's bewildering. I recently downloaded Tinder again after a self-imposed hiatus that lasted several years. When I opened the app and began to swipe, my inner monologue went something like this: *Nup. Nah. Nope. Too much beard. Serial killer. Why would you use your wedding picture as a profile? Nup. No, no, no. Weird eyebrows. ENOUGH WITH THE GUYS HUGGING SEDATED TIGERS. Nope. Nope. Which one even are you??? Put your shirt on. Nah. Maybe. Why can I only see half your face? Nup. Nah. Cute. Out of focus. Obviously dodgy. That's just a picture of your ute. Nope. Nope. Nope.*

There's nothing like a dating app to make you confront just how shallow you really are. But this is the world we inhabit: we can afford to keep swiping because there will always be more options. You *could* chat to the 15 people you've already matched with, or you could keep searching for someone better. How do you know the partner of your dreams is not just a few more swipes away? Or what if they're on a different dating app? There are apps that only match users with people they've recently been near—so there is now the added FOMO of knowing you may have just walked past the potential love of your life on the street and may never find them again.

That nagging 'what if' feeling has created a dating culture that all too often leads to empty and meaningless interactions. The majority of matches never lead to a message, much less a real-life date, and even if there is a conversation via message, it often comes to an abrupt stop for no apparent reason. The anonymity of online dating has made 'ghosting' an accepted modern phenomenon. I'm as guilty of it as the men I encounter, but it's exhausting and dehumanising. Imagine meeting someone in a bar and exchanging pleasantries about your passions and interests only to have that person walk off in the middle of the conversation, never to return. We have learned to treat one another as disposable commodities. It's partly due to the burden of choice — the constant search for something just a little bit better that will make us complete.

It's easy to believe that having a perfect partner, the right clothes, the smoothest hair, or the most intriguing wall art will project an image to the world that will make people — or at least the tribe we want to belong to — accept us into the fold. And that's exactly the way the advertising is tailored. Whether it's L'Oréal selling hair products 'because you're worth it', or Lexus, with their 'passionate pursuit of perfection', the aim is to push the idea that these purchases will fill the happiness gap. The advertising industry's entire business model is based on a single premise: you are not enough. But if you buy this product, you just might be.

The frenzied scramble for more has led to heaving crowds queueing outside Australian department stores in the early hours of Boxing Day each year. In the United Kingdom and the United States, Black Friday sales have become so popular there have been stampedes and outbreaks of violence when doors open at major retailers. The day of heavy discounting has sparked chaotic scenes, with police deployed to break up brawls between sales junkies fighting over cut-price widescreen televisions and high-end sporting gear. In 2016, there were several shootings, including one fatality, at snap sales across the United States. Google 'Black Friday violence' and you'll find a gallery of unedifying images that look more like refugees desperately scrambling for food parcels in a war-torn country than bargain-hungry shoppers looking for cheap electrical goods.

It's a consumerist culture that goes hand in hand with the 'crazy busy' mentality, as people work themselves into the ground to keep up with an insatiable need to own more stuff. The more aspirational we become, the more we want. And so we work more to achieve that luxury car, that designer dress, that exotic holiday, or the dream house. It still amazes me that home renovation has become its own genre of entertainment. But it's a fitting analogy for our times. Contestants spend three months frantically transforming a derelict block into a fantasy home, but then don't live in it. They sell it for huge profit and move on to the next one. As psychologist Michael Carr-Gregg observed, 'We've kind of fixed up everyone's bathrooms and gardens and houses, now we also need to look at the inside.'

I'm lucky to have been in a financial position to buy my own apartment. It's renovated and comfortable and I absolutely love it, but it's small, and I've often fantasised about a bigger home, with a backyard and guest bedrooms. I imagine I'd be happier if I could sit out in the afternoon sun, or have a walk-in wardrobe or enough room for a companion for Hamish. Then I spoke to someone who had what I wanted and I began to see things differently.

Steph is a friend who grew up with Nonie in regional Victoria. As I got to know her over dinner one night, we began discussing happiness and what we need to make us fulfilled. Her story was an eye-opener. In 2012, she was pregnant with her second child and living with her partner and their two-year-old daughter in a house they shared with her brother and his small family. The only area Steph and her husband Dave could afford to buy a small two-bedroom apartment was an outer-eastern suburb of Melbourne. They were fixing it up and planned to move in before the baby was born when Steph got a phone call that changed everything. A $15 home lottery ticket had come good. She had won a $1.1 million four-bedroom, two-storey home in one of Melbourne's most exclusive inner suburbs—fully furnished, mortgage-free, and council rates paid for the first year. The whole package was worth $1.4 million.

Steph was on a road trip with her mother and sister on the north coast of New South Wales when she received the call. 'I burst into tears because I couldn't remember buying the ticket and I thought it was a joke. I had my mum saying, "Just hang up. If it's a crank call, just hang up." By the time I worked out it was true it was completely overwhelming, and I spent the next 24 hours going between giggling stupidly to sobbing because it was such a life-changer.'

The house was in an area with an abundance of high-quality schools, and had a lush backyard packed with fruit trees and veggie beds. It was, said Steph, a 'dreamboat win'. Working as a nurse doing punishing shift work in a hospital emergency department, she was able to contemplate a career change. She no longer had to work unsociable hours, and later found her niche nursing in the drug and alcohol sector. Overnight, the couple became property investors, financially comfortable enough to rent out the apartment they'd planned to live in, and began looking at acquiring a second unit, with an eye to securing their children's future.

But then the unease crept in. When people heard about the windfall, they were divided into two camps. On one side were the friends who were thrilled, saying it couldn't happen to a nicer family. On the other were people who questioned why they deserved such good fortune. 'Initially I hadn't felt like there was any merit in it. I'd bought a ticket and I'd won a raffle. It didn't matter how big the prize was, the luck is the same,' Steph recalled. 'I was really surprised by people's reactions about deserving it because I hadn't contemplated it myself. But then it started eating into my thinking: well, was I deserving in a world where we were kind of doing okay as far as reaching life goals? Why us?'

It took some counselling for her to work through the feelings of guilt before she came to accept that the win was dumb luck, not divine providence. Suddenly, they were in a position they'd imagined they'd only be in come retirement.

Steph's mother had been buying these charity raffle tickets since Steph was a child. Steph would look at the floorplans of the luxury homes and pick out a bedroom, imagining how happy she'd be if the lottery came good. Decades later, when she was actually living the fantasy, she realised something was missing. One night, she turned to her husband Dave and said, 'We have everything we've ever wanted. Why do I feel like there's no joy in my life?' It was, Steph admits, 'a pretty big kick in the nuts' admitting to her partner — who was supposed to make up a big part of her fulfilment — that she was joyless. Yet, even with their unexpected windfall, life remained a mundane routine of child-rearing, work, and obligation. 'I felt like there was something wrong with me. I felt like I wasn't entitled to not feel joy because I had all this opportunity,' she said. 'After winning the house I think it gave me a different perspective. If you're joyless in life but you're working really hard towards something, it's because you've got all this extra burden. But if all of a sudden that burden's not there, why do you still not have joy in your life?'

It is the very essence of the hedonic treadmill. The plodding pursuit of a salve to soothe our woes. We think that our dissatisfaction comes from not having enough — from not being enough. When the journey is long and arduous, we imagine that reaching the destination will provide comfort. But as I discovered when my book was published, when you get to the endpoint and the discomfort remains, it can be deeply unsettling.

For Steph, it meant re-evaluating what she needed to have a meaningful life. 'I felt like I was always chasing after family and work and the roster of a household rather than spending time on myself,' she said. She got more counselling and worked with her therapist to have more realistic expectations of what happiness meant. 'I had it all. The three pillars — marriage, kids, the home — that's what we're meant to strive for. But you talk to any parent, and having kids is a bloody gauntlet of hard work. I think you have to be a little bit delusional to seek complete joy out of just having a child.' While winning the house did not bring instant happiness, she acknowledges it has given them financial security, which has been enormously comforting. And although the euphoric high that came in the months following the win has faded, she is still incredibly grateful. 'It's been four years now and there's one part of the house where, if I walk down the stairs, I still get this overwhelming feeling of how completely insane it is that I won this amazing house. That has never gone away.'

Listening to Steph's experiences reinforced what I was starting to realise: no amount of stuff could bring me the contentment I had long craved. There was no house big enough, car flash enough, or wardrobe expensive enough to make me whole. I started to focus on being grateful for what I had rather than wishing for more. And it helped me see that the noxious envy we sometimes feel for other people's 'perfect' lives is often based on little more than a story.

16

BE KIND, BE WELL, STOP F**KING SHOUTING

The man on the radio was screaming. I could almost feel the heat coming off his face. 'I'm so sick of you loony, leftie, pinko morons telling us what we can and can't say. Why don't you just shut up?'

It seemed like a rhetorical question, but the young woman on the phone, a high-school teacher, valiantly attempted an answer. 'We are taking a stand, as many teachers have done in the past, on human rights. Refugees are being tortured in offshore prisons and our students deserve to know what ...'

'It's propaganda! You're using the classroom to spread propaganda. This is child abuse!'

Modern life is so shouty. We have become so quick to anger—on talkback radio, on social media, on public transport, and in our cars as we honk our horns, trying to claim a tiny bit of this overpopulated planet for ourselves. In an age when facts have been downgraded to optional extras, and being right is a contest of who can shout the loudest, schoolyard name-calling is often rewarded. The 'Loony Left' whip themselves into a frenzy about trigger warnings and safe spaces, banning anyone they disagree with, while the 'Rabid Right' declares all-out war on political correctness and 'Generation Snowflake'. Boomers accuse Millennials of being vapid, self-obsessed fame-whores. Gens Y and Z fight back, slamming their negatively-geared parents and grandparents for locking them out of the property market, destroying the planet, and robbing them of a future. It's a perpetual orgy of outrage.

Then there's the outrage at the reaction to the outrage. Online, a vicious form of lynch-mob justice can see a person crucified for a minor misstep. There is no escaping the noise and fury. It's exhausting.

I turned off the radio as the ageing host continued his tirade about the 'communists on the Left trying to brainwash our children'. I was genuinely concerned he was on the brink of having a heart attack.

There was a time when I would have joined in. I would have taken to Twitter to point out all the ways in which this narrow-minded dinosaur was wrong. My witticisms about his ridiculousness would have been applauded by my followers and set me on a thrilling collision course with the conservative commentariat.

Sometimes I still weigh in. But not as much as I once did. And not with the same level of fury. The soul-crushing pointlessness of these arguments is too much. It's like standing at the top of an abandoned quarry and shouting into the abyss.

I used to think that by stridently highlighting my opponent's factual errors and deriding their ignorance, I was defending those who had no voice. When this approach was rewarded by those whose views were aligned with my own, it only emboldened me to go harder. During one particularly exasperating episode of ABC's *Q&A* that focused on marriage equality, I couldn't contain my frustration when several panellists invoked the 'slippery slope' argument to suggest that allowing gay couples to marry would lead to generations of fatherless and motherless children. With smoke coming off my keyboard, I took to Twitter to point out: 'Gay people are already having kids, you tedious imbeciles.'

Some weeks later, I was surprised to find my photograph on the front page of *The Catholic Weekly*, under the headline 'TEDIOUS IMBECILES', with an accompanying story about the 'invective' being unleashed on pro–traditional marriage advocates by biased, campaigning journalists. I duly shared the image on Facebook, joking that this was my most accomplished page one. Mum and Dad would be so proud. When *The Age's* editor-in-chief found out, he approached my desk. I was sure I was in trouble. Instead, he laughed and said, 'Next time annoy the Protestants, just to be balanced.'

After many fruitless online fights, I've come to see my problematic social-media activity as a canary in the coalmine for my mental health. If I find myself engaged in a three-hour online battle with misogynistic trolls or tone-deaf conservative commentators, it usually means I'm not in a particularly great place. I have learned to back slowly away from my phone or laptop, take a break, and ask myself, *What is this really all about? What will it achieve?*

The digital age has turned everyone into a keyboard warrior. When Twitter was first launched in 2006, it felt like a collegial global community—a marketplace of ideas and storytelling. Now, it can be a cauldron of venomous outrage, factional back-slapping, and outright bullying. This toxic echo chamber of righteous anger can make life even more fraught with anxiety.

It's hard to be calm when we're constantly on alert. A foolish mistake can go viral in seconds. An errant tweet is turned into a three-day shitstorm as the media cannibalises itself reporting on something someone somewhere said.

Guardian journalist and author Jon Ronson documents this in his book *So You've Been Publicly Shamed*, which paints a terrifying picture of a world in which people's lives can be all but ruined in an instant, often in 140 characters or less. Social media has become the modern-day village square, where villains are placed in stocks and booed by the mob. Except their crime is not theft or murder, but posting an ill-considered photo on Facebook. As Ronson describes it, shaming an apparent wrongdoer seemed exhilarating in the early days of Twitter, and he was intrigued by the phenomenon. He told *The New York Times*, 'When we deployed shame, we were utilising an immensely powerful tool. The silenced were getting a voice. It was like the democratisation of justice.' Now he's not so sure. Neither am I.

I've been part of many a Twitter witch-hunt and can attest to the intoxicating pull of a mass shaming. When the world is watching, united against a common enemy, it can be hard to resist the temptation to jump in and receive a round of back-patting from the crowd. It can make you feel as though you're part of something bigger than yourself. It can become almost performative. And when you feel like you're under attack, it can be a way of exacting some semblance of control.

For journalists and other public figures, the internet's anonymity has made online abuse a fact of life. Sometimes, the insults I receive are amusing and inventive. Like the time a reader got in touch to tell me my journalism was 'the written form of herpes'. Or the guy that said the points I raised in an opinion piece were 'dull and thudding and resembled someone carving a turkey with a clawhammer'. On other occasions, the comments have been gendered and violent. When I took an online-betting company to task on Twitter for its misogynistic advertising, I was attacked by angry rugby league fans whose objections took the form of calling for me to be euthanised; wishing I would die of AIDS; telling me, 'Bitch, shut the fuck up'; and suggesting that I 'just need some good cock up you'.

It can often be the most unlikely subjects that provoke a reaction. I have received repeated emails from a reader who hated me writing about binge drinking, and was particularly incensed with *High Sobriety*. Once, he wrote to tell me he hoped I got liver cancer. Another time, his message read, 'You are a pro-booze bitch pretending to be otherwise. Hope you drop dead soon from your own self confessed binge drinking you cunt!'

I try to picture the person who wrote this. What does he look like? Does he have children? Is there pain in his life? Would he say these things to my face if he saw me on the street? I don't reply to violent messages, but sometimes when I receive angry emails or personal insults, I will respond. My reply is always polite, and invariably the sender will write back and apologise, disarmed by the real person they find at the end of their rage. It's all too easy to fire a furious missive into cyberspace. The anonymity of the online age has dehumanised our interactions. It's the same removed dispassion that leads to road rage, prompting behaviour behind a windscreen most of us would never dream of if we stepped outside our cars.

With the rise of high-density apartment living, where people don't know their neighbours, and disputes over car-parking spaces, rubbish, and noise pollution abound, the passive-aggressive note-leaver has become a troubling, if amusing, phenomenon that neatly encapsulates the anger that sits so close to the surface. In a piece about the trend, *The Sydney Morning Herald* published some of their favourite anonymous notes from neighbours sent in by readers, including 'Congratulations, you've just won crappiest park of the week. Why don't you park across three spaces next time? You wanker.' And, 'NO DOG POO. STINK YOUR OWN BIN OUT.' And, 'SHUT YOUR FUCKING SECURITY DOORS.' In Melbourne, a producer for 3AW shared a typed note she and her boyfriend found taped to their front door one morning. Despite living what she described as a quiet 'nana's existence', going to bed at 9.00 pm to get up at 4.00 am for breakfast radio, the producer had a neighbour who saw things differently:

> You ALWAYS PLAY LOUD MUSIC ON WEEKENDS, as well as creating a RACKET with your loud bogan friends on your balcony. Also we shall be complaining about your BBQ TODAY, which MANY PEOPLE HAVE BEEN ANGRY ABOUT INCLUDING US. I know most of my neighbours and they will agree you are petty, bitchy freaks. Move out if you don't like it here and get a life losers.

All this anger can't be good for us. The temporary release of frustration might feel satisfying for a moment, but the rewards are short-lived. The temptation to vent is alluring in a world that can sometimes leave us feeling powerless. But after many pointless online battles, I've started to wonder what's really going on underneath. Invariably, I find that there is some underlying issue driving my fury and frustration. The unacknowledged child part of me is looking for recognition. It's as if I'm trying to wrestle back some autonomy over my emotions by asserting my rightness, looking for that elusive sense of belonging. It becomes compulsive, constantly refreshing the page to see how many strangers have validated my worldview. But the satisfaction doesn't last. I'm left feeling spent. All that righteousness comes with a side serve of shame. I like myself more when I'm not angry.

'Be kind and you will be well' has been the cornerstone of Eastern philosophy for centuries. Buddhists practise loving-kindness to all beings as a path to enlightenment. The Dalai Lama says, 'If you want others to be happy, practise compassion. If you want to be happy, practise compassion.' Now, the Western world is catching up. Recognising our shared humanity is more than just a sentimental ideal. Consciously practising kindness could actually change the wiring of our brains and make us live longer, happier, and healthier lives. Compassion is neuroscience's latest frontier.

The idea that all I might need to do to calm down and find happiness is stop fighting with Twitter trolls and go hug a News Corp columnist fascinates me. I'm sure those very same people would be the first to dismiss this notion as Leftist hippy nonsense dreamt up by a bunch of bleeding hearts singing 'Kumbaya' in a Tibetan prayer circle. But the science is compelling. Some studies have shown compassion can protect against disease and significantly increase lifespan. Brain imaging reveals that exercising compassion stimulates the same pleasure centres associated with the drive for food, water, and sex. Not only are we preconditioned to be kind, but it's essential for the survival of our species.

Dr James Doty, founder of Stanford University's Center for Compassion and Altruism Research and Education (doesn't it just make you feel better that a place like this even exists?) is at the forefront of this emerging mental-health movement, which, instead of focusing on pharmaceutical interventions, relies more on our innate human traits of empathy, altruism, kindness, and resilience. I spoke to him not long after I returned to work, and his insights helped change the way I viewed the world, and myself.

'We are seeing a revolution in how the mind works. As little as two weeks of practising compassion with intention has a positive physiological effect on the body. It can lower blood pressure, boost your immune response, and increase your calmness,' he told me over the phone from California. 'People are much happier and live a better life if they are able to maximise their genetic potential for being compassionate, and it has a significant contagion effect on others, motivating them to be more kind.'

This guy is no New-Age quack. He's a professor of neurosurgery and a former US Army major who spent nine years on active military duty. He is also friends with the Dalai Lama. Doty's centre was set up with the largest donation ever made by His Holiness to a non-Tibetan cause. Borrowing from Buddhist mind-training traditions, compassion practice uses meditation, visualisation, breathing, and mindfulness techniques to enhance mental health and foster connection by focusing on shared experiences. We can literally train our brains to be kinder. And that kindness has a flow-on effect. Doty said that when we recognise common fears or vulnerabilities rather than focus on our differences — be it with a difficult friend, an abrasive colleague, a noisy neighbour, or even a stranger on the internet — it calms the nervous system, boosting feelings of contentment and self-worth. 'There is no-one who has not, will not, or does not suffer. By trying to identify common traits which you share, it starts breaking down this barrier of defining someone as an "other",' Doty told me. 'You can see a dynamic happen when a person walks into a room with a sense of openness, kindness, connection, vulnerability, how the room reacts. It's much more positive than when a person is demeaning, unkind, rude, or aggressive.'

Since the bottom fell out of my world, I have tried to be more compassionate to the people I meet and consider the baggage that, like me, they may be carrying. It's not always easy when you're on a packed tram and the guy next to you is playing head-banging death metal at full bore with no headphones. But it's amazing how much a simple smile or eye contact with a fellow commuter can lift your mood. I try to remember that someone's irritable demeanour is not necessarily a reflection of their feelings towards me. When I visited a local café and the manager didn't acknowledge me as I sat down, and scowled before slamming a jug of water on the table and rushing off, my first thought was that I had transgressed. This had to be my fault. Then I was angry. Why was she so rude? But I'd been there many times before and she'd always been lovely. I looked around and saw that every table was full. There was a long queue for takeaway coffee. She had only one other staff member serving. So I waited. I was in no hurry. When she came to take my order, she said, 'I'm so sorry about the wait. I had two people call in sick this morning. I figured I could leave you a bit longer because you're a regular and you'd give me some leeway.' I smiled, told her it was no problem, and pondered how different that interaction might have been if I'd allowed myself to presume the worst of a woman who was doing the best she could. I left feeling better about myself and the world.

The work I've done with Veronica has had compassion at its heart. Learning to view other people's reactions to me through the prism of their own emotional preoccupations makes it easier to not always jump to the worst conclusion. One afternoon, walking back from therapy, I stopped and sat on a patch of grass in the park, feeling the winter sun on my skin as I absorbed the lessons from that day's session. Behind me, an elderly lady in a pink dressing gown, her white hair tied up in a messy bun, emerged from a row of modest, single-storey red-brick townhouses. She was yelling in my direction, making a shooing gesture with her hands. 'You're all the bloody same, you lot,' she barked. This was public parkland. I just wanted to sit for five minutes. I felt that sense of indignation rising in my chest and I turned to remonstrate in defence of 'my lot', whoever they were. But then as my gaze met hers I recognised a look of powerlessness in her eyes. It was a sense of fatigue, a weathered fragility. What events had preceded this moment? I gave her a nod and went on my way.

The more I'm able to offer kindness to others, the better I have become at forgiving myself. Regina is not so brutal as she once was. I'm allowed to be flawed. Failure and setbacks don't make me the problem child. It takes continued practice, but treating myself with the compassion and care I would a close friend has been enormously helpful. When my decisions have been questionable—drinking too much, binge eating my body weight in crap food, or midnight booty-calling that cute but shallow douchebro I promised myself I'd never text again —I try to be kind to myself instead of getting sucked into a shame spiral, which only leads to more bad choices.

The flow-on effects of practising compassion are not only good for emotional health but can also help our bodies. It reduces levels of the stress hormone cortisol by decreasing heart rate and arousal. Doty says that even as little as two weeks of compassion practice can have a positive effect on stress and immune function. When we're kind and nurturing to ourselves and others, oxytocin — known as the 'cuddle chemical' — is released. It's the same chemical emitted when a mother breastfeeds her child or we receive a warm embrace. That's why hugs feel so good. We're tapping into a primal, mammalian caregiving system that soothes emotional pain. Fledgling research shows that oxytocin, if administered in a nasal spray, can induce acts of altruism and increase bonding. Scientists are excited by its potential to create a kinder society.

In these deeply divided times, it's never been more important to understand our adversaries. It's much easier to brand people snowflakes or rednecks than it is to actually find out what's driving their fears and frustrations. The way we live in the modern world is making it more difficult to reach out to one another. We have evolved from tribal living — in which caring for the members of our tight-knit groups was vital to survival — to a more displaced, disconnected way of life in which community bonds have been eroded and many of us are separated from family by thousands of kilometres. Combined with the frenetic pace of modern times, it has led to a stressed-out, individualised society with a reduced capacity for empathy. Compassion is often the first casualty when our newsfeeds are filled with acts of violence and atrocity. When we remain vigilant to real or perceived threats, the fear and anger can drive our behaviour.

Doty explained to me that identification with a group gives us social connection, lowering fear and anxiety and fostering a sense of safety. When we have those strong social bonds, we're more likely to be of service to others. Without them, people will look for someone to blame, and quite often that is someone deemed to be different to us—an outsider or a newcomer. 'If the economy is doing well and people are employed and there are resources for everyone, then there's really never any issues regarding immigration,' he said. 'But as soon as a group feels a threat, especially those lower on the socio-economic scale, and they are concerned about loss of benefits or opportunity, they will often pick a weak group who can be perceived as taking resources from them.'

We're seeing this in the extreme political polarisation emerging in many countries across the world, including Australia, with the rise of the alt-right and its anti-fascist counter movement. The more closed off we become in the way we live, the more defensive we are in our positions, and the easier it is to find a sense of purpose, belonging, or control by pitting ourselves against the 'other'. We feel unhappy and aggrieved at perceived injustices and think that we can ease our discomfort by finding someone to shoulder the blame. But how many times have you felt happier by allowing your chest to swell with hate?

Thankfully, there are moves afoot to change things on a number of fronts. The corporate world, particularly large tech companies such as Google and Twitter, are running programs to help us understand one another better. Facebook hosts an annual Compassion Research Day to develop tools to resolve online conflict—a recognition that perhaps social media has been partly responsible for this 'us and them' culture and that making people feel safe and understood is not only good for business but will lead to a more cohesive society. Medically, Dr Doty's team have begun using the therapy for war veterans suffering post-traumatic stress, and for cancer patients. And a growing number of psychologists are using compassion-focused therapy in clinical practice.

I recently spoke with Sydney-born author Roman Krznaric, who was visiting Melbourne to discuss the empathy training he has conducted for some of Britain's top judges, as well as the violent offenders they sentence. He told me that while some judges initially believed that an empathetic approach could be viewed as being soft on crime, they found the training improved their awareness and decision-making. Ensuring that people felt as though they had been heard also improved courtroom management, making it faster to get through the system's caseload. 'Judges are often bringing their own stereotypes and prejudices to the table. They may be Catholics having to rule on issues of gay marriage, for example,' Krznaric said. 'Empathy can help shift some of their beliefs and be a tool for fairness. That imaginative leap is what helps us make a connection with another person who is different from us. We have all sorts of assumptions about people, and we're so often wrong.'

Tom Ballard pointed out in his Melbourne International Comedy Festival show *Problematic* that many of us on the Left view the world through our privileged inner-city bubbles. We support refugees, smile aggressively at women in hijabs, and demand action on climate change. In our hermetically sealed echo chambers, we can't fathom a worldview that would allow for the building of a nine-metre-high anti-immigrant wall, scale back women's rights, or challenge the veracity of climate science. We don't question what might be behind these positions. So when Donald Trump and Pauline Hanson are elected, we don't ask why, but instead shout that we are right and the people who voted for them are racist idiots. Only in the wash-up of the 2016 presidential election would commentators observe that Hillary Clinton describing Trump supporters as a 'basket of deplorables' might have helped him gain the keys to the White House.

The un-statesman-like behaviour of the 45th President of the United States has not only led to widespread condemnation and ridicule but has prompted many to label him as mentally unstable. Allen Frances, whose latest book, *Twilight of American Sanity*, is a psychiatric evaluation of life in the age of Trump, published a letter in *The New York Times* urging his colleagues to stop mislabelling the president as suffering from narcissistic personality disorder—a condition for which he wrote the DSM criteria. He argued that while Trump may be a 'world-class narcissist', this doesn't make him mentally ill because he doesn't suffer the distress and impairment needed to diagnose a mental disorder. It is, Frances believes, another example of the rush to explain normal human behaviour—as unpalatable and unhinged as it may seem—as abnormal. The temptation to medicalise actions, feelings, and personality traits we don't like, in others and in ourselves, is perhaps a form of self-protection, an act of distancing. It is also a way to dehumanise our opponents, which in turn makes it easier to justify hatred.

Perhaps change comes from turning to our enemies, not from them. After the US election, civil rights activist and CNN commentator Van Jones launched his 'Love Army', with the idea of using love as an act of political resistance, reaching out to opponents in a bid to unite people at a time of deep division. Through a 'summer of love' series of teach-ins, connecting people from all walks of life, Jones aimed to find common ground between groups with differing views and life experiences. He said the suggestion that love was a weak quality was wrong. Jones told *Rolling Stone* that the key to a more just America was to listen to Trump voters, particularly those who voted for him but didn't agree with his more controversial views. 'We can overreact to that and say, "If you vote for a bigot, you are a bigot." That's just not true,' Jones said. 'That kind of language—and that kind of approach—is actually helping Trump to build his coalition … You're giving away people who probably felt very conflicted voting for him. We need to build a bridge of respect, and part of it starts with actual dialogue.'

Jones faced criticism from many on the Left who said love was not enough to fight a regime that had introduced a ban on immigration from Muslim-majority countries, was winding back access to healthcare, and was taking a hammer to hard-won reproductive and LGBTIQ rights. How do you love the bigotry out of people? He countered by saying he wasn't trying to change racists—he was trying to keep racists from changing him. He told *Yes!* magazine:

> I'm going to fight for our side to quit being hypocrites, and reach out to poor white folks, and working white folks who may or may not even respect us as human beings. I don't care if they respect me as a human being. I am not taking a stand for the dignity of all people to try to change somebody else's mind. I'm taking a stand for the dignity and humanity of all people to make sure that my heart stays big in the era of Trump.

Retaining an open heart is challenging in the face of hatred. But it can also be healing. We saw it among the mourners in Manchester who stood together during a vigil after the Ariana Grande concert bombing and, rather than close down to hate, spontaneously burst into a rendition of Oasis's 'Don't Look Back in Anger'. It was there when conservative protesters tried to sabotage a same-sex formal for LGBTIQ young people in Melbourne by buying up the tickets and supporters responded by donating more than $40,000 in a matter of hours to ensure every kid could attend for free. And we saw it in Berkeley, California, when Al Letson, an African-American investigative journalist, threw himself on top of a neo-Nazi activist who lay bleeding on the ground to protect him from being beaten with poles by anti-fascist protesters. 'He was a human being,' Letson later said.

At the heart of these acts is compassion. It's a uniquely human empathy for others, and a belief that individual acts of kindness can make a difference. There is a place for anger and resistance, but I try to ration my fury these days. I almost never feel better after lashing out at someone, whether online or in the real world. When you peel back the layers of your own anger, you start to see that holding on to it only hurts you, and that under anyone's frustration there is usually an invisible battle the rest of us can't see.

17

LOVE THINE ENEMY

When I told friends who I was meeting for a drink, they all asked the same question: 'Why the fuck would you do that?' They were right to be sceptical. I was about to break bread with a woman who had publicly described me as a 'social-justice warrior straight out of central casting'. She routinely dismisses people with views like mine as 'frightbats', 'feminazis', and 'comically deluded, fringe-dwelling, virtue-signalling Lefties'. I was nervous.

Rita Panahi is an outspoken, right-wing columnist for Melbourne's *Herald Sun* newspaper and a social commentator on Sky News, 3AW, and Channel 7's *Sunrise* program. She has created a strong brand as a conservative provocateur, with some tipping her as heir apparent to Andrew Bolt, her hard-right tabloid colleague. With more than 150,000 followers on Twitter and Facebook, she is fast becoming one of Australia's most vocal media personalities. She prides herself on 'telling it like it is'.

Over the years, Rita and I have had many frank and robust Twitter debates. Her scorched-earth approach to public discourse has infuriated me. There is almost nothing we have agreed on. Her background could not be more different to mine: born in Arkansas in the United States, where her Iranian father was studying to become an engineer, she moved back to Tehran with her family at the age of three. In 1984, after the revolution that led to the installation of the repressive Ayatollah Khomeini regime, the family were accepted into Australia as refugees and moved to Melbourne when she was eight years old. It is her memories of life under the Ayatollah—when she and her schoolmates were made to chant 'Death to America' before each class—that helped inform a deep contempt for people who apologise for radical Islam, a topic she writes about with great frequency and fervour. She believes that political correctness is largely to blame for the Western world's failure to combat Islamic terrorism.

Another passion is her intense displeasure with the latest generation of feminists, whom she says obsess about trivial or imagined offences while 'ignoring the persecution of their sisters in the name of Islam'. In a column to mark International Women's Day, she wrote, 'It's clear the feminist movement has been hijacked by the regressive left with a level of hypocrisy and inanity unmatched in public discourse; just when you think these dolts have hit rock bottom, they find shovels and start digging.'

When I hit my own rock bottom I began to realise Rita was one of my red flags. Arguing with her was not productive; it was a unique form of self-harm. I'd see her tweeting about 'SJWs' (social justice warriors) and 'regressive left-wing flogs' and would be compelled to respond. It felt personal. I'd take to my keyboard and outline how wrong she was, mocking her arguments to the cheers of my followers. I could lose hours locked in combat with this woman I'd never met. As I furiously tried to make her see reason, my stress levels skyrocketed. Our followers would join in, taking sides, which only added to the sense of gladiatorial theatre. I had to have the last word. I had to land the killer blow. I simply had to be right. Sometimes the exchanges would stay with me for days.

When I took a break from social media to rebuild myself, I could see that in these moments I was not in control. The ship was being steered by the child part of me that was desperate to be applauded by the crowd. The more anxious I became, the more I took to Twitter for reassurance that I had value. Perhaps I was even a bit jealous of Rita's growing profile, rocketing me all the way back to the popularity contest of high school. Being seen and heard as I took her on would somehow give me autonomy in a situation where I felt powerless. But the anger was toxic. When you pick up a hot coal to throw at your enemy, you're left only with burnt hands. So often, anger is externalised shame.

When I returned to Twitter, I thought of what Professor Doty had said about the benefits of showing compassion for the 'other' and trying to focus on commonalities rather than differences. I still disagreed with most of what Rita said, but I could see our shared interests. We are the same age. We both love cats; we have a passion for the Hawthorn Football Club; and an enduring romance with the Italian Riviera. She has a wry sense of humour that is similar to mine, and on some issues, including abortion and gay rights, she is quite progressive. She is also a single mother, and I admired her independence. The more I practised compassion, for myself and others, the less I felt like fighting. I didn't imagine we would ever be firm friends, but I wondered if I could learn more about the world, and the people who view it differently to me, by getting to know Rita. And maybe I'd discover that, like me, her online persona was being driven by invisible battles.

I approached her on Twitter, and she accepted my invitation to catch up. When the moment came to finally meet, I was apprehensive. What if she didn't show? What if she wrote about the encounter in one of her columns? I could just imagine the headline: 'My Secret Meeting with a Feral Flog from the Loony Left'.

We met at a bar in Southbank, next to the *Herald Sun* offices, one evening after work, just as the sun was setting behind the Yarra. I was surprised how quickly I felt comfortable in her company. The conversation flowed easily. She is petite and energetic and has a warm, infectious giggle that makes her seem younger than her years. I felt secure enough to tell her that in an angrier moment during one of our many Twitter battles I had fantasised about the two of us presenting a Left vs Right political podcast. I even had a working title: 'Educating Rita'. She laughed, but seemed genuinely surprised that I had given so much thought to our online interactions. In her view, they had never been fights. The anger I felt was not an emotion she shared, although it is something people frequently bring up when they encounter her online.

'I'm often surprised when people say, "You're so angry" because I'm never angry on Twitter. Maybe it comes off that way because unless you're using a smiley face people can misread things,' she said. 'That anger accusation always comes from the Left, who, to be honest, I perceive as angry, and I'm thinking, are you projecting? Or is it just because my tone doesn't convey the mocking or the sarcasm?'

As we sipped our drinks—pinot grigio for me, port for her—I suggested that people may perceive her as angry because of the language she uses. Among her favoured terms for those she with whom she disagrees are 'irrelevant bile-filled dolt', 'moronic nutbag', 'self-loathing broken', and 'deranged leftie loon'.

She said I was mistaking mockery for anger. 'I just think some people deserve to be mocked. They are ridiculous, and trying to engage them … One, Twitter isn't the forum for serious discussion, and two, they're not worthy of that sort of discussion, they're worthy of being mocked and dismissed. They've said something that is insane or absurd and you're mocking that particular viewpoint.'

Mockery is an effective way to silence critics. In the kneejerk world of Twitter, it's a weapon used with blunt force. And it can be vicious. Recently, I found myself in the unfamiliar position of defending a right-wing Millennial commentator. I didn't know much about Daisy Cousens other than that she was a writer for conservative publications including *Quadrant* and *The Spectator*, and seemed to be a self-styled alt-right flamethrower who prided herself on 'triggering snowflakes'. She had recently praised Donald Trump on *Q&A*, saying the president was like the 'weird relative' who comes over once a year at Christmas and occasionally says embarrassing things but 'ultimately you forgive him because he is nice and gives you the best presents'. So yeah, she was an easy target for parody. Her crime, on this particular evening, was to publish a breathless, first-person account in *The Spectator* of her one and only meeting with the controversial and recently deceased News Corp cartoonist Bill Leak, in a piece that read as part eulogy, part erotic fan fiction. She described 'purring with satisfaction' after appearing on Sky News' *The Bolt Report*, and praised Leak as a 'gentleman, whose handsome face and unstudied smile left me strangely weak'.

I read it open-mouthed and cringing, wondering if it was satire. The late ABC veteran journalist Mark Colvin described it on Twitter as an 'astonishingly bad piece of writing'. That was about as polite as it got. Within minutes, Cousens was a national laughing-stock. High-profile figures played to the gallery of their large followings, dredging up everything she'd ever written and eviscerating it word by word. She was ridiculed in cruel and inventive ways, described as 'a cyst that had been left out in the sun', a 'thing', and a 'puffed-up nobody'. Her article was ridiculed as a 'bug-eyed, slack-jawed piece of teen romance tripe', 'thigh-slappingly, teeth-grindingly awful', and 'Enid Blyton meets 50 Shades of something that should have been burned on a pyre'.

Women on the internet have copped far worse. But there was something about the gleeful, almost tribal way people rounded on Cousens that made me wonder what the hell we're all doing in these moments. It was *Lord of the Flies* meets *Mean Girls*. People went trawling for old pictures of her, critiquing her looks, her youth, and her apparently vapid personality. Memes were created, satirical poems written in her honour. Someone dug up a column she'd written for an obscure overseas website in which she claimed to have turned down sex with a famous athlete. A frenzy ensued as a bunch of women — many of them staunch feminists, who themselves have been the target of vicious online trolling — tore apart the piece, joked about who the sports star could be, or declared that the incident simply never happened.

As I watched it unfold I tweeted: 'The Daisy Cousens pile-on is one of the harshest pile-ons I've seen in a while. It was a weird piece, but mob humiliation is pretty mean.' And so ensued a furious Twitter debate among my followers on whether Cousens should be defended or if in fact she deserved the ridicule because she'd set herself up as a right-wing provocateur and was therefore asking for it. People told me I'd backed the wrong side, implying I was a traitor to the Left for not joining in the public shaming. I added, 'Eviscerating a young conservative columnist who wrote something a bit silly is not witty or progressive. It's just bullying.

Maybe don't.' After several hours I went to bed, realising I'd only thrown kerosene on the flames. In the morning, I logged on and it was still going. People were incensed that I didn't share their fury.

Rita, who is herself a regular target for trolling and abuse, told me she 'couldn't give a fuck' about the flak she cops, and has grown a thick skin. But I wondered if she ever felt a degree of empathy for the people she disagrees with online?

'Sometimes I think they're genuinely not well,' she said with a laugh. 'I'll think, there is something much greater wrong with you than your opinion on this particular topic, and your reactions aren't normal. Quite often then you worry about how they're reacting. You might be thinking this is a hilarious little exchange, but they might actually be in some sort of a shame spiral. You just don't want to be adding to someone's pain or discomfort.'

She has, at times, felt guilty for retweeting ridicule or getting involved in a Twitter pile-on. When I told her about my mental-health battles, she was sympathetic and kind. It is not an attitude she extends to everyone. 'It's hard to have sympathy for people who are genuinely unpleasant. Or their persona seems to be. I'm sure if you probably met them you'd get a very different impression from what you see.'

Which brought me to why we were even there. I was curious as to how she viewed me. Online, she uses a broad brush to dismiss everyone on the Left side of politics as 'idiotic'. What did she hope to get out of meeting with this particular idiot?

'I've always thought you seemed like someone I'd be very happy to have a drink with or go to a footy game with or whatever. I've never seen you as the enemy,' she said. 'It's unhealthy only to have people around you who agree with you because then there's not much boisterous discussion or diversity of thought. We're not at war—this is Australia. It's not like parts of the world where people you disagree with you literally can't talk to because it ends in gunfire.'

She explained that she differentiates between the 'ordinary Left' and the 'lunatic Left', and went on to describe my place on this complex continuum. 'You're somewhere between ordinary Left and social-justice-warrior Left. I think lunatic Left is where you don't want to be. Regressive Left is very close to it, then you've got your social-justice warriors and your ordinary Left. So you're in dangerous territory, you're getting close to the regressives.'

When someone is essentially calling you intellectually backward, it's hard to keep an open mind to their broader point. But I listened intently and found that despite the slightly obtuse way her points were being delivered, there remained in her views some areas of common ground with mine. I couldn't disagree with her belief that the mainstream media is out of touch with the average punter, given Brexit, Trump, and Hanson came as a complete shock to almost every journalist who covered them. Whether it's coming from the Right or the Left, when we shut down debate, try to ban voices we don't like, and label people with opposing views as stupid or inherently bad, we only risk further alienating communities that already feel ignored. 'If you actually think that someone is evil then it gives you licence to not only dismiss their opinions but dismiss them as human beings,' Rita said.

This is the heart of the problem in our divided, digital age. When we separate ourselves into opposing camps and condemn the 'enemy' as fundamentally bad, we dehumanise the target, making it easier to join the social-media pile-on. Nowhere was this more apparent than when Yassmin Abdel-Magied, a Sudanese-born 26-year-old Australian mechanical engineer, author, and ABC radio presenter, found herself front-page news in 2017 after a seven-word Facebook post on Anzac Day, urging people to remember those in Australia's offshore detention centres who had fled conflict, went viral. Social media, Liberal MPs, and the News Corp papers went into overdrive, calling for her to be sacked, punished, or deported, in a frenzied orgy of blood-letting that was revolting in its ugliness. In the following three months, some 90,000 words would be written about Abdel-Magied in the Murdoch press, with the febrile reaction prompting daily death threats, rape threats, and harassment against a young Muslim woman whose greatest crime was to ask that people pause on a day of remembrance for our war dead to reflect on the plight of refugees fleeing war-torn countries. The abuse proved so extreme that she later announced she was moving to London, writing in *The Guardian* that she had become the most hated Muslim in Australia. In response, conservative commentator Prue MacSween announced on Sydney's 2GB radio that she was 'tempted to run her over'.

Leaving aside the transparent racism and Islamophobia that underlies the whole sorry incident, there is something deeply troubling about the anger running through these public shamings. As Abdel-Magied pointed out, the visceral nature of the fury weakens us all. It's a raw, naked rage that divides us into warring tribes, constantly scanning the surrounding landscape for someone to blame.

Rita upset some of her fellow conservatives during the Abdel-Magied furore by not calling for her to be sacked. She told me that in a democracy it is fundamentally unhealthy to silence opinions we don't like. In that regard, I share her concerns at the way some on the Left, in a bid to be inclusive and intersectional, have driven a burgeoning 'no platform' movement, banning speakers they don't agree with from university campuses or glossing over the tensions between radical Islam and women's or LGBTIQ rights. In some Muslim countries, women are being stoned to death for having sex outside of marriage and gay men are thrown from buildings. Rita's opinions might make some on the Left uncomfortable, but as a woman of colour and a former refugee who has lived under an oppressive Islamic regime, she has a perspective that can't be ignored just because it doesn't fit the ideological narrative of those who view themselves as progressive. You don't have to agree with her to listen.

'I think if you're a powerful woman and lucky to be living in the Western world then you've got an obligation to at least focus some attention on women who are genuinely oppressed and don't have a way out,' she said. 'I find the abandonment of feminists of that group really quite ugly because that's to me the biggest battlefront for women, instead of obsessing about sexist air-conditioning. I think it's a responsibility we have, to focus on those women who are voiceless. It could have been me. It affects family members of mine, and it was just luck that I'm not still there.'

Despite what her critics have claimed, Rita is adamant she's never written anything she doesn't believe in. This is not part of a brand she has built to feather her nest. Indeed, she is independently wealthy, with an expansive property portfolio, and could have retired at 30 had she chosen to, she told me. She writes on issues she feels passionately about. During our time together I try to get her to open up. I'm looking for those invisible battles—that soft underbelly we all have. She is guarded and doesn't give much away, but when I ask about her

10-year-old son, it's clear that this boy — who on Instagram she affectionately dubs #TGC (The Golden Child) — is the centre of her world. His future informs much of her writing. 'As much as I joke about and mock certain things, and certain trends that are occurring, I do worry about him going off to university and being faced with that oppressive campus culture where you're expected to think a certain way and you don't have that diversity of thought or critical thinking being celebrated,' she said. 'I would hate for him to go off and be exposed to that or be made to feel guilty because he's male or to be blamed for things he's not guilty of just because of the sex he was born into.'

After a couple of hours, we had to bring our catch-up to an end. She was heading to the studio to appear on Sky News' *The Bolt Report*. As a pre-condition of our interview I had promised to let her see the extract before publication. 'I'm trusting you,' she said, before adding, 'I screen-shotted the message. The one where you said you'd give me copy approval.'

I didn't blame her. We were from different worlds. Over a drink we had narrowed the gulf, but the apprehension remained.

No doubt I will continue to disagree with Rita on many issues. When she talks about the 'broken dullards of the regressive Left', it will make my teeth itch. And I'm sure my social justice warrior-ing will keep her in eye-rolls for years to come. But I'm tired of being angry all the time. I remain a passionate advocate for equality, inclusion, and the progressive causes that Rita might view as 'SJW virtue signalling'. But I'm no longer convinced that righteous fury is the best vehicle for change. The anger is corrosive. It diminishes me and my argument. I know it's not easy to remain calm and dignified when the public rhetoric is so poisonous — especially for those in marginalised communities who face constant attacks on their humanity and are still fighting for basic rights. How do you remain stoic and gracious when you're being told you're an abomination? A terrorist? A dole-bludging waste of space? And yet, history consistently shows that the antidote to hate is not more hate. We need dialogue and open hearts. As Van Jones says, we have to see the dignity and humanity in all people. And at the end of the day, branding someone a moron has rarely changed anyone's mind.

Meeting Rita won't heal the world, but it has helped change me. She's no longer just an avatar behind a series of tweets. I know that I won't find fulfilment in telling her she's wrong. I can't imagine ever ridiculing her again to win the admiration of my followers. My happiness levels do not improve by fighting with people on the internet. The anger I once felt when battling with Rita online—an out-of-control fury that would send my anxiety soaring and leave me empty—has dissipated. It's easy to throw stones at an ideology. It's much harder to hurl them at flesh and blood.

18

LOOK FOR THE HELPERS

It was Saturday morning in *The Age* newsroom and all was peaceful. I munched on a slice of fruit toast, scrolling through Facebook. This was production day, when all the stories we'd been working on through the week were pulled together, placed on pages, and prepared for *The Sunday Age* going to print that evening. I was sitting at the news desk—in the round configuration of chairs and desks we call the 'doughnut'—cracking jokes with my colleagues and hoping for an early finish.

It was our picture editor who first alerted us to the horror the world was about to witness. 'Something's happening in Paris,' she said, looking at the international wires. 'An explosion.'

Things got messed up really quickly. News filtered through like fragments of broken English on a CB radio. A bombing. No, two bombings. Maybe three. Shots had been fired all over the city. There were reports of hostages at a football stadium. Chaotic scenes were being broadcast on the bank of televisions above our heads. It was night-time in Paris, the darkness broken by the flashing blue lights of police cars and ambulances. I spoke to a pregnant friend, via Facebook, who was in Paris on holiday with her husband. They were in their apartment in the centre of the city, listening to the sounds of gunshots outside.

I tracked down Australia's then human rights commissioner, Tim Wilson, who was safe but told me his hotel near Notre Dame had locked its doors and he'd been instructed to stay away from the windows because of reports of grenades. 'They're now turning the lights out on the ground floor to try and make it look innocuous from the street,' he said.

Not long after this, President François Hollande—who was evacuated from the Stade de France at half-time during a football friendly between France and Germany after three suicide bombers blew themselves up outside—declared a state of emergency, closing the nation's borders and urging residents to stay home. He told his citizens, 'At this moment, unprecedented terrorist attacks are underway across the city of Paris.'

In the newsroom, our team of reporters and editors worked swiftly to keep our readers up to date online with a situation that was constantly changing. The first half of the paper was scrapped to make room for an event that was beyond comprehension. We knew that many, many people would be dead. I hadn't been back to full-time work long, only a few months. I was feeling fairly strong by this point, and coping well with life's demands, but this was still a shock to the system. And yet it was the job; anything can happen. Adrenaline powered me onwards. Then we heard about the Bataclan. The true horror of the terror attacks became apparent in the details of what happened inside that theatre. Three men with assault rifles entered the venue where about 1,500 people were watching American rock band Eagles of Death Metal. They opened fire on the crowd, methodically executing music fans with merciless precision, reloading three or four times. Twenty minutes later, 89 people were dead.

By the end of the night, 130 people had lost their lives in six different locations across Paris. It was only when I got home after a 12-hour shift that the reality of what had happened came into sharp focus. It was the striking familiarity that connected me to this terror in a way that made my hands shake. These were football fans, young people enjoying a glass of wine at a sidewalk café, music lovers slaughtered watching the same band I had danced to during their visit to a Melbourne laneway festival just a few years earlier. All innocent loss of life is tragic, but nothing unsettles the fragile human psyche quite like the recognisable. It reminded me that while once, avoiding terrorism meant staying away from the world's trouble spots, these days it seems nowhere is safe. And the gap between attacks grows ever shorter.

The collective helplessness is reflected in the futility of Twitter hashtags and temporary Facebook profile pictures. Buildings are lit up in the colours of the flag of the latest city to join a list none want to be on. We pray for Manchester, Paris, Brussels, Berlin, Orlando. Then we move on. And it all begins again. What worries me most is how quickly I can process facts that once would have been unthinkable. Watching people being murdered on live television is no longer the stuff of dystopian nightmares. I find myself taking inventory of the dead, weighing up the numbers, the ages, comparing the severity of the horror to that which has come before. It has become one amorphous blur.

In an age defined by an endless stream of bad news, it's easy to be dragged down by the mind-blowingly shitty things that people do to one another. For someone already prone to catastrophising, it can be difficult to gain perspective.

I shudder when I see viral YouTube videos of teenagers being beaten up in the schoolyard or red-faced men screaming racist abuse on public transport. When my Twitter feed is flooded with unfiltered pictures of lifeless Syrian children, I can't bring myself to absorb what I'm seeing. Friends take to Facebook, imploring the world not to look away, but I do. It makes me feel weak. I need to be stronger than this. And yet my heart can't take it. When I press play on that video, or read the accounts of people live-tweeting from the scene, I'm right there amid the panic and the terror. My anxiety spikes and I feel scared, despondent, worried for the world. So I have to stop looking.

For Generation Anxiety, the seemingly constant threat of terrorism and disaster has only exacerbated their sense of overwhelm.

After a suicide bomber blew himself up outside an Ariana Grande concert in Manchester, killing 22 people, many of them children and teenagers, the UK's National Society for the Prevention of Cruelty to Children issued, for the first time, advice for parents on how to talk to children about terrorist attacks. It included listening to their fears and not dismissing them as silly, not providing overly complicated explanations of events that could provoke fear or confusion, and reminding them that they're safe and surrounded by security. As educator Linda Lantieri discovered after the September 11 attacks, kids are resilient and can recover from even the most unimaginable trauma, but they need the skills to process it.

Online youth mental-health service ReachOut recently partnered with Twitter in a venture designed to help young people cope with the bombardment of bad news. They created a series of online factsheets offering tips on managing life in an era where unplugging is almost impossible. These included 'Dealing with Bad World News' and 'Understanding Terrorism'. ReachOut chief executive Jono Nicholas told the ABC that the world had fundamentally changed for today's young people, and when they're constantly hooked into their phones, it can feel as if bad news is following them around. 'Social media and technology is simply the way they navigate their day,' he said.

To preserve my sanity, I have learned to limit my intake of bad news. Switching off is a form of self-defence. It hasn't always been easy. My job as a journalist has been to bear witness. I haven't faced the persistent trauma that colleagues covering crime, the courts, and conflicts regularly encounter, but like any reporter, I've had my share of stories that shook me. After the Black Saturday bushfires that killed 173 people in Victoria on 7 February 2009, I spent a day assigned to the Alfred Hospital's burns unit, where the few people who survived the blaze were sent for treatment. I stood by the bedside of a man who was heavily sedated and bandaged from head to toe, and was told that when he came round he would learn that his entire family—including a two-year-old daughter—had perished. When Malaysian Airlines flight MH17 was shot down over Eastern Ukraine in 2014, killing all 298 people on board, I huddled together with my friends Rania and Nick in the pub to debrief after an exceptionally long shift that saw us trying to pull together pen portraits of the 27 Australians who died—tributes that seemed hopelessly two-dimensional in the midst of such loss.

Another journalist friend, Beck, who covered the devastating earthquakes that destroyed Christchurch's *The Press* building and much of the city, killing 185 people, told me, 'Working at *The Press* post-quake was weird because you were living it, working it. And then you'd go to the toilet and the poster behind the door had a list of coping mechanisms like, "Avoid too much media".'

Research suggests between 80 and 100 per cent of journalists have been exposed to a work-related traumatic event. Sometimes we witness horrific scenes without ever leaving the newsroom—the uncensored raw footage and images coming in from the coalface of a tragedy. On the scene, we see the same sights as emergency service first responders. Post-traumatic stress disorder among journalists with prolonged exposure to violence, misery, and tragedy is not uncommon. But the effects of terror, or the perceived threat of terror, can have a powerful impact even on those not directly affected. A survey conducted shortly after the September 11 attacks found that 17 per cent of the US population living outside of New York City reported symptoms of post-traumatic stress disorder. With the immediacy of social media and 24-hour television news, everyone now has a front-row seat to events that can have a profoundly damaging impact.

When my anxiety is heightened, watching the news can make it worse. It's not that the negative media coverage makes me necessarily fear I'll be blown up in a terror attack or abducted by a violent offender, it's more the sense of dejection that envelops me when I ruminate on the state of the world. As humans we are biologically conditioned to pay more attention to bad news because when we sense danger it triggers the fight-or-flight response, preparing us to go into battle. British psychologist Dr Graham Davey, who specialises in the psychological effects of media violence, states that negative news can significantly change an individual's mood, especially if the story emphasises suffering. Neurologically, our brain can actually perceive images of violence as a threat, which can make us feel warier of our environment. In addition, 'Viewing negative news means that you're likely to see your own personal worries as more threatening and severe, and when you do start worrying about them, you're more likely to find your worry difficult to control and more distressing than it would normally be,' he told *The*

Huffington Post. This exposure to bad news can become a self-perpetuating problem as we start to interpret what we see on TV as proof that the world around us is inherently threatening, making us more depressed. The images change our mood, which makes us more likely to hone in on things in our environment that are negative or threatening. Just as focusing on gratitude allows us to see the good in the world, consuming too much bad news can have the opposite effect.

The morning after my shift reporting on the Paris attacks, I woke up and kept reading. I consumed every story about the Bataclan, imagining myself—as I've done so many times before—standing on the sticky carpet of a darkened band venue, beer in hand, rocking out to my favourite tunes. I couldn't fathom how this could be the scene of a massacre. I turned to my Facebook page for light relief, but the first story that popped up was the tale of a lonely, doe-eyed dog tied to a tree in the backyard of a vacated bungalow. I fell apart. Then I banned myself from social media and all news for three days.

'If it bleeds it leads' has been a news-gathering maxim for decades, but these days, social media's immediacy and the insatiable 24/7 news cycle, with its onslaught of depressing information, can make it feel as though we're perpetually on the brink of the apocalypse. Events or details that we would once have been shielded from are presented in vivid detail. It's hard to fathom what has happened to us as a species when reading about the crowd of onlookers who encouraged a suicidal man to jump to his death from a multi-storey carpark, shouting 'get on with it' as they snapped selfies while police negotiators tried to talk the man down.

The rational part of me is reminded that this sensationalist and shocking view of the world is curated through Facebook algorithms and the perilous state of the media landscape. I'm seeing an edited view of the world, not a representative picture. All too often, footage is published just because it can be. The financial imperative to drive traffic to struggling news sites has led to a decline in editorial standards that has seen graphic or emotionally manipulative content published, with little thought given to the consequences.

As much as I've railed against the dumbing down of my industry, I must take my share of the blame. I've written countless stories that ensure the most poignant, heart-tugging details go straight to the top. Clickbait headlines and social media posts are crafted to reel readers in with snippets of human tragedy. It has become such a journalistic trope that Rania coined a phrase to describe the phenomenon: the 'misery hang'. It's the teasing headline that toys with our emotions but compels us to look — the online equivalent of slowing down to watch the aftermath of a car accident on the freeway. A few of us have taken to group messaging one another every time we spot a particularly blatant example of the genre.

He texted his mum he was fine. Minutes later, he was dead.

Michelle was in agony. Doctors said it was a temper tantrum. She died.

Ashleigh went out with friends to celebrate her twentieth birthday. But a fateful decision to walk home resulted in a terrible tragedy.

The more people click on this stuff, the more the formula is employed. And so the cycle of misery continues. Editors now have access to detailed metrics on every story they publish, and the dark stuff seems to rate pretty well. Maybe it's human nature to seek out the worst versions of ourselves, if only to be reassured that no matter what mistakes we've made, we are at least better than that.

But the bombardment of awfulness does not spur people into action. In fact, a constant stream of negativity can lead to a sense of 'learned helplessness', making us feel disempowered and fatigued by the apparent hopelessness of global events. A study of 2,000 people conducted by Denise Baden, Associate Professor in Business Ethics at the University of Southampton, found that negatively framed news causes disengagement, avoidance, pessimistic moods, and anxiety. Participants who were exposed to two environmental stories were much more likely to be motivated to act in an environmentally friendly way after watching a report that focused on the success of an ocean clean-up campaign than they were after watching a report that centred on damage to the ocean caused by pollution. Similarly, watching a story about the atrocities in Syria led to a 38 per cent reduction in mood for women and 20 per cent for men, while watching a report about peace talks between the United States and Iran had the opposite effect. Baden now tours universities, teaching workshops for journalism students on 'constructive journalism' — a movement that is helping to rewrite the script of how we perceive the world.

The UK website *Positive News*, run by editor-in-chief Seán Dagan Wood, is at the forefront of the movement, with its 'If it succeeds, it leads' inversion of traditional news priorities, and became the world's first global media cooperative after raising more than $450,000 at launch. It is now owned by more than 1,500 readers, journalists, and supporters. Dagan Wood wrote in the *Huffington Post*:

> We face colossal and escalating challenges as a global community: climate change and social inequality, to give just two examples. And on the individual level, people are

suffering across the spectrum of circumstances in which humanity finds itself. But at the same time it would be wrong, in our knowledge or imagination, to disown any one of their achievements, strengths, loves and joys. At the global level, there is also another side to the story.

When I dipped into the site, the stories were varied and topical, covering areas such as society, economics, science, and the environment, but all had a positive slant. In the days after Donald Trump walked away from the Paris climate deal there was an article outlining how American businesses were speeding towards a low-carbon future regardless of what was being decided in Washington. Another looked at how Iceland had radically cut rates of teenage drinking and substance abuse through investment in sporting programs and parenting classes. There is also a regular section called 'What Went Right', which charts a long list of positive signs of progress in the previous few months. After half an hour of reading, I felt considerably more hopeful about the future of our planet.

And there remains much to be hopeful about if we know where to look. Oxford University's Our World in Data tracks how global living conditions are changing over time. It looks at a range of measures, including poverty, violence, human rights, health, and literacy. Founder and researcher Max Roser created the site to counter the perception nine out of ten people share: that the world is not getting better. A recent Ipsos MORI Social Research Institute poll showed that across 14 countries, the public perception of rates of teenage pregnancy, immigration, and murder were much higher than they actually are. What the media focuses on and how it chooses to report it can play a major role in how people respond to events happening around them.

Roser points out that the news cycle doesn't reflect how the world is changing; it simply tells us what goes wrong in the world. It focuses on single events that are often bad — plane crashes, terrorism attacks, natural disasters, and election outcomes we're not happy with. Positive developments happen in a much more gradual way, and rarely make the headlines because the media is event-focused.

Roser says that the story we tell ourselves about our history matters and is a vital driver of change:

> Knowing that we have come a long way in improving living conditions and the notion that our work is worthwhile is to us all what self-respect is to individuals. It is a necessary condition for self-improvement. Freedom is impossible without faith in free people. And if we are not aware of our history and falsely believe the opposite of what is true, we risk losing faith in each other.

While Roser concedes that huge problems remain and we can't afford to be complacent, there is something comforting about the statistical evidence he provides. At the start of the twentieth century, 36 per cent of the world's children died before their fifth birthday. By 1960, this had dropped to 19 per cent, and in 2015, it was just 4 per cent. Progress on poverty has been even more remarkable. In 1850, 92 per cent of the world's population was living in extreme poverty — surviving on less than $US1.90 a day. A hundred years later, this had only dropped to 72 per cent, but in the last few decades the improvement has been steep. In 1990, 37 per cent of people lived in extreme poverty, compared to just under 10 per cent in 2015. Of course, it's horrible that one in ten of the world's citizens live below the poverty line, but the significant and continued advances paint a picture of progress that we can't always see when looking at global events in isolation.

Surely with all the terror attacks and global conflicts, though, we're living in a more dangerous world than our forebears? Not according to Harvard University psychology professor Steven Pinker, whose 832-page bestselling opus, *The Better Angels of Our Nature: why violence has declined,* analyses centuries of human existence and puts forth the hypothesis that we are currently experiencing the least violent, least cruel, and most peaceful period in our history. He maintains that every kind of violence — including murder, rape, genocide, animal cruelty, and homophobic and racist attacks — has declined, and we are now living in a more peaceful world than ever before. It's a view shared by Australian moral philosopher Peter Singer, who stresses that a person born today has less chance of dying a violent death than at any other time in human existence. If we look at the longer trend, we're becoming more humane, rather than less.

When I returned to Facebook after the Paris attacks, I asked my friends whether they ever felt overwhelmed by bad news and if so what they did to manage that. The response was a resounding yes. For my friend Jo, my question struck a raw nerve. It led to a profound revelation that came pouring of out her. She wrote,

> I've spent my life looking after people and believing that unless I do 'something', no-one else will and that it's my responsibility to fix things. On Saturday night we went to a 'Climate for Change' event at a friend's house and I came out feeling like if I didn't do ALL THE THINGS then it would be my fault if the terrible things foretold came to

250

pass. And so I got up yesterday morning and went grocery shopping and I walked around the shops and made sure that I bought only what we needed and nothing more so as not to be wasteful.

But it wasn't enough. She went home and wrote an imploring letter to her local MP. She tweeted Prime Minister Malcolm Turnbull and Opposition leader Bill Shorten, pleading with them to act on climate change. She still felt helpless. To counteract the anxiety, she lay on the couch and 'watched soothing, pleasant ABC fluff and felt much better for it'. Later, as she got into her car on the way to a family Passover meal, she had a revelation: she couldn't fix the world.

> I knew this already but somehow in that state of panic one develops a God complex and believes — much like the anxious flyer who thinks that it's the force of their anxiety that is keeping the plane in the air — that unless I personally do ALL THE THINGS about climate change that right this minute the permafrost will give way and a hole will open and swallow the Earth.

Her answer was to go back to the simple things. She would stop trawling the news. Instead she would retreat to the garden, cuddle her dog, eat delicious food, and bake.

Stopping to appreciate life's finer details was a common theme in my friends' responses. As Amanda put it, 'Sometimes I like to "live in the small". Really try and appreciate the small, good stuff. A nice daytrip to the markets, delicious dinner, a beer with a mate. I'm not saying a total disconnect with the larger world, but being happy in our own helps to contribute to the bigger.'

It can seem self-indulgent to pamper yourself when children are being massacred in war zones, and human rights abuses are being prosecuted in your own backyard. But I've found that if I want to make a difference I have to be armed with the energy to fight for change. As Veronica often reminds me, 'You cannot hold up a friend if your own arm is broken.' Allowing yourself to take a break and live in the small is not selfish, it's an act of replenishment.

Another friend had a simpler solution: 'I spend substantial periods of time watching videos of dogs greeting their owners. It works a treat.'

A woman I went to school with told me how she made a conscious decision to stop watching all news and reading newspapers when she was struggling with depression. 'I didn't carry the world's problems anymore, and even though I am constantly out of the loop, I don't mind that at all. It's preferable to the alternative. The wider world made me too sad to function as a person, so I had to take myself out of it.' Six months after making that choice, she went back to college and is now studying at university. While she doesn't believe her depression was caused by absorbing bad news, she found that opting out of the news cycle was hugely beneficial: 'When you are fighting the demons in your head, you don't need to be watching them on your TV screen or reading about another atrocity every day as well. I felt so utterly powerless that I had to do something, so I got out. Maybe that's not a responsible way for a grown woman to deal with the world, but it worked for me.'

When I find myself, like Jo, spiralling into a blind panic about the state of the world, I have to log off. And I've accepted that while I can make a difference in my own small way, there is much I cannot change. I have to channel my energy into what

I can control. So I try to break it down into bite-sized chunks I can swallow. I focus on 'living in the small' because it's the only way that works.

On the day of the 2016 US presidential election, I was sitting in Veronica's waiting room when it became apparent that Donald Trump was on track to win. As I watched the news come in, my anxiety escalated. Here was a man who was exposed as a misogynist, who had boasted about 'grabbing women by the pussy', and who wanted to ban Muslim immigration and build a giant wall on the Mexican border, reigniting a white supremacist movement many of us had hoped was all but extinct. Veronica and I spent the first part of our session talking about how scared I was about what this meant for humanity, and what it said about the divisiveness and fear that permeate our lives. I felt despondent that hate had won over hope. But then she said that these tumultuous events only served to underscore how important it is for us to strive to live well—to nurture our relationships and be present in every moment, even the uncomfortable ones. If we want to change the world, we start with ourselves. We have to be the change we want to see. That means not surrendering to hopelessness but trying to live with compassion, kindness, and a willingness to understand the fears of our neighbours. That may seem pointless in the face of overt racism and misogyny, but as Chido Govera taught me, the only thing we can control is how we behave in response.

My friends with children make a difference by raising their little people to be that change. A former high-school classmate of mine who now works in paediatric intensive care said she sees families coping with situations that most people can't even imagine, making at times heartbreaking decisions, but this also serves to give her markers for how to live:

> I see the resilience of the children and families, which makes you realise that there are things that we can't control. At the end of the day, especially if it's been a tough one, I go home grateful for what I have and give the kids a cuddle. So with the news, I take the attitude that there are things I can't do anything about, but I can bring my children up right, to be respectful, kind, and caring.

I don't think we should gloss over injustices or turn our heads from tragedy. But if a cycle of negative news leaves us paralysed by apathy and helplessness, we are effectively turning away anyway. Perhaps we need to look for the positives so we can have the strength to counter the negatives. On an individual level it can start with something as simple as a gratitude journal — training the brain to find the chink of light on a dark day. Even in the immediate aftermath of an atrocity it will be there. When something awful happens I turn to the famous quote from children's TV host Fred Rogers, who said, 'When I was a boy and I would see scary things in the news, my mother would say to me, "Look for the helpers. You will always find people who are helping."'

After tragedy came to Melbourne in January 2017, when a man allegedly drove his car at high speed through Bourke Street's pedestrianised mall, killing six people, including a three-month-old baby, and injuring 30 more, I took comfort from what happened immediately after the event. As bodies lay strewn across the pavement, pedestrians, café staff, and city workers on their lunchbreaks ran to help. In the midst of chaos and terror, when it was still unclear what was unfolding and whether this was the act of a lone assailant or the harbinger of a larger attack, countless members of the public put their own safety to one side and got down on their hands and knees to administer first aid and words of comfort to strangers.

One of the most poignant things I read was written by a young man, Henry Dow, who had rushed to the aid of a woman who had been struck by the car. In a Facebook post that was shared more than 17,000 times, he described how his legs carried him across the street to help, 'almost on autopilot, swearing under my breath repeatedly as it sunk in what had just happened'. As he rolled the woman on her side, supporting her neck and holding her hand, he heard gunshots. Henry didn't know it then, but it was police officers firing at the alleged perpetrator. Kneeling under a skinny tree on the footpath, he was helped by a man called Lou, who grabbed Henry's shaking hand and firmly told him to keep it together, that he was okay, and that they needed to be strong for this woman. The man was not, as Henry had presumed due to his calm and pragmatic demeanour, an emergency-services worker. He was a taxi driver. It was Lou's heroism that prompted Henry to write about what he witnessed that day. His words moved me to tears:

> We have all seen images and opinions flood the media over the past 24 hours. If you feel like shaking your head and feeling sad for the state of humanity, I implore you: Don't. There was no evil on Bourke Street yesterday; one sick young man did a terrible thing, and hundreds responded with the love and sense of community that makes Melbourne such a beautiful city, and Victoria such a great state. There was only kindness in the voices of the police who came to relieve us. I felt only love when an older man hugged me, having just told a father he had

lost a daughter. Many images and sounds will stay with me much longer than I might like, but I am glad to have seen, and hope I never forget, just how brave and loving strangers can be.

19

ENJOY THE SILENCE

I told myself that this would be the day I would finally calm down. Breathe, heal, relax, and renew. I was at a Sunday-afternoon workshop called 'Sacred Rest', which promised to provide 'the healing gift of restorative yoga'. Over two and a half hours, it would weave a gentle fusion of yoga, therapeutic breathing, divine guided meditations, and something called 'crystal bowl sound healing'.

My back was supported by a body-length bolster as I lay on a mat on the floor, arms stretched out by my sides. I was swaddled in two blankets. The teacher had placed a cool mask that smelled of lavender on my eyes. The lights were low, and a soothing soundtrack of *ommm*s and chimes played unobtrusively as she started to speak in that honeyed voice all yoga instructors seem to have. I could feel my mind slowing down. This was awesome. I was going to be the goddamn Mayor of Relaxotown. I would float out of this joint like a delicate bird, winging my way to tranquillity.

We were only five minutes in when it started. At first, just a faint whistle. But slowly it began to build. A wheeze. A louder, deeper whistle. Then a rasping, full-throated groan, punctuated with a snort. The bearded, heavyset man to my right was not only the Mayor of Relaxotown, he was the fucking sheriff. And he was holding us all captive with his insufferable snoring. I tried to block it out, but I could feel my muscles tensing as Regina began to scream, *YOU CAN'T EVEN RELAX IN A YOGA CLASS!! YOU'RE FUCKING MENTAL!!!*

That's when the other guy started. To my left, a young man with his mouth open like a fairground clown trying to catch a ping-pong ball had joined the symphony. I'd paid $50 to lie on the floor for two hours and be assaulted by surround-sound mouth breathers. The more annoyed I became, the more I felt like a failure for not being zen enough to rise above the irritation. Where was my loving-kindness for all beings? I should be able to accept this inconvenience and transcend to a higher plane like a good enlightened soul. Instead, my neck had frozen up in fury and I was sighing loudly as I fantasised about ramming wind chimes up the nostrils of my fellow yogis.

In the end, I moved to another corner of the room. Without the snoring I was able to unwind, and I left the class feeling more relaxed than when I'd walked in. But afterwards, I reflected on the experience and realised that part of my frustration came from this sanctuary of silence being invaded by unwelcome noise at a time when it feels there are few places left for quiet contemplation. On public transport, commuters watch videos without headphones or FaceTime friends on speaker phone. On a flight home last year, the couple in the row in front of me let their two children watch a movie at full volume on an iPad, and I wondered if this was now an accepted norm. The insidious hum of digital devices has even infiltrated our libraries, art galleries, and cinemas. In the United States, movie chain AMC Theatres has considered allowing audiences to use their mobile phones during films, with CEO Adam Aron telling *Variety*, 'When you tell a 22-year-old to "turn off the phone — don't ruin the movie", they hear, "Please cut off your left arm above the elbow." That's not how they live their life.' In a description that I fully endorse, film critics likened the move to the 'end of civilisation', and ultimately the chain backed down. As my good friend and *Age* entertainment reporter Michael Lallo wrote, 'Your right to feed your iAddiction ends with my right to enjoy a damn movie in peace. If you love multi-screening that much, why not stay at home with your TV *and* phone *and* tablet *and* smart watch and really make a night of it?'

The divide between private and public space is becoming more blurred as noise pollution creeps into places that were once considered sacrosanct. Friends have told me their horror stories of phones being used in yoga classes and at meditation retreats — even a loud Skype conversation carried out in the middle of a massage. Children using electronic games in restaurants and the maddening sound of music being played too loudly in libraries were also common bugbears.

The La Trobe Reading Room at the State Library of Victoria is one of my favourite places to seek silence. I go there to read, to write, sometimes just to sit. With its magnificent high-domed roof, green reading lamps, and geometrically pleasing hub and spoke of old wooden desks, it is my happy place. It used to be that just walking in there would bring me a sense of calm. But more and more it feels as if the silence that once made it a haven is no longer respected. Tourists traipse through, chattering as they snap photos, and students use the free wi-fi to FaceTime with friends. There is almost always the tinny sound of music being played too loud through headphones. I asked Matthew van Hasselt, the library's spokesman, why mobile phones and tablets were even allowed in this once silent space, and he said that the way libraries are being used has fundamentally shifted. 'When you have a generation who have grown up with devices and use them as a vital tool in their interaction with an institution—and we're seeing this in galleries and museums around the world—the answer isn't as simple as just turning it off because you're actually removing a really powerful tool for engagement in new ways that haven't previously been available,' he said.

In other words, get over it, grandma. I accept that my anxious disposition perhaps makes me more susceptible to noise irritation than others, but this constant background hum of technology is not just a problem for those in search of ways to find calm. At a recent meeting of the American Association for the Advancement of Science, a senior scientist at the US National Park Service warned that the constant use of digital devices and music played through earphones is putting young people at risk of 'learned deafness', leaving them unable to hear natural sounds such as birdsong, trickling water, and trees rustling. Kurt Fristrup warned that the innate human ability to pick up sounds that are hundreds of metres away was at risk of being lost through 'generational amnesia': 'There is a real danger, both of loss of auditory acuity, where we are exposed to noise for so long that we stop listening, [and] a loss of listening habits, where we lose the ability to engage with the environment the way we were built to,' he said. Fristrup likened excessive background noise to a fog, where you can only see what's directly in front of you: he said the 'rich natural choruses' that exist even in cities are not being heard because we have tuned them out. Today's children are at risk of growing up in an environment where silence is an alien concept.

The World Health Organization lists noise pollution as a serious health risk, ranking it as the second-largest disease burden globally, after air pollution. It can cause sleep disorders and contribute to heart attacks, learning disabilities, and psychological problems. The effects of excessive noise on children can be grave, impairing development and impacting on academic and cognitive performance. One study of more than 2,000 children from schools near various airports in Europe found a direct correlation between noise pollution and impaired reading comprehension and memory, regardless of socio-economic background. Our minds just aren't designed to cope with all this noise.

I have learned to sleep with earplugs in. As I live in a bustling inner-city suburb of Melbourne, the fastest growing city in Australia, the sound of traffic and construction work is constant. Since I bought my place eight years ago, the apartment boom around me has gathered such pace I can't remember a time before the skyline was dominated by towering cranes. Every vacant lot is being built on. The trams and trains are more crowded, and the cafés are overflowing. I know that I'm as much a part of the urban overpopulation problem as any of my neighbours, but still, the busier my suburb gets, the more crowded-out I feel, in space and sound. When I'm feeling anxious, the loudness only exacerbates my stress.

In a bid to dampen some of the noise from my traffic-heavy street, I invested in double-glazed windows, but that only provided a degree of respite. Nothing has been able to block out the obnoxiously loud motorbikes, which roar past my place with such ferocity the glass trembles. Victoria's Environment Protection Authority issued more than 5,000 noisy vehicle notices between 2014 and 2016. Sometimes it feels as if every one of those vehicles is right outside my window. A bike made before 1985 has a noise limit of up to 100 decibels—that's the equivalent of standing in the path of a jet plane as it takes off. It's the kind of noise you can feel vibrating in your chest. It does not help my nerves. One of the super-fun things about anxiety is it puts your body on high alert. The longer you live like that, the more your natural baseline for stress increases. It means my body is hyper-sensitive to factors such as light, pain, and noise. When I hear a thunderous engine revving up as I'm trying to relax at home, my body immediately tenses. Hamish jumps as if the bike has just driven through the hallway. It can send me into a white-hot rage.

The sense of powerlessness we can feel in our increasingly overcrowded and noisy suburbs perhaps explains the rise of the angry, note-leaving neighbour. When people feel their needs are not being considered, they can revert to irrational behaviours. As Veronica reminds me, when a response to a perceived injustice is disproportionately emotional, it's usually the aggrieved-child part of the brain that has taken over. Every time those Harley engines roar, I have to breathe deeply and recognise that the bike rider didn't get up that morning, pull on the leather strides, and jump on their bike with the express intention of disregarding the emotional needs of a Scottish-born crazy cat lady they've never met. My sense of righteous grievance is unlikely to change their behaviour and only serves to make me more stressed. But it's hard to remember that when there are few places of silent reflection left in the city and noise is coming at me from all angles. Noise pollution is an irritant that can aggravate our stress when we're already stressed. It's why that co-worker who hums incessantly or drums their fingernails on the desk can sometimes feel like the most excruciating form of torture.

My friend Michael Lallo shares my frustrations with the scourge of excessive noise. We often joke about how we're basically the same person. He also needs his plans scheduled with military precision. Whenever we catch up, it's always a contest to see who will arrive the earliest, so horrified are we by the prospect of being late. Even when we try to arrive on time, we somehow always find a way to be early. Like many people trying to navigate life in an impossibly loud world, Michael has spent a fortune on industrial noise-cancelling ear protectors to help him deal with a crowded open-plan newsroom where hot-desking has left little room for quiet contemplation. Despite these headphones being designed for runways, paper mills, and quarries, sound still seeps in, forcing him to also wear foam earplugs, which has led him to conclude that some of his colleagues are louder than jet engines. He recently messaged me an article from *Time* magazine, which described how people like us, who are infuriated by loud mouth-breathers or noisy eaters, may be suffering from a recently discovered brain abnormality called misophonia, a uniquely twenty-first-century condition that causes those afflicted to be pathologically triggered by certain sounds, sparking an extreme emotional reaction. It seems the cacophony of sound that punctuates modern life is pushing the anxious and the stressed to the brink of madness.

Michael and I have discussed how we'd like to be the kind of people who are unperturbed by noise intrusion and simply let the loud excesses of life in the modern age wash over us with Dalai Lama–like grace and virtue. But we're not. We're like Steve Carell's chronically confused simpleton Brick Tamland in *Anchorman*, who screams 'LOUD NOISES!!!!' when people start yelling, before curling up on the floor in a ball and praying for it all to stop.

So what can we do to get peace? When I find industrial life too loud, I try to escape to nature. I go to the local park, take trips to the beach, or spend time among the tall trees in our national parks. Larry Rosen, the *iDisorder* expert, told me that just being in nature, away from the over-stimulation of urban life, has been found to have an automatic calming effect on the brain. A growing body of research shows a strong link between access to green spaces and reduced prevalence of anxiety, stress, and depression. It's not just the opportunity to be physically active but also the emotional and spiritual nourishment these spaces provide. There is something innately soothing about being in the natural environment. In what some have dubbed 'ecotherapy', living among the greenery appears to be good for the mind and body. A Harvard University study of 10,000 female nurses found that those living in the greenest areas had a 12 per cent lower mortality rate compared to those in built-up areas. Researchers attributed this to a number of factors, including lower rates of depression and pollution, and higher levels of social engagement and physical activity. It may also be that disadvantaged communities have reduced access to green spaces, while wealthier people can afford to live in areas with an abundance of natural parkland.

I know now that if I am to maintain any semblance of calm I need to regularly switch off my devices, find quiet, and make space for my thoughts. Whenever I can, I take myself out of the digital sphere and into the natural world. As often as possible, I visit my friend Kath at her beach house down the coast. Closer to home, I leave my phone in my apartment and spend time at the nearby park, a small oasis of greenery in inner-city Melbourne where I sit listening to the wind whistle through the leaves of the ancient English elms and let my bare feet feel the grounding energy of the earth. Just being there acts as a circuit-breaker. It doesn't happen immediately, but eventually my mind slows down, and I am released.

However, even nature is being invaded by noise pollution. On a recent beach holiday with my friend Loretta, we were swimming in the ocean as the most beautiful purple sunset stretched out above us. It was a quiet, secluded spot and I remember feeling that this was one of those perfect life moments you wish you could bottle and take home. And then, overhead, a high-pitched screech and a robotic creature that looked like a giant angry mosquito was upon us. It was the first time I'd seen a drone in the wild, and I was horrified. Leaving aside the creepiness of a strange man sitting outside a beachfront villa wearing headphones and night-vision goggles, capturing footage of two women in bikinis swimming at dusk, it felt like a crime against nature.

There has been little time to contemplate the consequences of the march of technology for our shared public spaces or the etiquette and civic responsibility required to keep up with the changes. Anyone can fly a drone weighing under 2 kilograms for fun or for profit without approval from Australia's Civil Aviation Safety Authority. By 2021, the global drone market is expected to be worth $12 billion. In 2016, Dominos became the first company in the world to deliver food via drone to a customer when it dropped off a pizza to a home outside Auckland, New Zealand. The CEO said that drones, which can avoid traffic lights and congestion, were 'the future' for takeaway-food delivery.

Regulations state that drones should not be flown at night and must be kept at least 30 metres away from people, vehicles, or buildings. But realistically, there's little we can do in the moment if drones are impinging on spaces we once expected to be places for calm reflection. The Civil Aviation Safety Authority did threaten to issue a $9,000 fine to an enterprising

Melbourne man who, in possibly the most Australian crime ever committed, flew a drone to Bunnings to snatch a snag from a sausage sizzle and deliver it to a friend waiting at a nearby outdoor spa. But the organisation only knew about it because the culprit uploaded the footage to YouTube.

In the United States, there are already significant problems in wilderness areas. The National Parks Service banned 'unmanned aircrafts' in 2014, but despite the regulations the menace continued, with 325 citations issued since then for unlawful drone use. Rangers have reported that drones are having an impact on the parks' wildlife, affecting their ability to mate or escape from prey. Just as being plugged into our phones is creating 'learned deafness', for these animals, drone noise makes it harder to tune into the sounds of the natural environment. I'm sure this technology is a boon for all the budding David Attenboroughs out there, but surely our native wildlife would be better left in peace, free to roam, unstartled by the intrusion of flying robots?

We can't halt the march of progress, but just because technology allows us to do something, it doesn't mean we should. When I learned about the development of the 'selfie drone', my first thought was, *What fresh hell is this?* If you've ever tried to take a picture at a popular tourist spot and been whacked on the head by a backpacker trying to get the perfect angle with a selfie stick, you're going to LOVE this. It's a pocket-sized robotic camera that syncs with your smartphone and can take to the skies to snap your every move. Retailing at between $300 and $600, it's perfect for those panoramic Instagram pics and Facebook videos, but I'm not looking forward to a time when every scenic nature spot is abuzz with the hum of flying digital devices. If the selfie drone takes off (pardon the pun) it will be another case of the march of technology outpacing the law.

But this is life in the modern age. It is loud and it is busy. Our challenge is to make room for quiet among the noise. For me, with an inner world that is so often loud and unrelenting in its chatter, I have had to work hard to find that peace. It can be tempting to try to drown out the inner monologue with a different kind of noise. But instead of reaching for podcasts, music, or TV shows every time I have a spare moment, I'm trying not to be always plugged in and just let the gaps be there. Regular meditation is useful. I don't practise it nearly as much as I could, but even in sporadic bursts it helps slow me down. When excessive noise starts to irritate me I also take to my journal to get to the bottom of it. Often I'll discover that my fury at a neighbour's thumping footsteps is not really about the neighbour at all, which makes the noise easier to deal with.

But there are times I've craved silence so much I've contemplated heading to church to seek sanctuary. Travelling in Europe, I'm always drawn to the medieval cathedrals and abbeys not just for their stunning architecture but also for the echoing silence, and a stillness so complete it feels regenerative. Yet back home, as a devout atheist, setting up camp in God's house to escape my noisy neighbours feels somewhat uncouth. I can't reject organised religion then opt in just because they have good acoustics.

But then I found a spiritual space that welcomed unbelievers. It's a haven of tranquillity right in the heart of Melbourne's CBD. Mingary is one of those hidden secrets you can't believe you've stumbled upon. It's not really a church, although it's nestled inside one: St Michael's Uniting Church at the Paris end of Collins Street. Mingary means 'the quiet place' in Scots Gaelic, which made me feel as if this was perhaps my pre-ordained spiritual home. The church's executive minister, Dr Francis Macnab, opened it as a non-denominational 'peaceful escape from the hectic demands of city life' in 1999. In a softly lit room with a handful of wooden chairs and a traumatised rock sculpture in its centre, people from all backgrounds come to find quiet—it is a place to restore a sense of strength and vitality. Dr Macnab told me that Mingary is a sanctuary for people looking to connect with their inner silence, particularly those who have suffered trauma or tragedy. The room has been designed to evoke a sense of healing: 'There is the trauma of the past in the rock, there is the quietness of the present in the water, and there is the shaft of light on the east wall symbolising a new day for the future.' He added that for physical and mental health it was vital we take time to listen to our own inner space. Quietness is therapeutic, but takes cultivation.

When I first visited Mingary, late on a Friday afternoon, the sound of my boots click-clacking on the granite floor echoed around the space as I walked to a corner chair and sat down. Opposite me was a middle-aged man in a business suit with a shaved head, hands clasped, eyes shut. A gentle trickle of water flowed down the rock's face in the centre of the room. Dr McNab said it symbolised 'the flow of life, by which we are all constantly renewed.' The water landed in a bowl with two small rocks—a red rock gifted by the descendants of the Wurundjeri people of Australia, and a green marble rock from the Isle of Iona, in Scotland's Inner Hebrides. It was meditative to watch. My brain was busy, as it usually is, but the longer I sat, the more the chatter slowed. That inner space began to open up. I started to connect to that part of myself that is hard to hear amidst the noise of everyday life. Through the heavy wooden doors, I could still hear the sounds of the city. But the quiet was growing within me.

20

ALL WORK AND NO PLAY ...

There is a small park near my apartment with a running track around it. When things were bad, I would go there and make myself do laps. I walked religiously, wearing out the tread on my sneakers day after day like a slow-motion Forrest Gump. It didn't always make me feel better, but it never made me feel worse, and on the days when it felt I could rely on nothing, that was good enough.

Walking was a critical part of my therapy. I knew from experience that when I didn't move my body regularly, my mental health suffered. The endorphins released during exercise would lift my mood and help burn up some of the cortisol and adrenaline that heightened my stress. But I couldn't face the running, weight training, and boxing I usually enjoyed. I was too exhausted. And the thought of being around healthy-looking gym bunnies pushing themselves to the limit was like torturing myself with a vision of a future I couldn't reach.

So instead, Veronica prescribed a daily brisk walk for at least 30 minutes. It would get me out of the house, which was beginning to feel like a locked cell. Getting out of bed was a huge struggle, but I just had to make myself do it. Even on the days when I walked around the park with tears streaming down my cheeks, at least when I looked at my Fitbit at night and it said 10,000 steps, I knew I had achieved one thing.

And slowly, the walking began to improve my mood.

The evidence around exercise as a treatment for psychological problems is strong. Trials have shown that depressed adults who take part in aerobic exercise for 30 to 60 minutes a day improved as much or in some cases significantly more than those taking antidepressants. As Norman Doidge had told me, you can put your brain into a more receptive state to mind-training exercises through regular physical activity, which triggers neurotrophic growth factors, making it easier to consolidate neuroplastic change. I've learned over the years that if I want to give myself the best shot at staying well, exercise is an absolute non-negotiable.

The park I visited regularly was an off-leash dog park, which wasn't something I'd noticed until one day the fact announced itself to me in a manner that felt like divine intervention. In this instance, the supreme deity presented himself as a floofy little white dog, racing past me, fuschia-pink tongue lolling from the side of his mouth, ears flapping behind him like windsocks. Trampolining off the toes of my sneakers, he tore his way from the path to the grassy expanse of the oval with a look of such unadulterated joy on his face that it stopped me in my tracks.

My dad insists that cats and dogs don't smile. He is wrong. This ball of floof was grinning. He was so happy I suddenly realised I was laughing—a sound I hadn't heard for some time.

I took myself off the walking track to the boundary of the oval and sat on a bench bathed in sunshine. I watched the little dog run from one end of the ground to the other and back again as his owner threw a ball. He ran with the unbridled bliss of a creature who was just happy to be outdoors on a sunny day.

From that afternoon, the dog park became my go-to place when I needed a pick-me-up. Even if I didn't feel it within me, I could witness what it might be like to live in the moment and have zero fucks to give. I could remember that sense of abandon and the simple satisfaction of being able to roam free, unrestrained by the tightness of life's leash.

My favourite time to visit was just before dinner, when it was still light and people converged on the park as the sun dipped behind the trees. There was always a chatty, neighbourly atmosphere as people bonded over their dogs' playfulness. So although I remain a committed cat person, watching pooches of all shapes and sizes frolic in that park has become one of my purest pleasures. It reminds me that these joyful, untethered moments are possible if I cultivate the space to play.

Much like dogs, little kids view the whole world as a playground. They run at full tilt, dance without caring what anyone thinks, and find wonder in the things adults have learned to overlook. Children play simply because it's fun. Then they grow up and are told that playing is selfish, foolish, and indulgent. In a world that values busyness over downtime, play is an activity that so many of us have left behind. If you examine your life, how much of 'leisure' time feels just like work in another guise? Running around from jobs to social engagements, family obligations, and sporting commitments can feel like plodding along on a conveyor belt of duty.

As we get older, the child part of us that wants to run through a park like a dog off the leash is crushed under the weight of guilt, self-consciousness, and the chase for approval from the tribe. We forget what truly brings us joy and spend our time trying to please others. In therapy, Veronica made a point of placing the child at the centre of the work we did together.

She asked me to draft a list of all the fun things I liked to do and pencil in time every week to commit to them. I had to treat this time as I would if I were meeting a friend or going on a date; there was no cancelling. It had to be a priority. It couldn't be functional activities like going to the gym, which might produce fun as a by-product but still served the more adult purpose of keeping fit. And it didn't have to involve spending money. This was the stuff I liked just for the sake of it — the things we would do as kids without thinking twice about guilt, embarrassment, or the opinions of the crowd. It was hard at first to know what those things were, which made me realise just how disconnected I was from my own needs. But slowly, I began to compile a list.

On warm days, when the sun streams in my lounge-room window, I'll often find Hamish lying on the rug, a deliciously smug look on his face as he soaks up the rays. He looks so happy I've often felt like joining him. So I put 'basking in the sun' on my list of fun stuff, and the next time those life-giving rays shone down, I lay next to my cat and just drank in the warmth. I began to schedule in time to sing, smashing out show tunes from *Glee* and *Frozen* in my lounge room, and I took bike rides with no destination, just to see where I'd end up. One day, during a walk around the park listening to Gaga through my headphones, I felt an overwhelming urge to run into the middle of the oval and dance. I looked around and saw people everywhere. I bolted for the grass and cut loose anyway — a silent disco for one.

In those times of play, I felt so alive. It was as if I was welcoming home a side of me that had been in exile. This was an integration of the child with the adult, and in those moments I was whole. Veronica said it was a process of rediscovering my 'true' self. All too often, we follow the pack or pursue goals for others who want to live their dreams vicariously through us.

We do what is expected, not what is nourishing. Much of this is shaped by the issues we bring with us from childhood. 'We are born with a true self, but that self is subjugated in order to meet the demands and expectations of our parents, and to please them,' Veronica told me. 'We then repeat those patterns with the other significant people in our lives and that true self becomes more and more squashed, and obscured from sight.'

Therapy was about clearing away those demands and expectations and allowing room for my true self to emerge as I built a more balanced and fulfilling life. Making space for activities that were just for fun helped strengthen the connection with that emerging authentic side. It was so important to let myself off the leash. Just as I had when I was a kid—when my brother and I had a list of indoor games and another for outdoor games, which we consulted when we were stuck for something to do—I drafted a list of fun things and rediscovered my dormant playful side.

I first became interested in the importance of play during that precarious year between my first book coming out and the breakdown that followed it. I was looking for ways to try to slow down the speeding thoughts in my head—ways that weren't drinking or medicating myself. I wanted to feel free, to let go. Loretta suggested we try No Lights No Lycra, a dance class held in the dark, with no steps and no teacher, where being immersed in the joy of movement is the only objective. Dancing had always been something I loved, and the idea of being able to dance like no one was watching—while a challenging concept for my anxious mind—really appealed.

We went along on a chilly spring evening and I made a promise to myself to leave my inhibitions at the door. When the lights went down I had no idea what to expect. But the music started and it just happened: we danced. This was not alcohol-tainted, show-pony strutting at a flash city nightclub. We were sober, in a church hall basement in Melbourne's inner north on a wet Wednesday evening, with the lights off. The darkness acted like an invisibility cloak and everyone just let go, completely lost in the rhythm. I let my body move in whatever way felt natural. It was utterly intoxicating. More than 120 people had paid $5 to dance the way we did when we were kids. It was silly and freeing and joyful. Every song, whether sublime (soul diva Aretha Franklin) or ridiculous ('90s Eurotrash Aqua), was met with the same heady abandon. Bodies pulsed and swayed and leapt. For 75 minutes, the floor was a heaving mass of life. By evening's end, I was riding a high of euphoria. I walked into the crisp air, steam rising from my head, and realised I'd been blissfully lost in a state of play.

No Lights began in Melbourne with two dance students who wanted to offer a non-judgemental space to 'bring people together to experience freedom of self-expression and joy'. It has since gone global. I wondered what was driving this need to be free, and whether the runaway success of the movement is suggestive of a culture itching to find a way back to playtime. In an era where we're overloaded with work, technology, and seemingly endless bad news, it makes sense that there would be a collective yearning for simpler times. But I discovered that taking time to play is more than just a childish indulgence. It's a primal drive. And, according to a growing band of researchers, sociologists, and health experts, if we want to ease our emotional discomfort, it's exactly what more of us should be doing.

I spoke to Dr Stuart Brown, a pioneering play researcher and psychiatrist from the National Institute for Play in California—a not-for-profit committed to bringing the 'unrealized knowledge, practices and benefits of play into public life'. He told me there was an emerging evidence base that showed playtime in adulthood is the gateway to vitality, can promote a sense of belonging, and may actually be critical to human development. Bizarrely, his fascination with the subject began after extensive research into the backgrounds of violent inmates, including Charles Whitman, who killed 17 people and wounded 41 others in a shooting from the top of a tower at the University of Texas in 1966. The common theme among offenders, he discovered, was 'play deprivation' as children. The research backs up animal models that show play opens new connections in the brain, boosting social and emotional competency. Play deprivation can cause problems with mating, stress, and resilience, as well as immune system deficiencies. 'Although we can survive into adulthood without it, we don't survive socially, emotionally, cognitively with any kind of fullness without having a healthy play background that continues throughout life. It is a sustaining, important part of being human,' Brown told me.

Whether it's dancing in the dark, rolling around on the floor with a pet, or just belting out our favourite songs as we strum the air guitar, play for play's sake has been shown to have significant positive effects in education, parenting, workplaces, and even in fostering community cohesion. In Brown's book, *Play: how it shapes the brain, opens the imagination, and invigorates the soul,* he defines play as any activity that is deeply engaging, joyful, and done for its own sake, without consideration of time or an expected outcome. He writes, 'When we play, we are engaged in the purest expression of our humanity, the truest expression of our individuality. Is it any wonder that often the times we feel most alive, those that make up our best memories, are moments of play?'

Reading the obituaries of people who died in the September 11 terrorist attacks in 2001, Brown was struck by the thread that ran through so many of the tributes. Lost loved ones were remembered not for their titles or achievements but for the joyful times when they were in a state of play. After interviewing several thousand people, he found the most successful were those who had the opportunity to live their lives in harmony with their play nature: 'We know from a number of anthropological studies that in civilisations and cultures that incorporate a good deal of play there is increased co-operation, great altruism, more sharing and less violence.'

Dozens of cities are starting to integrate the play ethic into urban landscapes as a means to foster greater social interaction in public spaces. London's Swing & Be Free project put swings into bus stops, encouraging incidental fun for commuters. In Montreal, a giant collective instrument made of 21 musical swings was set up in the city centre. In Stockholm, a piano staircase in a subway underpass led to a 66 per cent increase in people using stairs over the escalator.

Google, Lego, and Red Bull are among the businesses prioritising playfulness as a building block of creativity and innovation. Workplaces are being reconfigured as adventure playground–style offices complete with scooters, hammocks, mini soccer pitches, lolly dispensers, and tyre swings. In healthcare, a 2011 trial of play therapy involving 35 nursing homes and 400 aged-care residents, using clowns and 'humour therapists', led to a 20 per cent reduction in levels of agitation among dementia sufferers and significantly reduced the need for anti-psychotic medication. The program has since been rolled out at 70 aged-care facilities across Australia. 'Smile Study' chief investigator Dr Lee-Fay Low, from the Dementia Collaborative Research Centre at the University of New South Wales, told me that nursing-home residents were often bored and lonely, with little chance to experience humour. 'Giving them an opportunity to play changes them. It gives you enjoyment, it gives you opportunity to express yourself, and helps you make a connection with other people, and those are critical things for mental wellbeing at any age,' she said.

But while once our playfulness would have been cultivated when we were kids, these days, overprotective parenting, shrinking backyards, and increasing pressure to achieve academic success are contributing to a reduction in play time for children. Even in kindergartens, children are often given homework and expected to reach academic benchmarks instead of listening to stories or playing in the sandpit. Brown is another proponent of moving away from the 'teach to the test' school culture. He wants to see play at the forefront of education, arguing that this feeling of 'flow' is the optimal state for learning.

If you've found your flow, you'll know it. It's state in which nothing else matters. It's the rapturous abandon of a virtuoso violinist's solo performance. Or an athlete pushing their body to the limit. It's when we're 'in the zone', so immersed in what we're doing that we're completely lost in the moment. Hungarian psychologist Mihaly Csikszentmihalyi, from the Quality of Life Research Centre at Claremont Graduate University in California, is the architect of this psychological concept. He believes accessing this state of transcendence is the key to a meaningful life. If we cultivate the skill and make space for flow, we'll have more productive workplaces, smarter schools, and contented communities. When he came to Australia to speak at a happiness conference a few years ago, he told me that the way we live in this age of technology is hindering the ability to find our flow: 'The constant interruptions make losing the self in whatever you're doing much more difficult. People need to learn how to turn off their cell phones and not be glued to their computers all the time.' If you want to bring more flow into your life, he recommends 'cycles of solitude' for days or weeks at a time — in which we're less socially stimulated, allowing greater focus.

While our culture obsesses over happiness as an end goal, flow is the act of finding joy just for the sake of it. It's doing the things we love without expecting a specific outcome or a reward. For me, this means less screen time and more time reacquainting myself with the little kid who just wants to dance or sit in a sun trap. Finding my flow is something I have to actively cultivate. But when it happens, it's a life-affirming treat. I've gone back to boxing, and when I'm hitting the pads, lost in a fierce combo of hooks, jabs, and uppercuts, it's one of the few times I can't hear my anxious inner monologue. It just stops. Time stops.

I'm learning not to feel guilty about making room for play. It's not selfish, it's a protective factor for my emotional health. As play researcher Brian Sutton-Smith says in his book *The Ambiguity of Play*, the opposite of play is not work, it's depression. So I continue to take myself on dates, dance with my nieces in supermarket aisles, and sing at the top of my voice while running. It doesn't mean I can avoid the necessities of adulting. I still have to do my laundry, pay the bills, and find enough work to service my mortgage. I still have periods of sadness and struggle. But the more I let myself off the leash and take care of that little kid inside me, the easier the grown-up stuff is to manage.

21

UNCOMFORTABLY NUMB

Nobody is the sum of their greatest mistakes. And yet it seems so much easier to focus on the times we fuck up than on our moments of goodness. Ruminating on every harsh word spoken to someone we love. Hating the part of us that eats until we feel sick. Letting anger be our decision-maker.

Shame is one of the most powerful human emotions. It's also one of the most corrosive. For me, it's Regina's voice turned up full bore, telling me that I am unworthy, I am a fuck-up, I don't deserve to be loved because I am bad to my core. Throughout my life I've spent an inordinate amount of time wrapping myself in shame's discomfort. It makes me think of the things I've done that I can't undo. Things that, no matter how hard I work at cultivating self-compassion, I just can't forgive.

The world's leading shame researcher, Brené Brown — whose books on vulnerability, imperfection, and courage have led me to conclude she is one of the wisest women alive — maintains there is a distinct difference between guilt and shame. Guilt allows us to measure our actions against the values we hold dear and use that emotional discomfort in an adaptive way. It's an internal alarm encouraging us to be better. Shame is destructive.

It tells us we're undeserving of love and uses our poor behaviour as evidence. Put more simply, guilt is recognising you made a mistake. Shame is feeling you are that mistake.

Brown's TED talk on the power of vulnerability is one of the most popular of all time. More than ten million people have seen it, and the transcript has been translated into 52 languages. She describes shame as a universal human emotion, at its core the sense that we are not enough: not thin enough, rich enough, good enough, smart enough, pretty enough, happy enough, and so on. It can be what drives our fear and our unhappiness, but also our anger. Being criticised can cut to the quick of that feeling of not being enough. Rather than sit with the discomfort, it's easier to defend ourselves by lashing out and looking for someone to blame. But sometimes the shame is turned inwards, in acts of self-sabotage.

Alcohol has often been the gateway to my greatest shame. I've said and done things I can't take back. I've made reckless decisions and caused great hurt to people I care about. There have been too many mornings where I've woken up with hazy memories and a nagging feeling that I made a dickhead of myself the night before, and had to sheepishly text friends to fill in the blanks. Sometimes, there is no fixing what I have done. As I struggled to return to moderation after my year off the booze, I came to realise that drinking to excess is directly linked to the feeling of shame. Booze had been my crutch since I was a teenager, when I was desperate to belong and my shame was at its peak, and in some ways I sought that familiarity. It's that perversely satisfying feeling of picking the scab on a wound my body is trying to heal. I know it's bad for me, but there's something comforting in the pain.

I didn't explore this in *High Sobriety* because I hadn't yet made the connection. It was only through my work with

Veronica that I started to see the extent to which drinking is linked to my core emotional issues. Alcohol can seem like a fast-track to happiness for all of us. Pure hedonism on tap. For an anxious brain, it's an easy way to find release. Those first few glasses of wine are freeing, a blessed hour or so of respite from a mind in overdrive. But there's the inevitable backlash the next morning, as my mind kicks the living shit out of me for daring to try to switch it off.

The way the body processes alcohol creates the perfect storm. When you're drinking, it's all fun and games. Booze slows down the nervous system, bringing a fuzzy sense of calm, merriment, and the urge to smile at strangers. But the next day, the system is depleted and needs a kickstart. Cortisol and adrenaline flood the body, helping to remove toxins but also sparking an antsy, restless feeling, which, for someone already prone to panic, is like waking up to find your world teetering on the precipice of a nuclear crisis. Then comes the speeding freight train of shame, guilt, and paranoia as every questionable decision you've ever made since the day you were born is replayed in a high-volume, Technicolor montage of absolute headfuckery. This is *hangxiety*. And it's the absolute worst.

Rationally, I knew that drinking as a way of coping with life's challenges was a terrible idea. I'd literally written a book about it. But despite all I'd learned during my year off the booze, I couldn't always put it into practice. Alcohol was the quickest, most familiar painkiller I knew. Before everything fell apart at the end of 2014, I was back to medicating my weekends. It was a vicious cycle of having a few drinks to slow down the chatter in an over-stimulated brain, only to cop the horrors of hangxiety the next morning. Hangovers cause depleted levels of serotonin, and a drop in blood sugars, which always brought a heavy dose of the sads. Since the year off drinking, my tolerance for alcohol was far lower, so it didn't take much for me to get drunk. And the hangovers were worse. Much worse. It was probably in part a natural consequence of getting older, but I was also starting to slip into a hole from which I would soon be unable to escape. The mornings after were really dark. I joked with friends about my 'Suicide Sundays', but it wasn't funny. This poster girl for sobriety was completely losing her shit. I felt like a fraud and a failure.

The human psyche often makes us unconsciously repeat problematic behaviour as a way of reliving the past. In therapy, after I'd stopped drinking to give my full focus to the work ahead of me, it became abundantly clear that I had a pattern of unwittingly bringing about the very outcomes that scared me most, turning my core beliefs about myself into a self-fulfilling prophecy. If I believed I was defective and unworthy of love, drinking to oblivion and making decisions that would alienate me from those I cared about was a superb way of proving that theory.

It was only when I read Jenny Valentish's brutally honest memoir *Women of Substances* that I could fully acknowledge the roots of my rocky relationship with alcohol, and see that they stretched back well beyond my first drink. Like me, Jenny is a British-born, Victorian-based journalist in her early forties, who fell in love with binge drinking at the age of 13. Since then, she's struggled with alcohol and drug use, and in her book she explores the unique pathways that women take into addiction and out again. I was immediately struck by the parallels in our stories: she'd been a fretful child, prone to catastrophising and overly fixated on morbid events. And just as I had when my book was released, she was feeling the pressure of talking about issues from her past she hadn't yet fully reconciled with her present.

In the book, Valentish interviews dozens of addiction researchers as she tries to untangle the complex origins of her drinking and drug use. She outlines how childhood temperament is a major predictor of problematic substance use in adulthood. Pessimistic children who find it hard to bounce back from emotional challenges will view their lives as a series of pre-determined negative events, setting them up to fail. These are the children most likely to become adults who struggle with anxiety and depression and turn to alcohol or drugs as a coping method. I read this chapter nodding my head, remembering all the times I thought, *Well, yeah, of course that would happen to an idiot like me* — like the time I fell into the water off the coast of 'Argentina' as a child, or the many occasions Chris or Jason had had to help fix a glitch in my laptop or phone because I became utterly convinced that I was so cyber illiterate that technology must have cursed me.

Valentish's research showed that if children also have difficulty regulating their emotions, they are at even greater risk of problems down the track. In homes where techniques of calming down are not modelled by a caregiver, it can be difficult for the child to know how to soothe themselves when they feel stressed. 'If these skills are not observed and learned, the habit of self-regulation will not be routed into the neural pathways. Failure to learn might be through parental neglect or through watching parents catastrophise minor issues,' she writes.

This gelled with what psychologist Andrew Fuller, one of the architects of the Kids Matter program, told me when I was looking at emotional literacy in schools. He said that if young people learned from an early age to recognise and regulate their feelings, we would see a reduction in violence and binge drinking—problems often fuelled by poor impulse control or a desire to mask anxiety. The kids who got really drunk or violent often had no idea how to form relationships. They were the same kids who were socially anxious and scared, and learned to resolve their problems by hitting someone or wiping themselves out with booze or drugs.

Valentish summarised the identified high-risk factors for problematic substance use as low resilience, poor self-regulation, low self-efficacy, and reactivity. When I looked at the list, I ticked almost all the boxes. And just as I'd realised that my shame and my alcohol use were intrinsically linked, Valentish noted that there was a danger this pattern can become comforting. 'There's a familiar cycle of disappointment and then—if you grow up to coddle yourself with drugs and alcohol—self-soothing. In time, defeat becomes a self-fulfilling prophecy. Things are not for the likes of you. Something simply cannot be done. There is no point.'

When I read this part of her book, I broke down. It was like looking in a mirror. Each time I've found myself back in a cycle of problematic drinking, that twinge of defeat has been acute. It's brought with it a repetitive narrative of profound shame. *Why can't I be better than this? Why did I have that last glass of wine? Why did I stay out till 3.00 am when I promised myself I'd be home by midnight? I took a whole year off the booze and I've learnt nothing. My happy-ever-after wasn't meant to go like this.*

Piling shame on top of guilt has never helped to change behaviour. And when I look more closely, I can see there are long periods of time where my drinking has not been problematic. I'm not helpless. I can make choices. Moderation is not beyond me. So why do I go through long stretches of having a healthy relationship with alcohol and then slip into periods where I'm drinking like it's an Olympic sport? And it isn't just me. The messages are still coming from people who struggle with moderate drinking and contact me after reading *High Sobriety*. People want answers. The most common question: how do you drink now? Have I managed to find a way not to slip back into old habits? It is unsettling how many of them seem to link their salvation to mine. Why are so many of us still soothing our emotional pain with alcohol?

The prevailing wisdom is that alcohol and drugs contain powerful chemical hooks that inevitably lead to dependency. The dominant treatment approach is to view addiction as a disease that has hijacked the brain. Once an addict, always an addict. Abstinence is the only cure. For people with a predisposition, just one drink or a single drug hit will be enough to send them hurtling back to dependency. This is what author and journalist Johann Hari thought until he embarked on a three-year, 50,000-kilometre odyssey that turned his idea of addiction on its head. His subsequent bestselling book *Chasing the Scream* charts that journey, and has huge implications not only for the war on drugs but also for the way we view ourselves and the shame we feel when we fuck things up during debauched bouts of self-sabotage. When I met Hari, he was in Australia for a series of sold-out talks on drug reform. His book advances a theory about addiction that spoke to me on a deeply personal level. Sitting down with him face-to-face in the foyer of *The Age*, I gained a fascinating insight into the nature of dependency and its link to our emotional health.

He told me how the chemical-hooks theory of addiction was born out of early twentieth-century experiments in which caged rats were given two water bottles, one containing only water and the other laced with heroin or cocaine. Invariably the rats preferred the drugged water, and would go back compulsively until they overdosed and died. But Hari wondered why most hospital patients who are routinely given high-dose medical heroin for pain relief simply stop upon discharge, with very few going on to develop addiction. He found the answer in a 1970s Canadian experiment called Rat Park. This time the rats, instead of being left in sparse cages, were offered a choice of clean or drugged water in a caged playground of coloured balls, wheels, playmates, and abundant food. They showed little interest in the drugged water, and none became addicted. Hari told me, 'It's not the chemical that's your cage. The overwhelming reason for addiction is the pain and isolation the individual feels. The opposite of addiction is not sobriety. It's human connection.'

Hari's theory that pain and a lack of connection create the ideal breeding ground for addiction helps explain why poverty, disadvantage, homelessness, discrimination, neglect, abuse, and trauma are so often linked to substance abuse. And why mental-health problems go hand in hand with drug and alcohol dependency. At any given time, around half of the inmates in our prisons are suffering from mental illness and struggling with addiction. The punitive 'tough love' approach only deepens a user's sense of shame and alienation. In places where compassionate drug policies have been adopted, the results have been astonishing. Portugal, which had one of the worst drug problems in Europe, decriminalised all drugs in 2001. The money saved on punishing addicts was used to fund comprehensive treatment services, job-creation programs, and training courses to reintegrate users back into the community. It led to a 50 per cent drop in injecting drug use, and huge reductions in street crime, addiction, overdose deaths, and HIV transmissions.

When you remove shame, you restore dignity and hope. Writing in *The Huffington Post* a few weeks after we met, in an article that was shared more than half a million times, Hari said human beings are bonding animals who need love and connection to thrive. 'But we have created an environment and a culture that cut us off from connection, or offer only the parody of it offered by the internet,' he wrote. 'The rise of addiction is a symptom of a deeper sickness in the way we live—constantly directing our gaze towards the next shiny object we should buy, rather than the human beings all around us.'

Whether it's binge eating a slab of chocolate, scrolling through my phone, or drinking more than I planned to, the compulsion almost always comes back to the same issue—a need to numb my pain with external distractions. It's the pull of maladaptive but familiar habits. It can't be a coincidence that the more difficult life becomes, the harder I find it to live with moderation. It's the desperate search for something that's always just outside of my grasp. In those times, I've come to realise that if my cage is a lack of connection, that disconnect is so often with myself. Drinking too much is just another example of the search for an external fix. But I don't have an easy answer for the readers who want to know, 'What happened next?' My love–hate relationship with alcohol is one I continue to negotiate. For the most part, I do an okay job. But when things start to get out of balance I know that I have to take a long hard look at the ways in which I'm caged. Breaking free means learning not to numb the pain but lean into it and face what's there.

The question I'm asked the most after 'How do you drink now?' is, 'How is Fiona?' It's another question with no easy answer. In the final chapters of *High Sobriety*, I describe the sudden and unexpected death of my oldest friend's five-year-old son two days before Christmas 2011. Jude was the kind of child who took your breath away. With a shock of messy blond hair and mesmerising blue eyes, he was a crazy kind of beautiful. When he died, I couldn't believe it wasn't leading the six o'clock news. In those first few days, shock gave way to grief, which came in a flailing, hanging-on-by-the-fingertips blur. As I prepared for the flight home, I found myself in the self-help section of a Melbourne bookshop, searching for ways to help my friend. My impotence was matched only by the abject futility of the titles I found: *When Bad Things Happen to Good People*; *Beyond the Broken Heart: a journey through grief*. It was like trying to fight a firestorm with a watering can.

I had no idea how to talk to the bereaved. Until then, I'd mostly avoided those who'd lost loved ones. I didn't know what to say, so I said nothing. In a culture that's distinctly uncomfortable with pain, this was a safe position. We don't like to look that kind of loss in the eye for fear it might swallow us. But then it happens to someone you love, and you can no longer avoid it. In the days leading up to Jude's funeral I spent a lot of time at Fiona's house, which seemed at once smaller without the presence of her knockabout wee boy and not nearly large enough to accommodate her family's loss. One morning, I walked into their home to find Fiona sitting on the living-room floor with her seven-year-old daughter, Isla, folding pieces of card. When I got closer I saw it was the order of service for Jude's funeral, his cheeky smile and pink cheeks beaming back at me from the front of every copy. I felt the breath leave my body. There were no words. So I got down on the floor and started folding.

Later, Fiona would tell me that she felt guilty for all the times she'd turned her head from other people's bereavement. She'd never once sent a condolence card or been able to talk to someone about a lost loved one. She'd only experienced small losses and had never considered how grief would feel. It was a shock to discover that it was an experience not just of deep emotional sadness but also of searing physical pain. 'In those early days I was thinking, *How on earth can I live like this?* I started to count out how many years I potentially had left to live, and it frightened me that I could live for 50 years and feel the same pain every single day,' she told me. 'I had to make a conscious decision to try to heal, and actively chose to get through the early months as best as I could.'

Fiona sought support online, finding people who had survived the loss of a child. She discovered that grief is a social experience. Just as she had joined baby groups to teach her how to bathe her newborn, where to buy nappies, and how best to manage sleep deprivation, she found people who were slightly further down the road with grief than she was. She credits these people, many of whom she has never met, with saving her sanity and helping her find a path to a new life.

It's not surprising Fiona was blindsided by the realities of grief. Unlike some cultures—in which wailing rituals, open caskets, and unbridled public displays of mourning are an important part of the healing process—in our buttoned-up Western world, grieving is something to be done discreetly and behind closed doors. Our fixation with happiness has taught us to airbrush death out of life's narrative. I read a piece by a psychotherapist who said silent mourning has become so normalised it has given way to a phenomenon of 'car grieving', where the soundproofed isolation of our car is the only safe place to express our most profound emotions.

When I came back to Australia after Jude's funeral, I felt utterly helpless and so far from Fiona at a time when she needed me most. I spent many mornings in the toilets at work sobbing.

Then I'd go back to my desk and quietly do my job. When I was a teenager experiencing death after death in my family, I felt the same sense of secrecy. Grief was not a public act. There was a time and place for mourning, and even then it was expected to be measured and muted. When my Dad clutched my hand and broke down at my uncle's funeral, I remember being more confronted by this public display of emotion than I was by the sight of the coffin.

But grief is not meant to be quiet. It can be a skin-scratching evisceration that rattles through every nerve ending and rasps on each breath. Denying it an outlet isn't healthy. And it's an insult to those we've lost. When you make space for it, grief can be the grandest monument to love. The exquisite pain is a measure of our loss. And yet, there are arbitrary time limits placed on the bereaved, dictating the point at which their pain is expected to have run its course. Fourteen days, if we're to go by the DSM's criteria. After that, the bereaved are no longer grieving—they're mentally ill.

For Fiona, one of the hardest things in the aftermath of Jude's death was feeling as though he was being erased. In the months after the funeral, once she and her husband David had returned to work, it was as if she was expected to move on. The silence was suffocating. Some people would say anything to avoid talking about Jude, terrified it would trigger more hurt. It had the opposite effect. She told me, 'I'm not over the death of my baby boy and I never will be, so the mention of his name doesn't remind me that he died; it lets me know that people remember that he lived.'

On 23 December 2018, it will be seven years since Jude died. As Isla navigates the challenges of high school without her little brother, Fiona's sense of loss remains ever present. By any measure, she will always be grieving. She does not have a major depressive disorder, although she would have met the diagnostic criteria many times since the death of her son. She is not sick. She has simply found a way to accommodate her pain.

Her explanation of how she had found ways to keep going simultaneously reassured and devastated me: 'I need people not to misunderstand my sense of being okay. They shouldn't decide that I've moved on, accepted my loss or, God forbid, replaced my precious son. Instead, people should know that it's possible to choose to be okay while at the same time living with a broken heart.'

In the lead-up to the first anniversary of Jude's death, Fiona swapped the traditional Christmas advent calendar for a journal that marked one thing each day for which she was grateful. Some days it was the simple things that not so long ago had seemed impossible. The familiar sights of her home town that in the acute phase of her grief had looked abnormal, almost surreal, like shifting shapes in a Salvador Dalí painting. Now, she could enjoy a walk across the Braid Hills, looking out across her beautiful Edinburgh, and it no longer felt like a foreign land. It was the city that was home to the memories of her boy, and for that she was thankful. There was the weekly Friday breakfast with her girlfriends, lunch with her mum, and the restored ability to laugh and mean it.

Ten months after Jude died, Fiona gave birth to a baby girl. It wasn't planned, but Marley's arrival was a gift. She brought great joy and made life busy. Isla said Jude had sent her to them. Marley has her brother's blonde hair and many of his traits. Of all the people in Fiona's life, Marley talks to her about Jude more than anyone else, even though she never knew him. 'It's probably because she doesn't worry about how I'll feel and consequently it doesn't feel forced or awkward. I love these conversations because they aren't about the pain, they're about him and what he did and which toys he loved,' Fiona said. 'That makes him alive again, just for that little while. I've lived with his loss for as many years as he was alive now, and I still prefer to talk about his life more than his death.'

In 2013, I took a beach holiday with Fiona and her family to Nerja on Spain's Costa del Sol—a resort town I'd last been to with her when we were 21. During that trip I saw up close how the loss of Jude permeates their lives on a daily basis in ways I hadn't even considered. On the beach one morning, a retired English couple started chatting to Fiona and David about Marley, who was still a baby, and Isla, who was nine. Noting the age gap, the woman asked, 'Will you try for a boy next?' I wanted to throw myself across the sand like a human shield, as if somehow I could deflect the words before they made impact. But they hung in the air. And then calmly, politely, Fiona replied, 'Oh no, I think we're done.'

At dinner that night I told David I was amazed by the way they had both handled the interaction. He explained it was a frequent occurrence. Another tricky question was, 'How many children do you have?' In that moment they're forced to decide whether they say 'two' and deny the existence of their beloved son, or tell the truth and embark on an awkward conversation with a virtual stranger they might never meet again.

When I spend time with Fiona and her family, I am always acutely aware that there is someone missing. But the fact that she and David found a way to survive has provided strength in moments when I thought I couldn't carry on.

It was during that Spanish holiday when my anxiety started to spin out of control. While lying on a sun lounger reading a potboiler crime thriller, I had a violent panic attack. The azure Mediterranean horizon tilted from side to side, and I gulped down more air than my lungs could take. It made no sense. I was on a beautiful beach with my closest childhood friend; I'd just published a book in Australia and was about to launch it with family and other loved ones at home in Edinburgh. I should have been happy. But I couldn't breathe. I felt so guilty when Fiona had endured so much worse. After a day or so of trying to hide it, I told her things were unravelling. I detailed the dread and the hyper-awareness and the panicked sense of wanting to run from my own brain, and although she'd never experienced anxiety in this form, she understood exactly what it was like to have to fight your way through the day moment by moment. She didn't tell me to pull myself together or try to soothe me with platitudes. Instead she listened, told me that what I was feeling must be really shit, and asked how she could help. Then she told me what someone had once said to her: 'If you're going through hell, keep going.'

I think we can thank Winston Churchill for that piece of wisdom. It's one I have come back to again and again. Some days all you can do is keep breathing. And then, one day, you get to bedtime and realise you didn't have to remind yourself to breathe that day. When you touch the bottom of your despair, it's possible to find reserves of resilience you never knew you had. And it can bring into sharp relief just how short our time on this planet is.

For Fiona, who was always an anxious flyer but stopped flying altogether after the September 11 terror attacks, losing Jude meant travelling again. She had to live the fullest life, even if that meant doing things that were outside her comfort zone. Turbulence, take-offs, and landings are still terrifying, but the fear no longer controls her. Grief has changed things in so many ways. 'I do live differently. I take more holidays and I let Marley sleep in my bed every now and again without worrying about the consequences. I spend more money,' she told me. 'However, there are times when I'm more vulnerable. I can be knocked more easily and I can't always rely on my emotions. I might see something that knocks the wind out of me and then I can struggle for some time. Christmas is always tricky, and so is his birthday. I have to prepare myself for that ahead of time.

'Having said that, I know I will come back up again. It's the rollercoaster, after all, and I know that I've felt the lowest that I could ever imagine and I came back from that.'

In Buddhism, the path to enlightenment starts with bearing witness to what we're experiencing—good, bad, or indifferent. By denying uncomfortable emotions or trying to push the discomfort away, we stay mired in our suffering and lie to ourselves about the realities of life. Grasping for happiness and certainty at a time of deep anguish and instability is like trying to throw a party while your house burns down around you. Having the courage to sit with suffering is not easy when every instinct tells you to flee from it or numb the ache with alcohol, Facebook, or buying stuff you don't really need. But as Fiona discovered in the most painful way imaginable, when the worst thing happens it can forge a form of clarity that only the deepest adversity can provide. When your world is tipped on its axis, the view can never be the same again.

As I look back to the days I was skirting the border between the living and the dead, I wouldn't wish it away. If I could change one thing, it would be to spare the people who love me the distress of witnessing it and carrying the weight of my despair. But I'm grateful for the experience. As the thirteenth-century

Persian poet Rumi said, 'The wound is where the light enters you.' It has opened me up and enriched my life in more ways than it has hurt me. Rather than catastrophising about setbacks, I now try to see them as opportunities. Every difficult experience, every challenging emotion, is a chance for renewal.

I'm not advocating a trite 'everything happens for a reason' approach to suffering. Nor do I want to suggest for a moment that those who have experienced the devastation of bereavement wouldn't do anything to have their loved ones back. Life can be random and cruel, and our struggles ongoing. There are experiences so traumatic they threaten to destroy the very essence of who we are. But just because we feel like we're broken doesn't mean we are. In Japanese, *kintsugi* (golden joinery) is the ancient art of repairing fine pottery with powdered gold. When the cracks are painstakingly filled with luminous golden seams, it shows that nothing is ever beyond repair. As a philosophy, *kintsugi* is the act of embracing imperfections, wearing our emotional wounds on the outside. Rather than trying to hide the bits of us that are scarred, we make them part of a masterpiece. When we put the pieces back together, they might not look the same, but they can still shine. The broken becomes beautiful. When I view my life's most difficult events through the prism of *kintsugi*, I can see that the problem child is not a problem at all. She is the gold that holds the vase together.

For Fiona, the golden seams in her life are the love she has for Jude and the unexpected legacies he left behind. In those early months, there was no room for observing her pain; it was a simple case of survival. But now, things are different. 'I do embrace that suffering and I can scale my levels of happiness by having those early months as a baseline. I think I'm better able to appreciate the things that make me happy and feel grateful for them,' she said. 'I definitely live in a less careful way, not trying to micromanage decisions as much as I did. I'm also more keenly aware of people who are living in pain for prolonged periods of time. Watching the news, I'm more closely connected to the pain of the people who are digging in rubble for their families or watching their children die from malnutrition. It's not a feeling of removed sympathy but empathy, a very human connection.'

When I couldn't imagine living through another minute, I would listen to American Tibetan Buddhist and author Pema Chödrön's meditations. Her book, *When Things Fall Apart*, gifted to me by a thoughtful colleague at a time when I could not yet see that I needed this wisdom, has become my Bible. Chödrön points out that '[t]o be fully alive, fully human, and completely awake is to be continually thrown out of the nest'. Life is not a straight road to the fairytale ending. It is a twisting, complicated route populated by speedbumps and landmines, scenic views and beautiful sunrises, and a whole lot of beige, mundane days we will instantly forget. Whenever I feel like I'm falling, I listen to Chödrön's wisdom, and find solace as she guides me to connect my pain with the hundreds of thousands of other people around the world who are suffering the same pain in that moment. It doesn't remove the anxiety completely, but it always provides comfort, and a reminder that although what I am feeling is difficult, it is normal. It is human. My brokenness is not evidence of dysfunction—it is proof that, like all of us, I am a wonderfully flawed work in progress.

22

DANCING ON MY OWN

I know it's hard to see right now, but life will be easier again. There will be things to look forward to and joy to be found. You will travel again and see new places, watch spectacular sunsets, drink a glass of wine in a piazza, and soak up the local atmosphere. You will enjoy the sun on your skin and feel that life-giving energy. You will have vitality, and your warmth and fun and vibrancy will return. You will laugh until your sides hurt and you're gasping for breath. You will have amazing sex and be touched and held. You will feel the love of your friends in equilibrium, without neediness or expectation. You will run again and box and enjoy exercising. Your appetite will return and food will be your friend. Sleep will be a welcome embrace, not something to fear. Your home will feel like a sanctuary again. Watching the Hawks will be a joy. Reading a book will be something you can do without effort. And you'll be able to veg out in front of the TV and watch movies without your mind racing. Work will be rewarding and collegiate and challenging in ways you will enjoy. There will be new opportunities and possibilities you cannot yet even imagine. I know you can't see it now, darling, but there is a future. It's not too late. This

is just your tired mind playing tricks on you. Try to hang on.
We will get past this, I promise.
13/07/15

A year after I wrote this journal entry I sat in an Italian piazza, drinking a glass of Sangiovese and feeling the life-giving energy of the Tuscan sun warming my skin.

I'd written those words when I was struggling to make it through each hour. Twelve months later, living was again an experience to savour, not a torment to endure. I had just taken voluntary redundancy from *The Age* after more than a decade on staff. It was a tough decision based not on my health but on the bleak future facing media companies all around the world as an industry struggling to sustain itself faced savage cuts and rapid change. I was sad to leave, but had no regrets about my decision to move on. I was excited about the future and all its possibilities. Yet I wasn't quite ready to start the next chapter of my career. It had been a pretty brutal couple of years, and although I was feeling stronger and infinitely more hopeful, I needed some space to regroup.

The holiday was, in part, a birthday gift to myself for my fortieth, which I'd celebrated with a huge party in Melbourne with Mum and my friends a few months earlier. Then, as winter cranked up in Australia, I headed home to Edinburgh for a few weeks and on to Italy for a month. My entire Italian trip, barring a few days when Mum would join me in Venice, would be a solo adventure. It was the first time since I was a 20-something backpacker that I'd spent an extended period travelling alone. I flew into Florence and then travelled through the towns and villages of Tuscany, and on to the coastal majesty of the Cinque

Terre, before visiting Verona and finishing in Venice.

Having lived alone for years, I knew how to enjoy my own company, but I wasn't prepared for the challenge that *this* much of my own company would bring. The travelling itself wasn't difficult. I loved the independence, was comfortable finding my way around, and wasn't afraid to ask for directions when I was lost—which, given my woeful navigational skills, was often. I could muddle through with my handful of Italian phrases, and I felt confident in my ability to find company when I wanted it. The biggest hurdle was the alone time—the endless space to think and think and think, and then think some more. When you're taking in the sights with no one to share them with, it can make you occasionally forget you're alone. You see something you simply *must* remark on and before you know it you've blurted out, 'He looks like an Italian Billy Connolly' or 'Holy cow, I can see that lady's arse cheeks', while chuckling maniacally to yourself.

Not having my friends around to defuse some of the more toxic thoughts was also difficult. Those endless 'what if' anxiety loops were a little harder to break. In the first few days there was a constant running commentary, bombarding me at a million miles an hour with unhelpful and often wildly inaccurate information. It was like listening to Channel Seven's Brian Taylor call a footy match but with less 'WOWEE, how about that foot candy!' and more, 'I am definitely lost. I will never find the hotel again. Rabid Italian dogs will pick over my bones as I die here in the street.'

Back home, when I was able to verbalise some of those thoughts and get the benefit of my support crew's wisdom ('Seriously, Starkers, you don't have a tumour, you just had a big lunch'), I felt lighter. The chatter was easier to tune out. In

Italy, I was on my own. Just me and my thoughts. My many, many thoughts. In some ways it was freeing, and allowed me to know myself in a different context, without the reflective gaze of familiar faces and surroundings. But it also meant that there was nobody to steady me when I walked down a cobbled Tuscan laneway, having a panic attack so fierce it felt like vertigo, as if the sheer force of it could knock me off my feet.

Grappling with the challenges, I messaged my friend Kath, who had spent a long time travelling overseas, to ask if she found solo adventures tricky. Her response motivated me:

> I did, but I also found it very liberating. Relying on only myself for making myself feel good is a great skill to have. I worked out what I needed in my life to make me happy and decided to just do that instead of my perception of what other people thought I should do. I also learnt to think only good things about other people and I assumed that they were thinking the same about me. I've lost that a little bit now and still doubt myself, but travelling solo made all that go away. I was in control of me.

I followed her advice, tapped into my play nature, and began to discover what I liked. Unlike a group holiday—when so often choices are made by committee—I could afford to be entirely selfish. When there is nobody with you, it allows you to focus on what you want—not what you think you should want or what other people might enjoy, but just your own desires. Once you figure that out, you then need the courage to follow through, without apology or guilt. I opened up that playful, childish part of me and learned that some of the things that make me the happiest aren't always valued in our frenetic modern world, but are vital to my sense of self and wellbeing. I love watching the world go by, listening to the sound of rain on the roof, not rushing, sleeping in, or reading a book for hours on end. I also really like cheese, soft lighting, never having to share my dessert, and binge-watching low-rent reality TV shows.

I stopped scrambling out of bed at the crack of dawn every morning to tick off the sights like the other tourists, and instead stayed under the sheets, read a book, and ate croissants as the sun streamed in the window. I listened to the sounds of horses clip-clopping past and a pianist playing a Baroque concerto under the archway below. I started to notice the richness of life, and realised it comes in the details. It does not come, as Hollywood would have us believe, in the happy-ever-after but in the happy-in-between. It's in the finest points, the simplest pleasures, that there is peace. The first bite of a perfectly baked lasagne. The afternoon sun warming anxious muscles. A sky so blue and vast it feels painted on. If this was mindfulness, then for a few moments each day I was nailing it.

Alone, I was more attuned to the world around me, noticing things I might have missed had I been lost in conversation with a travel companion. There was the little blonde girl, arms outstretched, trying to catch the cool spray from the misting fans outside a wine bar. Another girl chasing bubbles, calling out, 'bubbles, bubbles, bubbles' until she collapsed on the cobblestones laughing. Boys running full steam at a flock of pigeons across an empty courtyard. In a piazza filled with cafés, I watched an army of waiters and shopkeepers assemble with military efficiency to move their tables, chairs, and trinkets undercover at the first rumblings of a thunderstorm. When the rain came down, they sang out to one another across the square like a family of birds in a call-and-response melody. I marvelled as team after team of groups dressed in white ran feverishly past my sidewalk café, snapping pictures en masse, in something called 'The Selfie Run'. I googled what this was but couldn't understand the Italian website, so just presumed it marked the end of civilisation as we know it. I also developed a newfound ability to start a conversation with strangers out of absolutely nowhere. Top tip: children, dogs, maps, or interesting-looking food are all easy segues into small talk with total randoms ('Oh, I see you're having the wild boar, how adventurous,' and so on).

I found it freeing that I could choose when I had company and when I didn't. And most of the time I chose solitude. But despite being content with this choice, I often weathered the anguished looks of strangers as I dined alone. To some of my fellow travellers, a 40-year-old women eating pasta on her own in an Italian beauty spot represented a glimpse into an existence we have long been taught to fear: one that relies only on the inner self for validation and comfort. A life untethered—liberating in ways, but without the anchor of another to reflect our worth.

Several times I approached restaurants and asked for a table for one, only to find myself ushered into a poky corner out the back or by the bathroom door. When I asked why I couldn't have the vacant table closest to the ocean, or the one with the view of the rolling Tuscan hills, the wait staff would tell me it was reserved. Five minutes later and a couple with no reservation was ushered to the same table. It felt as if my aloneness was not only being viewed as abnormal, it was being actively discouraged.

Solitude is a terrifying prospect for so many of us because we're told that it's not the natural order of things. Our cultural markers repeatedly remind us that coupledom is the ultimate fairytale ending. Whether it's through media, advertising, or government policy, women are judged particularly harshly for being without a partner or child—described as 'spinsters', 'unlucky in love' or, as in the case of former prime minister Julia Gillard, 'deliberately barren'. An entire beauty and magazine industry is predicated on teaching girls that their most pressing life priority is to ensure they don't die alone. Even the notion of 'failed' marriages suggests that coupledom equals success, while being unpartnered is a sad consolation prize.

An extended period of single life is like being among the long-term unemployed—the longer you're out of the game, the harder it is to return to the workforce. With technology adding to the pressure, modern dating is a non-stop rollercoaster ride of hope and expectation played out at breakneck speed. There's always that heady buzz of anticipation—like unwrapping a Christmas present—as you imagine whether this will be the person who makes your heart dance. Then, the crushing low of realising that although the gift is wrapped in shiny paper, the box inside is empty. For a long time after the eight-year relationship that brought me from Scotland to Australia ended in an excoriating storm of grief and bewilderment, I wasn't looking to 'find someone'. It took all my will to find a way back to myself. Then, when I was capable of sharing the rebuilt me with the world, I discovered that meeting a man to spend my life with was a more complex matter than just being ready. It's a labyrinthine equation of circumstance, timing, emotional maturity, sexual chemistry, vulnerability, and trust, and a thousand other variables so that at times it feels like buying a ticket for a cosmic lottery. No app or 'online compatibility matching system' can manufacture the inexplicable spark that ignites a great love.

A few times I thought I'd come close to finding it. After my book came out, I fell for a man who seemed to adore me. He was charming and attentive and sexy, with a smile that made my head sway and my insides somersault. He told me I deserved everything. It was a painful unravelling to realise he couldn't—or didn't want to—be the one to deliver it. After that, I met someone who was willing and able to give me everything. It was refreshing and lovely, and I wished I could dive in and meet his affection with equal enthusiasm. But that thing—a spark, an energy, some sort of unspoken kismet that twists you inside out—wasn't to be.

'Oh, but perhaps you're too picky,' I've been told, by well-meaning purveyors of unsolicited advice on the single experience. Yet I know what it feels like to be trapped in a union when one party isn't fully there. It's an aching emptiness that feels like the slow death of your soul. I won't do that again. I remain open to love, but for the past few years I've actively taken myself out of the dating game. My full-time commitment has been reconnecting with the parts of me I'd neglected. When you're constantly searching, it takes you away from yourself, and from all the people who make your life sing. So I stopped chasing.

Since I gave up the hunt, I've enjoyed single life so much more. I love my freedom and independence, and I'm incredibly proud of what I've achieved on my own. My apartment is a self-made sanctuary. I even have a recurring nightmare in which I can't breathe because a man moves in, takes my artwork off the walls, and shifts my furniture around before telling me he's allergic to cats and he's serving Hamish an eviction notice.

But if I was to listen to the messages society sends me as a 40-something woman, I should be unfulfilled. My life is an oddity; an existence to be pitied, not celebrated. Solo life is an aberration. It's a narrative that flies in the face of reality. There are more single-person households than at any point in our history. We prop up the economy, and yet every year at Budget time our government acts as if we don't exist. The norm may be the 'working family', but things are changing. According to the Australian Bureau of Statistics, lone-person households are projected to show the biggest percentage increase over the next 25 years. That means the number of people living alone will rise by up to 65 per cent, from 2.1 million households in 2011 to 3.4 million in 2036. We're going to have to redefine our view of solo life if this trend continues. A community built with people who can't stand or have never experienced their own company is not a healthy one. And yet, in an age when we're constantly connected, spending time alone has become a foreign state of mind. It's a perverse irony that the selfie is ubiquitous at a time when being in touch with our true self is a skill many simply don't possess.

For younger generations—who have never known a world before smartphones and social media—true aloneness is such an alien concept that some will do anything to avoid it. In one recent study from the University of Virginia, two-thirds of college students chose to administer themselves electric shocks rather than be left in an empty room with nothing but their own thoughts for just six to 15 minutes. It seems anything, even physical pain, is better than nothing.

There is a global push to destigmatise solitude, and a raft of research which suggests that, rather than run from it, we should actively seek it out. Embracing alone-time can improve mood, creativity, and memory, and lower stress and agitation. A study from the University of Illinois found that teenagers who spent between 25 and 45 per cent of their non-classroom time alone were academically more successful and less depressed than their socially active classmates. Research out of Harvard has found that people who perform tasks alone retain memories better than those who work in pairs.

I spoke via email with Sara Maitland, author of *How to Be Alone*, who lives in a home she built on a remote moor in south-west Scotland—where there is no mobile phone coverage and the nearest supermarket is 30 kilometres away. I imagined her living there in the wilds, like a character in a moody Nordic crime drama, and found the idea both terrifying and somewhat appealing. Maitland said that she did not seek solitude, 'it sought me' following the breakdown of her marriage. After a year of living alone in a small country village, she realised she had become 'phenomenally happy', not because she was glad to be separated from her husband but because it allowed her to become more attuned to nature, and to foster creativity, deep self-knowledge, and a profound connection to her own needs. She told me that solitude is a description of fact, while loneliness is an emotional response to it, and the expectation that loneliness accompanies single life is no more than a cultural assumption. 'We live in a culture that tells young people that being single is a disaster. They were not brought up with any training in being alone and enjoying being alone. Like social skills, solitude needs practice,' she said. 'Look at the language we use. "Loner" used to mean "heroic adventurer"—the Lone Ranger, for instance. Now it means "dangerous weirdo" and very probably "sexual predator" ... Office culture favours the team and the open-plan office. Not having a partner is seen as a tragedy.'

Maitland believes our culture places too much emphasis on couples and the family, and would like to see single life afforded more respect, to help normalise solitude for young people. 'We could start by never using isolation as a punishment for children.

It should be a reward. Not "Go to your room" but "You've been so helpful this morning, would you like some time of your own now?" But equally, by not giving them a mobile phone too early or a computer in their room, we could encourage them to get outside alone.'

I agree that practising solitude is a healthy pursuit, but we can't disregard the very real sense of loneliness many people feel in a fast-paced society that is big on connectivity yet often pulls up short on human connection. A 2016 Lifeline survey found about 60 per cent of the 3,100 respondents said they 'often felt lonely' and 83 per cent felt loneliness was increasing in society, with the suicide prevention charity's chief executive saying their helpline received more calls about social isolation and loneliness than they did about mental-health issues. The health risks of loneliness include increased chances of heart disease, stroke, and early death, particularly when that isolation has not been a choice. We need those intimate connections to thrive. I'm acutely aware that my network of close friends and family has insulated me from the loneliness that pervades everyday life for many people in this age of anxiety.

Dr Stephanie Dowrick, author of *Intimacy and Solitude*—a book that really helped me embrace that sacred solo space—told me that when aloneness is involuntary, whether through rejection or divorce or bereavement, people can feel shame and powerlessness. 'It's that sense that "everybody else has got someone to love them and I don't". In those moments, we forget that almost everybody has had some experiences of not being chosen. Tiny children feel it, very elderly people feel it, and we have to go through many processes as we mature of really reconciling our relationship with ourselves so that when we are with other people we're not overly needy.'

The key, it would seem, is how we view being alone, and the sense we can make of it. Being unpartnered does not necessarily mean being isolated. The loneliest I've ever felt was in a long-term relationship that had become loveless and dysfunctional. I was so disconnected from myself I'd forgotten who I was. Dowrick said, 'I think if people understand aloneness and solitude with a little bit more subtlety, and if they see that they have more power than they may know about how they may experience these times, then even aloneness can be a useful catalyst and times of solitude can be utterly nourishing.'

This insight helped me feel less self-conscious when I noticed the stares of fellow diners on my travels in Italy. In the scheme of things, their opinion of me was of as much consequence to me as mine was to them. And what do we ever really know about the strangers we briefly cross paths with while holidaying? We get only glimpses of their lives — stolen snippets of their joy, their frustration, their ridiculousness. And we judge, painting a picture of their lives on a canvas that can't be stretched past that moment. No future, no past, just the terse words they exchanged with their child or the kindness they offered a street beggar. Sinner or saint, the sum of their humanity fossilised in the second we encounter them.

So I tried to judge people less, and in turn accepted, with compassion and an open heart, the discomfort that my table for one might cause strangers. But I also became profoundly aware that having a partner does not in itself make that discomfort disappear. Just as I found that my problems did not vanish by transporting them to a beautiful city on the other side of the world, I noticed that for many partnered people, holidays can amplify the distance in a relationship. In Lucca, an achingly beautiful walled Tuscan city, I wandered through a rabbit warren of narrow cobbled streets and occasionally found myself stumbling into someone else's personal hell. For every couple kissing on a tandem bike at sunset, there was another wondering why they ever thought the person standing next to them was a suitable life partner. One morning, strolling along Via Fillungo — one of Lucca's liveliest pedestrianised thoroughfares — I noticed that the Australian couple walking next to me were having a bad day:

> *Him*: Well, it's your bloody fault. We could have been out walking yesterday, but you were bloody sick in bed all day.
> *Her*: You could have gone out walking without me. Nothing to stop you going out on your own.
> *Him*: You don't get it, do you? You just don't bloody get it. This was meant to be a holiday where we spent time together.
> *Her*: Can you slow down? My feet are hurting in these sandals.
> *Him*: FUCKEN HELL! First I'm too slow, now I'm too fast. I can't fucken win.

I left them there as we walked past the stunning Basilica di San Frediano, its Romanesque beauty only serving as cruel counterpoint to their discomfort. Who knows what happened next? But it was a reminder to me — the solo traveller, who sometimes felt that she must be crazy to still be anxious among all the splendour — to be kinder to myself and accept that being alone can sometimes be a blessing.

I felt the strength of my solitude most keenly during a hike between Levanto and Monterosso — two beach villages separated by the clifftops of the Cinque Terre. The guidebooks said it was a 7.12-kilometre track. That didn't seem like much from the outset—I used to walk that far from my apartment to work some mornings. But this was mostly uphill, through steep, rocky terrain. It would take me up to three hours. At first I imagined it as a great odyssey of self-discovery, like that undertaken by author Cheryl Strayed in *Wild*, where she frees herself from grief and self-medication by trekking through the wilderness to find wholeness and a brand-new life. This would be just the tonic I needed.

Then I realised I was back in the happiness trap. Focused on the endpoint rather than the journey. It was just a walk through the hills. It didn't need to be life-changing. And also, Cheryl Strayed hoofed it some 1,700 kilometres from the Mojave Desert along the Pacific Crest Trail. I was taking a morning stroll from one Italian beach town to another.

The path started just off the promenade by the water in Levanto. It climbed steeply up too many steps for me to count, and then I was on the trail proper. Almost immediately, the views down to Levanto were breathtaking. As the path got steeper, I realised it wasn't going to be a stroll. I began to sweat like Pauline Hanson in a Bankstown kebab shop. As I climbed, I became more concerned by my attire. There weren't many other walkers on the trail, but every 20 minutes or so I'd see a couple pass, and invariably they were dressed as if they meant business—serious hiking boots, khaki shorts, backpacks, and walking poles. Meanwhile, I was wearing my runners, a cotton beach skirt I'd bought in Byron Bay as a backpacker circa 2001, my bikini top, and a fedora.

The climb was hard. It was bloody hard. For more than an hour it was an uphill slog over rocky ground on a dusty track that often disappeared, making it difficult to know which way was forward. I began to question whether I was as fit as I thought I was. But the more I walked, the more determined I became. I was not going back. There was no going back. I just kept breathing, stopping for a rest and some water when I needed to, admiring the views before me. I was struck by how grateful I was for my own company and the rejuvenation that can come from solitude. I stood looking out on to the stillness of the water and breathed deeply into the space and the quiet. It felt as though this hike was a metaphor for the last few years of my life. Or maybe all of my life. Or maybe everyone's life. You climb and you climb, and it seems never-ending. You struggle to catch your breath, to the point where all you can do to keep going is put one foot in front of the other and remember to breathe in and out. Then, just when you think you can't keep battling uphill, the path levels out and there is air in your lungs again. You find your feet, you reset; you feel stable, and so proud of yourself for not giving up.

But then, as you are starting to find your equilibrium, a lizard darts out and it scares the shit out of you and you nearly lose your footing and you think, *Where the fuck did that lizard come from?* You keep going, rattled but undeterred. You get back into a rhythm. But then another, bigger lizard appears out of nowhere and you're like, *ENOUGH WITH THE FUCKING LIZARDS!* You keep going. Climbing again. You round the corner and the track is blocked by boulders. You worry that perhaps you're lost. Then, a very subtle signpost appears, a splash of red paint on a small rock, that lets you know you're on the right path. You reach the summit, and even though you know there will be more pain and more climbing in the future, you're grateful that your body and your mind are strong enough to have brought you here. The vista opens up before you and it's beautiful and expansive and worth every drop of sweat and twinge of pain. You run down the hill towards the end of the track, skipping over rocks as if you are jet-propelled, arms outstretched like a bird opening its wings. And in that moment, you are so grateful that despite the climbing and the struggles and the pain and all the fucking lizards, you made it here to see it.

23

FALLING BACK TOGETHER

Early on in therapy, Veronica told me the word 'should' was banned in her room. It's a word loaded with shame and impossible expectations. The happiness fairytale in all its inglorious fakery. When 'should' becomes the driving force, we forget what it is that truly brings us joy. Believing that I *should* be happy when I'd reached society's preordained goals was the beginning of my unravelling.

In the first week of my solo trip through Italy, I had a timely reminder of the pitfalls of 'should'. The morning after I'd enjoyed the best lasagne of my life in a little hilltop Tuscan village on a night that was as close to perfect as I can remember, I woke up feeling exhausted and struck with unexplained melancholy. I was perplexed. How is it possible to have such a truly unique life moment and rebound with utter inertia? I spiralled headfirst into a bottomless well of 'what ifs' and doomsday scenarios and concluded that this was just further proof of my brokenness. From my bed, I could see the majestic ninth-century Duomo di San Cristoforo perched on a hill above Barga's historic old town. It was a divine and tranquil view, with the ivory curtain fluttering in the breeze as the birds sang me good morning. I just wanted to stay in bed and watch through the balcony doors.

But *should* got me up and propelled me into a day I wasn't ready to face. I convinced myself that staying in bed past 9.00 am — even though I was on holiday with nowhere to be, and most of the people in this sleepy hamlet didn't get going until around midday — was tantamount to giving up on life. I should be out there, amongst it, seizing the day, seeing the sights.

After some aimless wandering, I settled on a spectacular spot for lunch, looking out towards the lush green hills, a patchwork blanket of terracotta rooves dotted throughout the valley below. But this only made the panic worse: *If I'm looking at a view this stupendous and I still feel anxious I must be really fucked up. I should be feeling on top of the world and instead I'm scared and sad.*

And in that moment, I remembered why Veronica had banned 'should'. That one word is the departing platform for every destructive train of thought. It can kill a lovely moment stone dead. Had I been less intent on trying to recapture the feelings of the previous night and more accepting of how I felt right in that moment — good or bad — the anxiety might have passed. Instead, I put my discomfort under a microscope, examining its every groove and crevice in search of my madness. But I was not broken. I knew how to pull myself back from this precipice. Being in the Tuscan countryside was not by itself going to soothe my soul. I needed to keep doing the things I knew kept me well. So I vowed that when I was tired I'd allow myself to rest. And I stopped having the kind of holiday others might enjoy and started experiencing the one that worked for me. And if that meant lying in bed reading books for a day, then that was okay.

Things improved almost immediately.

Many of life's rituals can trip us up when viewed through the lens of 'should'. If we're to believe the hype, Christmas should be the happiest time of year for those who celebrate it, surrounded by loved ones as we delight in the festival of gifts, fine food, and general merriment. In reality, for many people it's an unholy nightmare. The expectation of unbridled happiness only leads to more misery for those who either don't have family to spend the holidays with or would rather be strapped to an operating table and slowly waterboarded than confined in an enclosed space with their relatives for a whole day.

I've never really enjoyed New Year's Eve, or Hogmanay, as we call it in Scotland. For a long time I tried to enjoy the enforced frivolity, but the occasion always left me disappointed. It felt as though every painful memory and regret came to visit as midnight neared. *Tomorrow is just another day*, I'd repeat to myself, but still I felt pressure. On the first day of the year somehow we're meant to be reborn, like Christ rising from the dead. As the clock counts down to midnight, the expectation sits so heavily—looking forward and back at all that could have been, should have been, might still be but probably won't. The passing of time, the fading of youth, another year with our dreams unrealised.

I remember that Mum would always cry on Hogmanay when the bells brought in the new year. We'd hug, and her face would be stained with tears for the family she'd lost—living and dead. Their ghosts would join hands with us as 'Auld Lang Syne' rang out, and I'd wonder, in the naivety of my youth, why all the adults were so sad at a party. Then I grew up and realised that dead relatives were only part of the New Year's Eve shitshow. Packed bars, extortionately priced drinks, taxi-less streets, and a 5-kilometre walk home were all included in the package deal.

In Edinburgh, where every year hundreds of thousands of revellers pack into the city centre for the biggest street party in the world, I just wanted to stay home, keep warm, and avoid the crowds. But my youthful need for acceptance always drove me to a party. Invariably I'd feel disappointed, crushed by the burden of 'should'. The older I got, the more I realised that the greatest adventures can't be pre-planned. On Hogmanay, like so much in life, the build-up to the event is bigger than the finale.

My epic breakdown gave birth to a renewed perspective. It became easier to see what made me happy: what I had to let go and what I had to cultivate. Friends who left me feeling like a lesser version of myself were not really friends. No matter how hard I tried, yoga was never going to be something I loved. Going to the movies alone was a treat. Wearing Ugg boots and trackies out to breakfast was totally fine because who gives a fuck what anyone thinks of my fashion choices? And New Year's Eve was a circus I didn't need to join. How many times had I gone out on the last night of the year simply because everyone else was? What if I just didn't?

So I decided to stay home.

I booked a late-afternoon massage and then ordered in pizza, put on a pair of new pyjamas and my favourite tunes, and lit candles in celebration of the year I'd survived. I watched the last light of 2014 stream through the blinds, casting a dynamic rainbow over the black screen of my TV. I breathed in and out, long and slow. I ate a few pieces of chocolate. I patted Hamish and felt grateful for his gentle company. I took guilty pleasure in intermittently checking the Uber surcharge as the clock ticked closer to midnight. And then I journalled, not about the person who I wanted to be in the next year but the person I already was. I wrote:

I am compassionate and generous. I am turning my fear into wisdom. I am a work in progress and always will be. I am imperfect. I am the new normal. I am a loving and thoughtful friend. I am a much-loved daughter, aunty, and sister. I am a crazy cat lady. I am someone. I am learning to be okay with not being okay. I am love. I am opening up. I am courage. Endless courage. I am funny, vibrant, warm. I am passionate and principled. I am healing.

Spending New Year's Eve alone is now my annual ritual. Four years in a row I've stayed home and gone to bed before midnight. I stay off the internet, make space for myself, and re-establish that inner connection with the little kid who just wants to be prioritised. It's the ultimate date night, and it's always nourishing.

These moments can't be reserved for one night of the year. If I want to keep myself from falling down the well again, I'll have to maintain that connection for life. I often go to dinner or the movies on my own, just to remind myself that I'm worth the effort. I try to have regular detoxes from social media and spend less time on my phone. When I was in Italy, taking that break gave me the headspace to read 20 books. I actively schedule in dates with myself and make sure nothing gets in the way.

In a 'crazy busy' world, the notion of taking time to unwind and 'just be' can seem indulgent or even impossible. But it doesn't have to be a ten-day silent meditation retreat or an afternoon at an expensive day spa. It can be as simple as a five-minute walk in the park or an hour without looking at screens. We all wear so many hats — mother, daughter, father, brother, partner, sister, employee — that it's easy to lose sight of who we are, what we really want, and what we need to sustain us as whole people. We're more than just the roles we fulfil or the expectation heaped upon us. Actively practising time alone can be re-energising, allowing more presence for the important people. Making space to put down the devices and just stare at the wall, inviting boredom to visit, can also be the breeding ground for greater creativity and inspiration. It's hard for ideas to flourish when your brain is constantly distracted.

Sometimes, when I have trouble making that inner connection, I have to remind myself that beneath the noise and the frenzy, there is a quiet clarity. When I was at a low point, my friend Dana gave me the gift of a small bronze figure to keep my spirits up. Wide bottomed, big bosomed, and flat footed, with a little pot belly, this tiny statue looks like a mini Buddha. When I try to stand her up on a flat surface, she often topples over. But sometimes she stands tall. I've come to think of her as my warrior child. When I doubt myself, I hold her in the palm of my hand and remember that this warrior spirit lives within me. When I'm face-down on the hallway carpet, it's her strength that helps me get back up. And in many ways, it's her vulnerability that makes her strong: the willingness to embrace imperfection, accept change, and lean into pain. It's a strength that comes from the courage to let those emotions in. Just feeling her weight has become a trigger to tap into the sense of resilience I've cultivated. It allows me to reassure myself and counter the irrational thoughts that spring to the top of my mind. There are days when that's still a struggle, but practising this ritual is helping carve a healthier track through the forest, a new pathway in my brain.

In those early days, I found the notion that I could rescue myself preposterous. When Veronica urged me to believe in my own strength, it felt as though she was telling me I wasn't getting better because I hadn't been trying hard enough. I was cast adrift, floating through space with nothing to anchor me. At a time when I was desperately unhappy, I just wanted someone to take the pain away. But one day, I was hit with a realisation that terrified me: we are all alone. Every one of us. We come into this world as individual entities and leave it the same way. We can love and be loved but ultimately, nobody can live or die for us.

Over time, the terror gave way to comfort. I felt liberated by my aloneness. It's one of the few things all humans share. Every time I found a way to push through an impossible day, my strength grew. My aloneness became my anchor.

One weekend, during those months off work, I'd gone to Kath's beach house on the coast to seek some quiet and spend time in the summer sun. But a couple of days in, I was struck down with gastro, spending most of the night and the next morning in the bathroom. It only made the anxiety worse as my narrative about being 'defective' kicked in and I ruminated over why I couldn't catch a break. I just wanted to go home. So I made the decision to drive back to Melbourne.

It was one of the worst journeys I can remember. Stomach cramps came in stabbing waves, doubling me over the steering wheel. It was a 42°C day with a roaring northerly buffeting the car, forcing me to grip the steering wheel tightly just to stay in my lane. Driving had been a challenge for some time, but under these conditions, the panic attacks were worse than ever. As I drove onto the West Gate Bridge—nearly 60 metres above the Yarra River, on a ten-lane freeway with no emergency stopping lane—my heart was thumping, my knuckles white, my t-shirt drenched in sweat as the wind howled its disdain. The panic was so violent I wanted to run, abandoning the car, my body, my brain, in the middle of that bridge. But there was nowhere to go but forward. Every time the terrified part of me said, 'I can't do this. I'm going to die out here,' I had to reassure her she was strong. When I got to the other side of the bridge— 2.5 kilometres of concrete in the sky—I was still crying but I punched the air and yelled into the ether because goddamn it, we made it.

I accepted, then, that as enormously grateful as I was to my friends and family for seeing me through the toughest times, they couldn't do the work for me. Even if they sat with me every minute of every day, holding my hand and telling me I was loved, they couldn't make the panic or the doubt stop. They couldn't make me believe that Stark was strong. It was up to me.

That's not what Hollywood has taught us. Tom Cruise has a lot to answer for on this front. It's that one line: 'You complete me.' Ever since he uttered those three words to win back his on-screen wife Renée Zellweger in *Jerry McGuire*, it has been repeated ad nauseam as the ultimate romantic gesture. Finding that special person is like slotting in the final piece of an otherwise imperfect jigsaw puzzle—it's a sweet notion, but it's not particularly healthy. The implication is that we're not enough on our own. Until we meet someone, we remain incomplete, wandering around mournfully seeking the lost piece to make us whole. It's a concept that has kept women's magazines and dating sites in business for years and will continue to do so, but fundamentally it's a con. One thing the last few years has taught me is that wholeness is an entirely internal affair. If we want to ease this yearning, this sense of existential bereavement, we have to stop chasing happiness externally and figure out what we're really searching for. We all need deep connections to others to nourish us and help foster that critical sense of belonging. We need community and a sense of meaning and collective purpose.

But without that connection to ourselves, no matter how much love and validation we get from partners, friends, children, parents, or internet likes, it will never be enough. If we don't believe we're worthy, it's like pouring water into a leaky bucket.

I'm still thankful every day for the people I love, but learning to first turn inwards for reassurance has allowed me to find hope even when things feel hopeless. And in many ways, relying more on my own strength has deepened the relationships with the significant people in my life. No longer do I expect them to rescue me. The burden of my completeness—or my emotional health—is not resting on their shoulders.

It seems like sweet serendipity that the interview with the philosopher that sparked that newsroom meltdown, and was the precursor to my own enforced solitary confinement of five months off work, should have held the key all along. As Damon Young told me in that conversation: the art of solitude is the capacity to confront and accept your own existence without needing others around to entertain or distract you. He pointed out that so many of the problems we all wrestle with in this highly charged digital age stem from our inability to practise solitude and a reluctance to shift our view from the external to the internal.

'When you don't have the time or energy to cultivate that sense of a separate self, you're far more likely to seek it in the crowd,' he said. The anger and division we're seeing in the world and the need to point the finger often comes from a feeling of disconnection from ourselves. 'It's a lot easier to define yourself against some nasty "other" than it is to figure out what you think and feel. It's a way of keeping you preoccupied and stops you asking those awkward questions about your own cruelty or pettiness.'

When I think about all the things that add to my stress—drinking too much, fighting with conservatives on the internet, getting lost in a deluge of bad news, impulse-buying things I don't need, or obsessively checking social media—they can almost all be ameliorated by pausing and connecting to that inner landscape. What is driving the behaviour? What part of me have I neglected in that moment? In what way am I fearful or trying to fill a gap? As Young told me, we are social animals, and while we need intimacy and camaraderie to be healthy, we are also creatures of imagination. Solitude restores that connection to our complicated, whimsical inner world: 'Much of what we do and think is opaque to us. The self is a puzzle. Solitude is absolutely vital for trying to become more intimate with this weird self that we are.'

I can confidently say that I'm more comfortable with my weird self than I've ever been. Last year, as a Christmas gift to myself, I bought a canvas tote bag from The School of Life. Printed in large capital letters on the side are the words *EMOTIONAL BAGGAGE*. The tag inside reads, *Everyone has it; the trick is to carry it elegantly.* It's a reminder to me that the broken can be beautiful. I wear my scars on the outside because I am no longer ashamed. Regina is still with me, but she's mellowed. Her barbs aren't so sharp. And now, she's joined by a warrior child, whose grit reminds me I'm strong even when I feel weak. I suspect she was always there. I just had to turn Regina's noise down long enough for her to be heard.

I'm not 'cured' of my anxiety, and I don't imagine I will ever be. I struggle. A lot. There are still days, sometimes weeks, when the darkness overwhelms me and I have to fight hard not to be dragged back into familiar patterns. I may well fall down again in spectacular fashion. That is part of being human. No amount of therapy or mindfulness can help you dodge the curve balls that knock you flat on your back. But I know that I can get back up. And there are days now when I'm just so content with the life I have. Days when I feel whole. I am learning to live in the small. At my fortieth birthday party, as I looked across a room filled with people who loved me—my village of helpers—I was no longer worried about the advent of middle age. It was a privilege just to be alive.

Without the tough days I'd have nothing to measure those beautiful moments against. I'm no longer searching for the fairytale ending. Underneath it all, I trust that whatever's thrown my way, I'll survive it. Life can swing from happy-ever-after to happy-never-after and back again more times than we can count, and that's okay. What I know now is it's possible to struggle and still be strong.

Veronica, who I continue to see, often reminds me that nothing of value comes without sacrifice: 'A good life does not just happen; nor is it inherited, earned, or bestowed upon us. Rather, it is forged with our own will. It requires concerted effort.' Whatever lies ahead, I've come to see the last few years not as a breakdown but as a breakthrough. Everything has changed. From my new perspective, things are different, rearranged. As Jason said to me when I was trying to rise from the embers of my immolation, 'You're not falling apart, Jill Stark. You're falling back together.' The cracks remain, but those gold seams have enriched my life in so many ways.

Not long after I'd recovered from the episode where I couldn't imagine staying among the living, I was having breakfast on my own at a café near my apartment. At the next table I saw a woman in gym clothes, hand to her face, wiping away tears. She looked scared and confused, and I could sense her hopelessness from where I sat. I recognised her pain—that feeling of falling, that feeling that nothing will ever be okay again. I wanted so much to walk over and give her a hug. But she had a friend who was holding her gently by the arm, staring into her eyes, with a tenderness that brought a lump to my throat. It was the purest love. My friend Fiona was right: suffering is not a solitary experience. While nobody can walk the road for us, that doesn't mean others don't feel our pain, or our joy.

We are all profoundly connected. The trap is in feeling we're somehow different: broken, defective, more unfixable than the countless people around us fighting their own battles. It's in believing there's something wrong with us if we're not perpetually happy. Acceptance is not surrender; it's empowerment. It's the act of trusting ourselves but also looking for the shared humanity in the people we meet. It's in recognising that there is no such thing as normal and that we are all, in our own way, a little bit mad.

24

THINGS I'VE LEARNED

If you've read this far, you'll know I'm not a fan of unsolicited advice. Nobody knows you better than you. Rest assured that if you're struggling, I'm not going to suggest you 'just don't worry about it' or offer links to a seven-day wellness retreat in a remote hinterland log cabin. But I do know what works for me. So that's what I'm sharing. Just a few things I've learned that help* keep me grounded.

- Thoughts are not facts.
- If that thing you're freaking out about won't matter this time next week, it probably doesn't matter.
- Breathe. Slowly and deeply. Five times. Repeat.
- Patting a cat is soothing. Dogs are also good.
- Lists are your friend. If all the things you have to do are forming a gluggy hairball of confusion in your brain, write them down. Then number them in order of urgency. Only move on to number two once you've completed number one. And so on.
- Fighting with strangers on the internet is bad for the soul.

- Sometimes you just have to cry until all the crying is done.
- The more you resist those painful, icky feelings, the longer they'll hang around.
- You are stronger than you think.
- Putting yourself first is not selfish. If you've got nothing left in the tank, you can't help others. Learn to say no.
- No one person can fulfil all your needs. Different people in your life play different roles. Choose the right person for the right role.
- That last glass of wine is rarely a good idea.
- Ugg boots and a collection of comfy pyjamas are a solid investment in yourself.
- Respond to that voice in your head telling you you're not enough with compassion, not anger. It comes from a place of fear. Reassure, don't chastise.
- Try to think the best of people. Even when they're being dicks. Everyone has a struggle we can't see.
- You're not in high school anymore. You don't have to take part in the popularity contest.
- Get outside. Move your body. Walk around the block. If you're not feeling it after ten minutes, give yourself permission to come back. (Nine times out of ten, if you make it to ten minutes, you'll keep going.)
- 'Should' is a word that unravels everything. Get it in the bin.
- Watching YouTube videos of baby pandas sliding down a slide is never a bad idea.
- Be wary of Twitter. If it's becoming a toxic cesspit, make for the exit.
- Schedule in regular digital detoxes. Screen-free weekends are a good way to start.

- Turn off the news sometimes. Go watch your favourite fun TV show.
- Kick your shoes off and let your bare feet touch the grass now and then.
- Take yourself on dates. Be brave enough to watch a movie or go to dinner on your own.
- If you wear a bra, take it off as soon as you get home. Best. Feeling. Ever.
- Sing at the top of your voice.
- Leave your phone at home sometimes. It will be okay.
- Keep a gratitude journal by the side of your bed. Every night, write down three things that went well that day. Celebrate every small win.
- Don't go more than two days without a shower. Change your clothes even if you're not going outside.
- Those perfect moments filled with joy can't be bottled. Don't chase an encore. Appreciate it for what it is: an exquisite snapshot in time.
- Dance. As much as you can. Wherever you can.
- Accept love without question. Don't hold back on telling the people you love how much you care.
- Accept the shitty days. Don't attach a significance to them they don't merit.
- Listen to the rain on the roof.
- Know that this moment will pass. You can survive. Hold on.

* Just because I know what's good for me doesn't mean I always do it. I am, after all, a work in progress. Give yourself permission to not be perfect.

25

REACHING OUT

If you or someone you love needs help, there are lots of great people out there who can lend support. I know that reaching out isn't always easy, but you'd be surprised how others respond if you allow yourself to be vulnerable and share how you're feeling. Often, those around you will have experienced something similar themselves.

So start the conversation. Make the call. If you're not okay, tell someone. The system isn't perfect and it's underfunded and overstretched, but it's filled with compassionate, caring souls who work their backsides off to make sure that when you're ready, there's someone there to listen.

If your need is urgent, call 000 or dial any of these numbers for free, confidential, 24/7 support and counselling:

> **Lifeline:** 13 11 14, lifeline.org.au
> **Kids Helpline:** 1800 55 1800, kidshelpline.com.au
> **MensLine:** 1300 78 99 78, mensline.org.au
> **Suicide Call Back Service:** 1300 659 467,
> suicidecallbackservice.org.au

If you're after information or counselling, or just want to get in touch with people going through similar issues, these organisations can offer advice and help you find a therapist or doctor in your area:

> **beyondblue:** 1300 22 4636, beyondblue.org.au
> **SANE Australia:** 1800 187 263, sane.org
> **Black Dog Institute:** 02 9382 4530, blackdoginstitute.org.au
> **Australian Psychological Society:** 1800 333 497, psychology.org.au

If you're under 25, try these organisations:

> **ReachOut:** 02 8029 7777, au.reachout.com
> **Headspace:** 1800 650 890, headspace.org.au
> **Orygen Youth Health:** 1800 888 320 (triage), 03 9342 2800 (general enquiries), oyh.org.au
> **Project Rockit:** 0435 150 280, projectrockit.com.au

And if you're after LGBTIQ-specific counselling, try these numbers:

> **QLife:** 1800 184 527, qlife.org.au
> **Switchboard:** 1800 184 527, switchboard.org.au

TO THE HELPERS

It took more than four years for this book to be written, from idea to manuscript. But the road to get here was one I'd been unknowingly travelling down my whole life. So many people have walked it with me, and at the risk of sounding like an airbrushed Insta-dickhead, I really do feel #blessed.

At *The Age*, I was fortunate to work in a newsroom that has always thrown its arms around its own in tough times. Thank you to Andrew Holden, Mark Forbes, Cameron Houston, Mel Fyfe, Adam Morton, Mick Coulter, Beau Donelly, Marilyn Vella, Michael Bachelard, Chris Johnston, Penny Stephens, Miki Perkins, and many others for supporting me during those difficult days. And to Duska Sulicich—the best boss who ever lived—you will never know how much your love, patience, and support helped get me back on my feet.

I am grateful to all of the friends, experts, and colleagues who shared their expertise and personal experiences on happiness, mental health, and the human condition in this book, but particularly to Hong Vo and her family for allowing me to share Martin's life with the world. May we learn from your loss and do better at building a future where young people are seen *and* heard.

At Scribe, my sincerest gratitude to Cora Kipling — not just a kick-arse publicist but a caring friend — and Henry Rosenbloom for his enduring patience and faith in me and this book, despite having to wait so long to see it finished. I am also forever indebted to Julia Carlomagno, the most insightful, diligent editor, whose commitment to this project went above and beyond. Thanks for taking my teary phone calls and for ignoring my repeated requests to 'burn this fucking piece of shit book in a fire'. And to Allison Colpoys for her patience and talent in coming up with such an elegant and striking cover.

During those final months of writing and editing I was lucky to have friends who offered me their homes as an escape from the city. Amelia Chappelow and Vincent Taylor, thank you for the Clubhouse, with its glorious sunsets and family of backyard kangaroos. And Kath Cinque, I don't know if I'd have finished this book without your beautiful beach retreat or your loving friendship. Warmest thanks also to my dear friends Brigitte and Simon Belleville, who looked after me with such care and kindness in those difficult early days and continue to add great richness to my life.

I am so grateful for the village of helpers who had the courage and compassion not to turn away when things were bleak, but rallied to my side, tenderly guiding me through the despair, the catastrophising, and the many hours of ugly crying. Rachael Bettiens, Carmen Hawker, Dana Meads, Jen Vetilleschi, Mary and Matt Goodman, Mari-Claire Lewis, and Jesse Hogan, you made me soup, held my hand, did endless laps of the park, brought care packages, listened, and generally gave me hope that the storm would pass. And Hamish (as if my cat wasn't going to get a mention), you're as batshit crazy as I am and often treat me like your personal butler but you're a constant source of love, comfort, and lols.

I know that not everyone struggling with mental-health issues has a support crew, so I'm incredibly grateful to have a family who has always had my back. Thank you to Neil, Ker, Daisy, and Orla Stark for your love and generosity. To Margaret Ross and Robin Stark, for every supportive conversation, card, email, text, and bank transfer over all of these years; for your boundless love, and for believing with every ounce of your being that your daughter was strong enough to overcome anything. It's taken me a while to believe it too, but here I am. Thank you. And to my amazing goddaughter Charlotte Brennan, who continues to face her own struggles with grace and courage. I am so proud of you, darling.

To my journo family, Rania Spooner, Tammy Mills, Nick Toscano, Tash Boddy, Sarah Danckert, and Ben Butler, who are always with me through the good times and bad: cheers for all the intense political discussions, raucous singalongs, inappropriate jokes, and Sunday-afternoon sessions at the Castle. Our trips to Tang have nourished my soul (if not my liver) at times when I've needed it most.

Also, a huge thank you to Marieke Hardy for a generous gesture of trust and friendship that eased the burden and gave me permission to press pause.

To my brother-from-another-mother, Michael Lallo, it was those long chats over cups of tea in *The Age* café many moons ago that not only sparked one of the most meaningful friendships of my life but also raised my emotional consciousness and set me on this journey. Thank you for your love, insight, and punctuality.

And to Loretta Curtin, whose whole-hearted friendship has been a joy for more than 15 years: thank you for our conversations about courage and vulnerability, for your tenderness, and for connecting me with a doctor who saw the real me. That doctor, Fiona Enkelmann, has my eternal gratitude for her patience and compassion. May we see more carers like you in our health system. Thanks also to Belinda Bailey, a compassionate and wise early guide when I was looking for answers.

To my childhood friend, Lisa Gilroy: despite the geographical distance, I feel the strength of our closeness and shared history every day and it has sustained me. Likewise, Fiona Hunter, some days you were my reason to get out of bed. Thank you for sharing your wisdom and your pain, and for all that you and your beautiful boy, Jude, have taught me.

Veronica Clarke, you have been more than a psychologist. You have been my guide, my rock, my lamplight through the darkness. How do you say thank you to someone who has saved your life? I suspect you would tell me that gratitude is shown through deeds, not words. And so I hope that every day that my heart is full and open, every day that I live authentically, stand by my values, and resist the urge to be dragged back to old ways, it will go some way to repaying the faith you have shown in me.

Finally, to the three people who shouldered the most weight.

Chris Vedelago, my flannel-wearing, gangster-chasing, potty-mouthed, most excellent partner-in-crime, thank you for steadfastly refusing to let me give up on myself, for loving me even when I am a complete pain in the arse, and for finding a way to make me laugh in moments where the simple act of existing seems impossible.

Jason Ball, admit it, the psychic lady was right. Meeting you changed everything, and I'm so glad it did. I doubt I'd be here today if not for your love and support, and all that I've learned from our friendship. You more than anyone carry the burden of my crazy. Heartfelt thanks for having the compassion and courage to stand by me through it all. Your trust in me helps me trust myself.

And my dearest Leonie (Nonie Nones) Wilson, what a privilege it is to be loved by someone so caring and wise. Someone who knows me better than I know myself. Thank you for your kindness and patience, your unconditional love, your thoughtful handwritten cards, and for confiscating the shovel when I can't stop digging. You are, quite simply, the best.